Scotland's Last Frontier

A JOURNEY ALONG THE HIGHLAND LINE

Alistair Moffat

BIRLINN

*For Kate, Sam, Holly, Chloe, Stephen,
Charlotte, Tim, Louise, Will and all the
Moffateers. You were all much on my mind
as I wrote this book.*

This edition first published in 2015 by
Birlinn Limited
West Newington House
10 Newington Road
Edinburgh
EH9 1QS

www.birlinn.co.uk

First published in hardback in 2012 as
Britain's Last Frontier. A Journey along the Highland Line

Copyright © Alistair Moffat 2012
Introduction copyright © James Naughtie 2012

ISBN: 978 1 78027 331 0

British Library Cataloguing-in-Publication Data
A catalogue record for this book is available from the British Library

Designed and typeset by Iolaire Typesetting, Newtonmore
Printed and bound by Bell & Bain Ltd, Glasgow

Contents

❋

List of Illustrations

✸

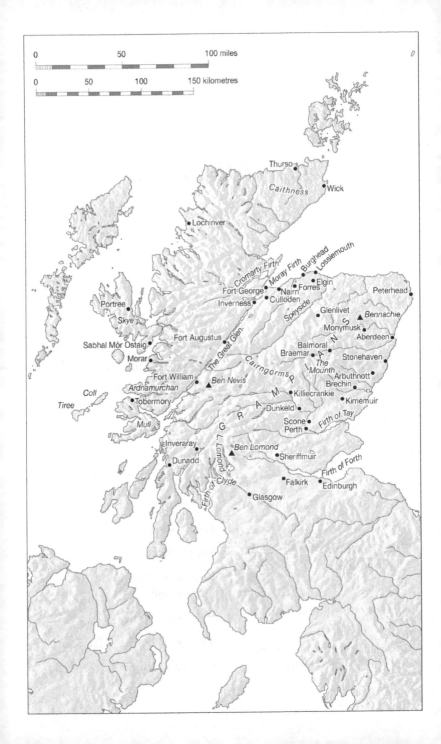

Acknowledgements

Writing in the early morning, filling pages with scribbled long-hand in a pool of angle-poise light, focusing closely on the unspooling of an idea or a narrative, those quiet hours are the best of it. What sets apart the writing of a book from all of the other things I do is that it is a solitary activity, something that is entirely my responsibility and, for the period of its writing, something under my sole control. And I like that, wish I could do more not less, and when it has gone well, there is no satisfaction better than that experienced at the end of a good day at my desk. For once, an evening glass of something seems deserved.

But after I change, edit, score through and finally type up my pages of scrawl, the work of other people begins. My agent, David Godwin, is simply the best, not only one of the calmest, most civilized and cheery of men but also now the author of his own book, a beautifully written little gem on the travails of handicap golf. Now we are all sure he feels our pain.

Jan Rutherford of Birlinn made this book happen and it would not have been published without her. Jan's good sense, warmth and boundless patience have been invaluable. Her colleague, the excellent Andrew Simmons, is the complete professional as he steers manuscripts deftly through the process of production. Nothing is ever a problem to Andrew and it is a pleasure to work with him. And my old friend, Jim Naughtie, surely the busiest man on earth, has done me proud and found time to write a superb introduction to this journey. Thanks, Jim.

And finally to the Moffateers – Kate Andrews, Sam Fowles, Holly Patrick, Chloe Hill, Stephen Kelly, Charlotte Baker, Tim Foley, Will Lord, Lovely Louise and all the others, my deepest thanks for your support. While writing this, I took time out to run for Rector of the University of St Andrews, my alma mater. Calling themselves, the Moffateers, these sparkling young people were the core of my campaign team. It was a wonderful time – and we won! By a mile! Forty years after graduating from St Andrews and 36 years after being married there, Lindsay and I have a better reason than nostalgia to come back, and there are moments when it seems as though we never left.

I hope the completion of that journey has meant the enrichment of the one chronicled in this book.

Alistair Moffat
October 2012

Introduction:
A View from the North-east Lowlands

James Naughtie

IN SCOTLAND'S NORTH-EAST, where I was born and raised, the significance of what Alistair Moffat describes as Scotland's Last Frontier – the line that marks in both a physical and cultural sense the boundary between Highland and Lowland Scotland – is palpable. It is borderlands such as these, where different landscapes, languages and cultural attitudes collide, that really make us think about who we are.

In this book, Alistair takes us on a journey through place and time – from the Clyde valley to the North-east lowlands of Aberdeenshire, from the prehistoric peoples of the Moray Firth to J.M. Barrie, the creator of Peter Pan, to explore the histories and cultures on either side of the divide.

In my own home patch, the best place to start to grasp all this is not by the shores of the North Sea or on the farmland that has given the place its character. Much better to step beyond its boundaries and look in. Head for the hills. The walker who approaches the massif of the Cairngorms from the north-west, through the Rothiemurchus Forest, perhaps having come from a little further south through the deep folds of Glen Feshie, sees, opening up in the side of the mountains, a great cleft, where some mighty force has parted the rocks. The effect is surprising because the four mountains that create the plateau appear from almost every angle to be a solid mass, a great obstacle in the sky.

Their height is not the whole explanation because they are modest by the standards of Europe's high ranges, displaying no spectacular towers of rock or jagged peaks and appearing unlikely to harbour deep gorges, although all that is an illusion. Their visual power comes from the obvious fact that they create a barrier that divides the landscape. No one coming from the north or the west can believe that what lies beyond is the same territory. The hills feel like an end, not a beginning.

They give notice that the high places, the geographical space that we know loosely as the Highlands, will soon be left behind. If there are traces on the other side, they will soon disappear. And, therefore, the V-shaped opening in the massif is enticing, as if it is a passage which will lead to secrets being revealed. The path that leads through it is known as the Lairig Ghru, one of the greatest mountain walks in our islands, and it fulfils its promise because, in the course of only about 25 miles, the crossing is made from Highlands to Lowlands. The Lairig Ghru rises to a modest but often intimidating height of about 835 metres (2740 ft) above sea level. Up there, a subarctic cold can grip you without warning and an icy, unforgiving wind sometimes forces even the sturdiest travellers to take shelter for the night. But it is here that you can observe the sudden drama of our most northerly frontier and its power.

The Lairig Ghru is a walk rather than a climb but a rough one. There are boulder fields and bleak channels where a vicious wind can swirl in without warning and scree slopes where a drenching mist can drop down in a few minutes. You pass the Tailors' Stone which, legend says, marks the grave of a band of tailors who were said to have promised to dance at both ends of the Lairig Ghru in the course of one Hogmanay night. They perished on the journey, even that great stone having failed to given them enough shelter in the storm. A little further on is the rough bothy at Corrour where walkers can bed down safely for the night and the source of the River Dee that flows all the way east to Aberdeen. The walk, which people are told to attempt in one day only in the summer months when wild weather is intermittent rather than the norm, is a kind of challenge. The knowledge that cattlemen were still using the pass as a drove road in the second half of the nineteenth century, walking their beasts to market by the shortest route to the south, is not much comfort these days. It is tough. So, coming from the north-west, you sense a promise that the hard slog will be worth it in the end and that the rough places will pass away. And so it proves. Descending towards the rich pastures of Aberdeenshire, with only Byron's 'steep frowning glories of dark Lochnagar' to remind you of the mountains, the Highlands are behind you.

The countryside that stretches east along the Dee and north-wards to the Moray Firth coast about fifty miles away is flatter, more intimate, and the voices are different. They speak of a distinct piece of territory that, for all its contrasts – fishermen and farmers have always gone their separate ways – is a sheltered part of Scotland, surrounded by mountains and sea, that has a confident sense of itself.

Growing up in the North-east was to understand instinctively that there was a dividing line – geological, linguistic, cultural – that was a natural part of our firmament. It is represented by those mountains in the Cairngorm plateau, the northernmost spur of the Grampians, and by the history that has made the frontier between Lowlands and Highlands such an obvious fact of life. The North-east has always seemed the far north from a Glasgow or Edinburgh perspective but its people think the Highlands are just as far away. They are themselves and the reason is that they are aware of the boundary.

When Johnson and Boswell were heading for the Western Isles in 1773, they had a mixed time of it in the North-east. They found little to interest them outside Aberdeen. They found Banff especially unappealing and, in Cullen, Johnson ordered a dried haddock to be removed from his table. Boswell makes clear that, after they left Aberdeen, where they had been very comfortable, they wanted to get on the road west as quickly as they could. They travelled round the coast and cut in to Elgin, only to find an inedible meal set before them. Never mind, Johnson was still interested in the spare ruins of the cathedral whose fate, typically, he interpreted as 'another proof of the waste of reformation', noting that it had first been desecrated by a Highland chief 'in the intestine tumults of the barbarous ages'.

Boswell noted in his journal that they had travelled about twenty miles westwards from Elgin to Nairn, having indulged their imaginations with pleasant thoughts of Macbeth's witches along the way at Cawdor and Auldearn, when they first smelt peat fires and heard Gaelic spoken (Boswell referring to it as 'Erse', its Irish counterpart). They knew then that they were in the Highlands.

That translation, away from the lowlands to somewhere different, would still be evident to anyone born in the North-east two hundred years after that journey. Growing up in Banffshire – administratively abolished in 1975 but alive in the minds of everyone who knew it as home – was to understand the difference between east and west. Towards Aberdeen there was a familiar landscape, on which the small family farms of the higher, rougher ground gave way to the bigger, richer, pastures of the plain of Buchan. As surely as the cattle were taken to market in Aberdeen or the slaughtered meat, like the whisky, was loaded on the trains that took it south the centre of gravity was in the east. The voices were the same and the music of life in village and farm was familiar. Rough though life had been for generations on some of the inhospitable land and at sea in search of the herring, the place had a harmony of its own – it demanded to be treated as a distinct territory, different from anywhere else.

That feeling was encouraged by the fact that, when you turned west, things started to change. In my childhood, I was aware that somewhere on the way to Elgin voices began to alter. A Highland softness would modify the broad vowels of Banffshire and Aberdeenshire and the cadences would shift upwards. By the time you were beyond Elgin . . . well, you were on the way to

Inverness, where people wore the kilt in the street, churches still held services in Gaelic and the rhythms of life took on a Highland pace. My home village was almost equidistant from Aberdeen and Inverness, roughly fifty miles each way, and they were worlds apart.

The cultural distinctions that became a part of our lives are testimony to the persistence of that great divide, without which the North-east, in particular, makes no sense. Its ability to hold on to a kind of territorial identity that has proved surprisingly robust in the face of the ravages of recent times (some of them well-meant and some of them beneficial) is remarkable evidence of a clear-headed set of distinctions that have lingered in the collective mind. They had the force of a divide.

My village was Rothiemay on the banks of the River Deveron, which runs for about 60 miles from the Cabrach moors near Dufftown to the sea at Banff. The river has often been considered a poor relation to the swanky Spey, which is the faster and the broader of the two, but locals will point out that the British record for a salmon caught on the fly (61 lbs) was on the Deveron. For much of its course, it defined the old boundary between Banffshire and Aberdeenshire and therefore meandered through some of the best farming territory in the North-east. I used to know many of its banks and stones so well that I believe that now, several decades later, I could find my way across it in a dozen places without a guide. The river was a place of excitement and calm and a journey along its course – I remember once a daft expedition on a ramshackle raft that had been built without consideration for the rough patches of white water that would pull it apart – is an introduction to the countryside of the North-east, so resonant for anyone who knows it and so particular.

I used to have, on a wall above my desk, a photograph of a cattle pen, showing a vast black beast behind its bars, and tied to the front rail is a simple red card bearing the legend, 'Turriff show – First Prize'. This is an emblem that conjures up glorious pictures, and memories, and it is an image that will bring to anyone of North-east farming stock something of the ecstasy felt by the Earl of Emsworth when P.G. Wodehouse allowed his black Berkshire sow, Empress of Blandings, to win the silver medal in the fat pigs' class at the Shropshire Agricultural Show for three successive years. The Turriff Show – like its great rival, the Keith Show – remains a place of cultural pilgrimage in reminding everyone of the story of the farms that were the life of the place and they bring to mind the markets, greatly reduced in number, that were the weekly focus of interest in a dozen and more towns across the North-east. When oil and gas began to turn the economy of the North-east upside down in the 1970s, much of this history began to reek with nostalgia – as if the profound changes that had been happening for a generation had been highlighted by the arrival of a industry controlled from far away. Because the truth is that, for the farmers and fishermen of the North-east, the glory days were long gone.

Those of us who grew up in the 1950s and 60s are aware that these old ways were in decline. The steam drifters were celebrated only in historic photographs, and the North Sea would soon be as much a European political battlefield as a place of threatening storms. The patterns of farming had changed and, although the Aberdeen Angus beef barons and the big farms of Buchan and Mar would still prosper, the tradition of family farming that had been in place for a couple of centuries was in decline.

The memories, however, ran deep. In the heart of the North-east – say sixty miles north to south and the same east to west – this was the character of life that would not pass away, whatever came along. The place was defined by the traditions of the land and, on its coastal strip, by the demands on fishing communities that were drawn together by the knowledge, day by day, that they would continue to suffer even as they prospered. So its characteristic, even at times of great change, was a feeling of solidity. Like the granite from Rubislaw quarry that built 19th-century Aberdeen, life seemed to promise an element of permanence.

The simplicities, of course, are not so simple. Take the

language. One of the most outstanding and resilient elements of the culture of the North-east is the Doric tongue, the broad dialect with its own rich vocabulary that acts as a barrier to outsiders and is still a matter of pride in many communities, despite the natural winnowing away of its distinctiveness in an age of mass communication. Yet it should not be imagined that it was always so. At the end of the middle ages, Gaelic was still spoken everywhere in the North-east except on the coastal strip, running from Buckie round Buchan Ness and through Peterhead south to Aberdeen. Norse and Anglo-Saxon were the components of the mixed tongue of the people who went to sea and later became the predominant voice of the region.

The name of my own village, Rothiemay, derives from Gaelic *Ràth a' Mhuigh* and many of the farms that make up the parish are a rich inheritance from that source – Auchinclech, Auchencrieve, Retanach, Corskellie, Avochie among them.

So the divide that is now so obvious – the shift in language to the west, the gravitational pull to the east – was not always so simple. It confirms that the best way of thinking of the North-east is to think of it as territory that has always been on the frontier. Highland clans never held sway here – it was the lowland families like the mighty Gordons who shaped its history – yet, in the upper glens of Banffshire, remote places stretching beyond the fabled Scottish chateaux of whisky, in Dufftown, Aberlour and around Glenlivet, Gaelic was still being used at cattle markets into the nineteenth century. The glens, pointing towards the Cairngorms, had not lost their Highland character. But their very remoteness showed how much had changed – from the time Gaelic was outlawed after the collapse of the Jacobite rebellion in the rout at Culloden in 1746, the North-east began to take on the character that its people, say, a hundred years later would recognise.

In the '45, it was a part of Scotland that was splitting apart. Prince Charles Edward Stuart believed, with his characteristic excess of vanity, that he could count on broad support across the North-east but some of those who had supported the first fight against the Hanoverian crown thirty years earlier were unwilling to rally to his cause. By the time he marched north after his failed effort to take Stirling Castle in January 1746, with an army that was shrinking, bedraggled and ripe for defeat, he found that even the 3rd Duke of Gordon, whose family had faithfully served in 1715, was unwilling to follow him and had turned to the king. Other members of the family did retain their historic Stuart loyalty and raised two battalions, which were duly battered at Culloden, but the idea that the North-east would stand alongside the Highland clans, despite the strong residual Catholic loyalty in those days in Banffshire and Aberdeenshire, was outdated. Even Aberdeen, where the two colleges, Marischal and Kings, showed strong Jacobite sympathy, apparently caused little difficulty for the Duke of Cumberland, the king's commander, when he rested there before heading west to put Bonnie Prince Charlie's troops to the sword.

In the century that followed, the divide with the Highlands deepened. In the North-east, it was much easier to accept the assault on the culture of the Jacobites that many further north and west resisted because there was a way of life that was substantially different. It had not been broken and its customs outlawed. The development of the land proceeded in a different way and there would be none of the clearing of the land that became one of the scars of the 19th-century Highlands story. Gaelic would disappear almost entirely within a couple of generations and the North-east feeling of separation – from the west as well as the far south – would intensify.

This was the inheritance of the twentieth century. The North-east spoke differently and its farm life was of its own devising – there was no domination by sheep, as in the borders, and the challenges of the landscape (meagre hill grazing, a tempestuous east wind) meant that techniques and practices were developed that were exported far and wide. Beef cattle were profitable, their superiority unsurpassed and, into the period after the First World War, both on the land and at sea, it was a time of expansion, modest prosperity and a settled way of life.

The village in which I grew up would have been recognisable to a generation just after the First World War. There were fewer than 50 houses in the Milltown – the village proper – and a spreading parish of about 700 people. On our short street, running from the church past the school to the working meal mill at the riverside, there were a working bakery, a good general store, a post office, a skilled shoe- and bootmaker and a proper dispensing chemist. I still have some of the Victorian glass jars from the shelves of Geo. Pirrie and Sons, Chemist, and they remind me of a happy, settled time. That pattern would change and, by the mid 1960s, the baker, the chemist and the shoemaker had gone, but the memory of a community that had confidence and a connection with the past is powerful – the parish was flourishing, like the land.

Such obvious features of a past life have a way of becoming boasts and no one, I hope, would wish to argue that there was greater wisdom, enlightenment or innovation in the North-east than anywhere else in Scotland. The case is a different one – these lands have a particular mix in their history and the way their communities grew illustrates an important consequence of Scotland's geography. They have gone their own way.

Looking at the Highland Line or the last frontier, running with the geological fault from the south-west to the North-east, it is easy to see Banffshire and Aberdeenshire as a vantage point, for they are neither one thing nor the other. Not being drawn to the remnants of a Highland culture and style yet separated from the rest of the Lowlands by a particular social and linguistic history and by the accident of the mountains and the sea gave the land its shape and the people their character.

I have long suspected that one of the aspects of this pride – and a certain gallous bravado underneath the dour exteriors that North-east men and women are supposed to cultivate – is the lurking knowledge that even the Romans found us a little difficult. I can still recall the excitement at school caused by the realisation the battle of Mons Graupius (AD 83–84), the climactic battle between Agricola and his northern enemies, had been fought on our own doorstep. There is nothing remarkable about this. After all, anyone living in London is tramping the streets of a Roman city – just as in Bath you can see the water gushing into their baths or at Inchtuthil in Perthshire you can pick up a nail from their carpentry store – but the excitement at the presence of Roman legions somewhere north-west of Aberdeen, at various points along where the A96 now runs was strangely thrilling. Everyone goes to London sooner or later but not everyone comes to Rothiemay or Grange or Sillyearn – yet they did, in their legions.

Is there anyone who would not be excited by the thought that he had capered in fields on summer evenings *without knowing* that, on that very spot, Romans were settling down for a few nights, preparing to find a way across the river? (I could have shown them the best place, easily.) It is the thrill of discovery after the event that gives it a special edge. Had we learned the story in a textbook, we might have absorbed it as one more fact for the memory, like the one that Mary, Queen of Scots spent a night in the castle above our village on her way to somewhere unknown (or perhaps not). The Romans raise all kinds of different and intriguing questions.

Why had we not known this before? Tacitus, Agricola's son-in-law, was historian-in-residence on the conquering march that led to Mons Graupius but he is tantalisingly sparing in his descriptions – as if deliberately making trouble for future historians. Some have suggested he wasn't there at all. He can certainly not have heard the words he attributes to the leader of the Caledonians, Calgacus – '. . . *solitudinem faciunt pacem appellant*', famously translated as 'they make a desert and call it peace'. But we are stuck with him as our only guide and we know this – they didn't get much further

There are some traces some miles to the west but they fade away quickly. No one has been able to show that they had much interest in going into the Highlands. It is as if the experience of the North-east was enough – the line of mountains, whose eastern side they'd followed north-eastwards through Perthshire and into the Mearns, was not to be crossed. Like the hills and mountains themselves, the Roman passage leaves its mark on the landscape. Theirs was a Lowlands invasion – the Highlands were beyond.

Though an understanding of the history is still sketchy, we know enough of the Roman story to be fairly certain of that. Rather like the stone circle in Rothiemay. Dating from the Neolithic period, this set of stones was perhaps laid out to mirror a particular arrangement of the stars and still is puzzling. From it, we get a sense, in our own secure surroundings, of the backstory. There are Pictish stones here and there, across the parish where I grew up, marked with snakes and broken arrows, crescent symbols, crude representations of what appear to be an eagle and a wild beast. I have not read any convincing explanations of precisely how old they are or who put them there – everything written about them is hedged around with enough uncertainty to leave the mystery greater than the fact.

I crawled around them as a boy, unhindered by fences or warning signs. They sat in fields of corn or gave shelter to sheep on windy days. They remain for me, simply, the markers of a particular place. The people who lived there tilled the same land that was being worked when I was a boy and produces the same crops today. The Romans came, we know, and went. How and why, we are not so sure.

These are the foundations of a territory that is home, the special traces of a history that is unique. As the Romans discovered, the North-east is the deceptive land that divides Highland and Lowland Scotland, apparently spreading out in its own space but connected at different times in its history to both west and south. From there you can understand how important the great divide is in the story of Scotland – its sheer physical insistence, the cultural and linguistic significance, its ability to separate quite small corners of the country and allow them to live in their own spheres.

Whether you come by way of Rothiemurchus, where they spoke Gaelic until not too long ago, and walk through the remnants of the old Caledonian Forest to start the ascent of the Lairig Ghru towards the south or land in the North-east from some fishing boat on a stormy sea in a tiny Banffshire harbour or take one of the long drove roads from the south to reach Deeside and rich pasture, you will know that you have come to a place that has carved out for itself a shape and a spirit that is it is own.

Author's Preface

�֍

THIS BOOK IS INTENDED as a companion to a journey, one that can be made in the mind as well as in person. It is a journey along the line of what was British history's last frontier, a border between two cultures that ended its political life as recently as 1746 in bloodshed and genocide. At Culloden, the last battle was fought between two armies who could both claim to be subjects of the kingdom of Great Britain and Ireland. And when the charge of the clans failed and the killing began, memory also began to fade, disappearing into the mists of romantic fancy. This journey aims to stir what has been forgotten, to tempt the history of what is sometimes called the Highland Line out of the shadows, to remember how divided Scotland once was and how those divisions and their unlikely legacies formed the modern nation.

This is not a straightforward story with a continuous narrative thread that weaves a sequence of pivotal events together in a clear chronological order. Instead, what follows is a gathering of impressions, of atmosphere, but continuity is served by the loose but logical geographic arrangement of a journey of discovery. The tale begins at Culloden, not far from Inverness, and proceeds in an easterly direction through the tumultuous events of the lost kingdom of Moray before turning a sharp right at Stonehaven, where the mountains almost reach the sea, and then it hugs the foothills of the southern Highlands all the way to Glasgow and the Firth of Clyde.

Occasionally the route strikes into the mountains, in a cultural as well as geographical sense. In an overwhelmingly monoglot Scotland with only 58,000 people, just over 1 per cent of the population, having any Gaelic, few are able even to pronounce the names of the lochs and the glens correctly. Locked in incomprehension, the way of life of Highlanders has been documented by many outsiders without a word of their language. It is at best opaque, at worst impossible, for Lowlanders to understand. And, more than that, there exists an atavistic instinct to brand people whose language one does not comprehend as babbling savages. Throughout Scotland's history, such attitudes have been regularly on show and this book attempts to look in both directions across the frontier.

Over the long story of this dramatic divide, perspectives have been shifted as much by the imagination as by politics or economics. For that reason, the work of four great Scottish writers has seemed more than usually important. Three lived close to the Highland Line and set some of their narratives in the shadow of the mountains. Lewis Grassic Gibbon, J. M. Barrie and Neil Munro all add colour and humour, while Sir Walter Scott has a lot to answer for.

In thinking about our history, neatness, inevitability and homogeneity ought all to be resisted. The past was never tidy and, at various turnings, it was by no means clear that all roads would necessarily lead to the present. And most importantly this story of the last frontier tells us that Scotland is only one version of history.

Roads to Culloden

✳

THERE ARE MANY Scotlands. Edinburgh and Glasgow would shudder at being thought similar. Galloway is a place apart, guarded by its sheltering hills looking south to the Irish Sea. The Borders sometimes prefers to share a history with Northumberland, perhaps because the last few miles of its great river flow through England, while Tayside, Angus and the Moray coastlands all have pungent and readily recognisable identities. But the deepest, most profound internal divide in Scotland is that between Highland and Lowland. It is Scotland's last frontier.

Running from north of Glasgow almost to the sea at Stonehaven, what geologists call the Highland Boundary Fault is very obvious. At the Pass of Leny in Perthshire, the road rises suddenly from the boggy flatlands of the meandering River Teith and plunges into the mountains. It narrows and winds as cliffs close in and the landscape changes utterly. Ben Ledi rears up on the left and, across Loch Lubnaig, the ranges of the Lomond Mountains dominate. Forests darken their flanks and the marks of people fade almost to nothing. Few houses or fields can be seen and the row of telegraph poles by the roadside seems somehow forlorn, holding up a fragile thread connecting two Scotlands.

From many vantage points in the south, the Highland Line can be clearly seen, a front rank of sentinel mountains rising abruptly from the plain. Commuters on the Edinburgh bypass can often make out Ben Ledi and sometimes Ben Lomond looms out of the morning haze. And yet the high country behind the mountains is not really familiar at all. Few Scots can pronounce its geography. The lochs, rivers, passes and ranges are named in Gaelic, a language fast fading and now spoken by fewer than 50,000 Scots, many of them the wrong side of sixty. Ben Ledi is one of the simpler names but, like many Gaelic words, it is not pronounced as it is spelled. Those who named it called it Ben Letty not Leddy and behind it rises Beinn Bhreac. Deeper into the mountains, the older spelling of Beinn is now standard on maps but Bhreac is a challenge. In Gaelic, the *bh* combination is said as a 'v' and it means 'Speckled Mountain'. The English word 'freckle' is cognate with *bhreac*.

As much as geology and geography, language used to change when the Highland Line was crossed. To the north, Gaelic not only described the landscape, it spoke of a different way of life, acted as another lens through which the world could be seen. On the high plateaux and in the narrow glens, herdsmen reared their beasts and lived in a society structured around clan and kinship. To the south, ploughmen tilled the flatter and more fertile land and had stronger cultural links with England than with the north of Scotland. Road signs unwittingly acknowledge the tremendous influence of language difference when they declare *Failte do'n Gaidhealtachd*. They translate it as 'Welcome to the Highlands' but a more lexically tight subtitle would be 'Welcome to the Land of the Gaels', the people who speak Gaelic.

This is overwhelmingly a story of mutual misunderstanding – even incomprehension – between two speech communities and it is also a story of conflict between two cultures. Those who live to the north talk of the land below the Highland Line as the *Galltachd*, the 'Land of the Foreigners'. And Lowlanders who attack support for Gaelic often call it a foreign language even though it is clearly native and was probably spoken in Scotland for many generations before the coming of Northumbrian English in the seventh century. Gaels occasionally talk of *miorun mor nan Gall*, 'the great malice of the Lowlander', while Gaels themselves are sometimes characterised as lazy, sulky and with a historic sense of entitlement. These attitudes have changed somewhat in recent times but they remain a recipe for misunderstanding and, for many centuries, supplied sparks for bloody confrontation.

History happens at the edges and a persistent theme of this book will be the exchanges between Gael and Gall, between Highlander and Lowlander, between two sets of suspicious neighbours. Too often commentators and historians have felt compelled to take sides. Guilt at the treatment of Gaels during the long period of the Clearances has informed attitudes, not always helpfully. Romance, especially the sort so brilliantly confected by Walter Scott, has wreathed the mountains in impenetrable mist and ignorance has further clouded the picture. And yet something has changed. In the last few years, many Scots have gratefully adopted the iconography of the Gaels so that most weddings now resemble clan gatherings, football crowds are tricked out in tartan and politicians feel compelled to march through the streets of New York wearing a kilt.

My own fascination with the differences between Lowland and Highland may have been an early symptom of changing attitudes and it began a long time ago and a long way away from the mountains and glens of the north.

On a sunny spring day in 1964, I travelled across that invisible frontier, from one Scotland to another, from familiarity to an epic, melancholy strangeness, from the homely geometry of the fields and farms of the Scottish Borders to the shores of the mighty Atlantic where the mountains rise out of the ocean into huge Highland skies. It was a transformative journey and a day whose memory has never left me.

Led by our Latin teacher, Mr Goodall, a party of a dozen schoolchildren departed from Kelso Station in the Easter holidays on what was to be a journey of firsts and lasts. It was the first time I had ever gone far from home without my parents and the last time passengers could catch a train at Kelso. The station closed in June 1964 and our trip immediately became a footnote, frozen in a small corner of history.

Kitted out with rucksacks, anoraks (not yet a term of mild abuse), waterproofs and walking boots, we gathered on the platform for the great adventure, an advance into the unknown. There was a definite sense of expedition, a journey into an interior where nothing should be taken for granted. Perhaps there were no Mars Bars or chip shops, perhaps they had never heard of The Beatles and certainly not The Rolling Stones. Rucksacks were checked and rechecked by touch, fingers fumbling through the narrow neck amongst socks, a spare pullover and an old yellow sou'wester my dad had forced me to take even though I would have had to be rescued by a lifeboat before I would ever wear it. Maps flapped around as we waited on the platform and we worried about storms, gales, days of never-ending rain. Dubbin had been strongly advised by Mr Goodall. Slathered on and rubbed into dried-out boots each morning, it would keep out the wet. Rub-a-dub-dub. Pots of it were purchased by everyone except Ronald Barker. Following his father's advice, he declared that spit and polish would work just as well. No doubt about it. An Assistant Postmaster in Kelso, Mr Barker strode straight-backed past our window every morning, his shoes gleaming, his socks dry, his demeanour oozing military certainty. After a run of rainy days, we took turns to let Ronald use our Dubbin.

After what seemed like an age, a steam train from Berwick-upon-Tweed puffed into Kelso Station, hissing and grinding to a stop. 'Change at St Boswells for Hawick and Carlisle. This service terminates at Edinburgh Waverley.' The stationmaster walked up and down the platform, a whistle in his mouth. We clambered into compartments, shoving rucksacks into the netting shelves above the seats and arguing over who should face the way we were going. The whistle blew, the carriages shuddered and the journey into the unknown began.

Glamour was waiting on the platform at St Boswells. When Sheelagh Drummond and Sandra Black boarded the train, the expeditionary force was complete and attention refocused not on the view out of the windows. By late morning, we were chugging into Edinburgh Waverley and, on the onward service to Glasgow Queen Street, those who hadn't already eaten them unwrapped their sandwiches. I'd never been to Glasgow before and it was deafening. Because our connection to Mallaig was tight and probably because Mr Goodall wanted to keep the party together, we did not leave the railway station. Incomprehensible tannoy announcements, the slamming of carriage doors, clanking trains and the jarring chatter of thousands of people in a hurry made my head spin.

After perhaps only ten or twenty minutes, as the train taking us north left the sprawl of the city, there was a sudden revelation when the Firth of Clyde opened. And across the glint of the water, not far distant, stood the mountains. In a moment, it seemed, we had passed out of the oppressive, detailed racket of Glasgow and into a place of elemental majesty. The schoolboy talk stilled as we gawped and Mr Goodall smiled. We found ourselves in a Scotland none of us had ever seen before. As the train rattled north along the shore of Loch Long, towns, villages and houses disappeared and we plunged into dense forest before crossing the isthmus to Loch Lomond. *The White Heather Club* and occasional renditions of 'The Bonnie Banks' had not prepared us for such a vast emptiness. There seemed to be nothing and no one in the landscape except a scatter of yews on a far mountainside. To children raised in the market towns, the tree-lined lanes, the tidily hedged fields and the farm places of the Borders, the grandeur we saw at Crianlarich, on Rannoch Moor and in the glowering shadow of the Nevis Range was almost intimidating.

At Fort William we were allowed out to pee and buy crisps and sweeties. Fort? What fort? Where were the Indians? Children habitually accept a great deal without question but I do recall wondering why the trains had stopped at a fort. What kind of fort? From our recently acquired telly I knew what Fort Laramie and the forts garrisoned by the US Cavalry in *Boots and Saddles* were like. And they weren't like Fort William.

Even though the train had hugged the shores of several sea lochs, our first powerful sense of the Atlantic opened before us at Arisaig. It must have been late afternoon by then and, despite a tendency to sun-tinted recollection, I do remember bright blue skies when I first looked out over the ocean. I had never seen the Atlantic before. At Morar, the sands are blindingly white and on the western horizon lie Eigg, Rum and the Sleat Peninsula of Skye. When at last we reached journey's end at the little station next to the large hotel and the even larger viaduct, we assembled on the platform, a little dazed and quietened by all that our train windows had passed. But here we were out in it, in the landscape, in the heartlands of the Highlands at last.

The youth hostel at Garramore was a half-hour walk to the south along a single-track tarmac road. I have never forgotten it. Having crossed the famously short River Morar and passed below the viaduct, we began a walk that has lived in my memory for almost 50 years. As it rose and turned to reveal white beaches or the limitless blue-green ocean, it showed me how heart-breakingly beautiful the Highlands can be. Scattered along the roadside were a few white cottages and a road end for at least one farm but we saw no one and met no traffic. And yet the land and seashore seemed friendly, always there was a sense of people and how they had shaped this utterly lovely place. Having travelled to several continents since I first saw the road from Morar to Garramore, that small stretch of coastline in the western Highlands remains, for me, unquestionably the most beautiful place in the world.

It seemed then a different, otherworldly beauty, very different from the domesticated, pleasing order of a Borders landscape. And, though the sun shone every day we were at Garramore and gales did not make the Atlantic roar on to the shores of white sand, it was, nevertheless, spare, unfussy, somehow Edenic. I had never seen anywhere like it.

After a few days, we moved on to another youth hostel. Further north, Ratagan is by the side of Loch Duich, not far from the picture-postcard castle at Eilean Donan. Soon after we arrived it began to rain. For days. Youth hostels had a policy of expelling residents in the morning and not allowing them back in until the late afternoon. As the endless rain fell steadily out of leaden skies, testing the resilience of Dubbin-ed boots and waterproofs (but not my sou'wester – only Noah's Flood could have persuaded it out of my rucksack), we mooched around, eking out our coffees in the café at Shiel Bridge. It was closed on a Sunday so, in desperation, I decided to go to church.

A mile or two further along the shore road by Loch Duich, there stood a church and my memory is of a large corrugated iron hut. People materialised, it seemed, out of nowhere and inside it was packed. Raincoats steamed gently in the warmth. At an unseen signal, all went still and an old minister stood up and began to address the congregation in a language that was not English or a Highland version or indeed like anything else I had ever heard before. With a mane of white hair and a jutting jaw, he resembled the actor Finlay Currie when he played God in a Scottish accent in a Roman epic I had seen recently at the Roxy. And then the minister turned to me to welcome a visitor first in Gaelic and then in English. With a mischievous smile, he told me that I could find a hymn book in a pocket attached to the back of the chair in front of me.

And then it began. A tall, cadaverously thin man stood forward from the congregation and started to sing. It seemed like chanting at first and not conventionally melodious, with no recognisable tune. Each time the man completed a line, the congregation appeared to sing it back to him, except that they had made it different. And immensely powerful, almost hypnotic. It was the first time I had heard the Gaelic psalmody.

Soaring and swooping like flocks of birds, the psalms seemed perfectly suited to the land that made them, the steep mountain-sides, the limitless horizon of the ocean and the drama of the winds, the rain and the blinding sunlight. Even though it was to be many years before I understood the words, the emotion behind them was entirely intelligible. As the rise and fall of the singing and its apparent seamlessness reverberated in the little church, it felt as though a history and a culture hidden to me was beginning to open.

Many years later I did an immersion course in Gaelic and became a supporter of the Gaelic-medium further education college at Sabhal Mor Ostaig on the Isle of Skye. It is now part of the University of the Highlands and Islands. There I met a lovely man called Donnie Campbell. Gaelic was his first language and I remember him watching Scotland play football on TV in his cupboard-sized office. When a rare goal was scored, he celebrated and exhorted the team in his native tongue, entirely unselfconsciously.

Sabhal Mor Ostaig

In English, and on a map, the Big Barn at Ostaig lies to the west of a leafy road running through the Sleat Peninsula of the Isle of Skye, surely one of the most beautiful places in the world. The Big Barn is, in reality, a small farm steading where a very big idea was made real. In 1973, the merchant banker and entrepreneur Sir Iain Noble came up with the notion of a further education college teaching through the medium of Gaelic. With the help of others, he brought Sabhal Mòr Ostaig into being and it has grown in scale and importance ever since. Under its inspirational principal Norman Gillies, the college chimed its ambitions perfectly with the announcement in 1989 of a government fund to make additional Gaelic TV programmes. Expansion followed, the Scottish ITV companies contributed significant sums and SMO, as it is known, became much more than a renovated farm steading on a stunningly scenic island coastline. A large new campus, the Arainn Chaluim Chille, named after St Columba, was built across the road, beautifully located on a height above the Sound of Sleat. By 2010, there were more than a hundred full-time students and many more part-timers and people on short courses. From a small beginning, the Big Barn has inserted itself into the centre of Gaelic cultural life – an extraordinary achievement.

Once we talked of Highland history and he told me a moving story about the battle at Culloden in 1746, the last act of the Jacobite Rising. Donnie told me that, before they charged across the moor into the gunfire, the clansmen had recited their genealogy. When the government army heard the chanting of what is called the *sloinneadh* the 'naming of the generations', they believed that the Highlanders were singing psalms. Instead each man counted back through his genealogy – *Is mise macIain, macRuaridh, macIain Mor* 'I am the son of John, the son of Ruaridh, the son of Big John'. Many could count back through more than a century. And once the names had been named, once the clansman had said out loud who they were and where they came from, they prepared to charge, to defend a way of life.

Donnie Campbell's story has stayed with me as a singular and dramatic illustration of difference, of the cultural as well as the political and geographical division marked by the Highland Line. And, since our journey along it starts in Inverness, it seems appropriate to begin with the nearby battle of Culloden, the climacteric event in the 18 centuries of recorded difference between Lowlander and Gael.

In the early evening of 19 April 1746, a horseman was galloping towards Edinburgh. Three days before, he had watched the Highland army of Prince Charles charge over the heather moor near Culloden House and engage with the government troops led by the Duke of Cumberland. As the rider clattered over the cobbles of the West Port, he shouted news of a victory to those who turned to watch him pass through the Grassmarket. There the scaffolds General Henry Hawley had ordered for the execution of rebel soldiers and sympathisers only a few weeks earlier still stood and the rotting corpses of the condemned swung in their chains. Kicking on his tiring horse, the rider made for houses where he knew his astonishing news would be welcome. The Prince and his brave Highlanders had triumphed once more! The hated Cumberland had been defeated in battle near Inverness.

Capital Cleaning

The most northerly city in Britain, one of the fastest growing in Europe with a 10 per cent rise in population since 1991 to reach more than 61,000 now, Inverness is booming. A true Highland capital, it was recently ranked fifth out of 189 cities in a quality of life survey. In 1746, after Culloden, the Duke of Cumberland thought it a disgusting collection of hovels and ordered that its streets be cleaned. When Edmund Burt asked a town official why this had never been done before, he was told it rained often. And, when officers in the government army wrote home, they complained that Inverness was very dirty indeed, much more so than London, which had no public street cleaning either. Like the capital city, Inverness was a port and ships from France and Holland docked regularly with cargoes of wines, weapons, lace, silver, silk and spices. All of these luxury goods are a reminder of how populous the Highland hinterland was in the 18th century for they were intended not for the burghers of Inverness but for the clan chiefs and their wealthier tacksmen. They, in turn, exported the products of their clan lands through Inverness – wool, hides, salt beef and cereals. Some chiefs had houses in the town but social life seems to have been sparse with only one tavern (perhaps The Gellions – still serving drinks now) and one coffee house for around 3,000 inhabitants. The social focus of the Highland capital was really the Clach na Cuddain, *the 'Stone of the Tubs', so called because washer-women rested their heavy tubs on it as they came back into town from the banks of the River Ness. Probably a prehistoric standing stone, it is a reminder that not everything in 18th-century Inverness was unwashed.*

The *Caledonian Mercury* reported that Jacobite supporters were delighted and 'balls and dances were held by the disaffected ladies'. But Edinburgh was not a city sympathetic to the Stuart cause and it had closed its gates to the Highland army only seven months before. A young David Hume had translated his progressive philosophical convictions into action when he joined the muster of the militia to defend the walls.

What the impetuous horseman had seen 300 miles to the north at Culloden was the beginning of a battle. Had he waited less than an hour before galloping off, he would have carried very different news to the disaffected ladies and gentlemen. After a lethal preliminary of government cannon fire that ploughed through the ranks of the Highland army and a fatal period of dithering by Prince Charles, who had taken personal command of the army for the first and last time, the clansmen on the right had broken into the charge.

Probably already on horseback, the courier will have seen the Atholl Brigade, Clan Chattan, Clan Cameron and the Appin Stewarts tearing across the moor, screaming their war cries and clashing their broadswords into the ranks of redcoat bayonets. Steel rang against steel and Highlanders ran through the gaps in the government lines where the cannon had been emplaced. Gillies MacBean, a captain of Clan Chattan, broke through the front rank, killing several men. John MacGillivray also breached their lines, killing 12 men before breaking through the second rank. He was finally cut down by the men of the reserve battalion in the rear.

The premature joy of the courier, circling on what was probably a skittish, terrified horse, was understandable. Not only was it difficult to see through the smoke and chaos of a thousand-metre battle front, there was every reason to believe that the Highland army's ferocious charge would once again prove irresistible. In a matter of only ten minutes, the clansmen had scattered Sir John Cope's army at Prestonpans in September 1745 and at Falkirk, only a few weeks before Culloden, the redcoats had again turned and run as the claymores had whirled over the heads. Battles can turn on moments and James Wolfe, a young officer who would later find a brief but fatal fame on the Heights of Abraham in Canada, watched Barrell's Regiment stand their ground:

They were attacked by the Camerons (the bravest clan among them), and 'twas for some time a dispute between the swords and bayonets; but the latter was found by far the most destructible weapon. The regiment behaved with uncommon resolution, killing, some say, almost their own number, whereas forty of them were only wounded, and those not mortally and not above ten killed. They were, however, surrounded by superiority, and would have been all destroyed had not Col. Martin with his regiment (the left of the second line of foot) moved forward to their assistance, prevented mischief, and by a well-timed fire destroyed a great number of them and obliged them to run off.

Over on the left of the Jacobite lines the MacDonald regiments failed to engage properly with the government troops, having been driven back by intense musket fire. In the centre, boggy ground had forced the charge of some clans to veer right and they collided with the Atholl Brigade, forcing them against the drystane dykes of an enclosure. Firing by rank, the government troops held firm, stopped the careering momentum of the charge and drove the Highlanders back. They had no other tactic, the charge had failed, the battle was lost and a great slaughter began.

An accurate version of events far to the north finally reached Edinburgh just after midnight on 19 April. The *Caledonian Mercury* reported that the celebrations and dances of the disaffected ladies suddenly ceased when 'their mirth was interrupted about one on the Sunday morning by a round of great guns from the Castle'. Government messengers had finally entered the city and informed the Governor of the Castle that the Duke of Cumberland's army had routed the rebels. When they heard the salvo, the commanders of Royal Navy warships lying at anchor in Leith Roads answered with one of their own. And, as a further example, the Governor handed down a severe and humiliating punishment to one of his own gunners for drinking the health of Prince Charles. After a frame of halberds had been set up in a triangle, the man was stripped of his shirt and tied to the uprights. The drummers rolled up their sleeves, picked up the cat-o'-nine-tails and lacerated his back with 300 lashes. To silence lingering Jacobite sympathies, the gunner was drummed out of the Castle and made to stagger, bleeding and half-naked, through the streets for all to see.

Far, far worse had been seen on Culloden field. Prince Charles had been led away by his lifeguards to become a fugitive in the heather and eventually a bitter, resentful exile in Italy. His men were less fortunate. Perhaps as many as 2,000 Highlanders died on that terrible day – many of them slowly and in agony. Cannonballs maimed as often as they killed outright and the same was true of musket balls and wounds from bladed weapons. Often pinned under dead comrades, many bled to death, passing in and out of consciousness, sometimes screaming in terminal agony. Government burial parties reported many wounded Highlanders still alive in the evening of the battle and veterans believed they had never before seen such carnage. It temporarily unhinged some men and an officer reported: 'The moor was covered with blood and our men, what with killing the enemy, dabbling their feet in the blood, and splashing it about one another, looked like so many butchers rather than Christian soldiers.'

In Edinburgh, it was the turn of the Whigs, the supporters of the House of Hanover, to celebrate. As Jacobites closed up their houses and quietly slipped out of the city, the Edinburgh mob assembled. Fuelled by drink as well as hatred, they made effigies of Prince Charles and the Pope and hanged them. Any unfortunate suspected of sympathy for the Stuarts was set upon and worse. And a day was set aside by the bailies for public thanksgiving. The more genteel Whigs held parties and dances.

Culloden was a catastrophe for the clans and clan society and certainly fatal for the Stuart cause. But, as much as the battle was decisive, it was the appalling aftermath that changed the Highlands utterly and attitudes as well as actions turned history against the clans.

Amongst the aristocracy and the gentry, there appears to have existed something approaching a genuine political divide, more than a simple loyalty or sense of obligation. It occasionally pulled families apart. When the Jacobite Earl of Kilmarnock found himself surrounded by government cavalry after his regiment had fled Culloden field, he had no option but to surrender. As he passed through the lines of the Royal Scots Fusiliers, tears streamed down the old man's face and a young officer came forward to hold a hat in front so that others might not see his distress. It was Lord James Boyd, Kilmarnock's son.

The fate of other Jacobite aristocrats was less chivalrous but the gulf between them and their Whig counterparts was as nothing compared to what was to happen to ordinary Highlanders and their way of life. For these people, stocksmen, fishermen, and farmers, Culloden was a cultural and economic disaster.

Once the execution parties led by General Hawley had bayoneted the wounded who lay on the moor, even more destructive work awaited the government army. In order to extinguish the threat of Jacobite rebellion completely and to secure his family's hold on the throne of Great Britain, the Duke of Cumberland set in train a systematic programme of mass punishment, plunder, rape and killing.

Flogging the Forces

To prevent looting after victory at Culloden, at least by the enlisted men, the government army used the medieval threat of the cat-o'-nine-tails. This was a whip of several strands with small slivers of bone or metal attached so that the lashes administered ripped out lumps of flesh from the backs of the guilty. This brutal punishment was part of a long tradition in the British army and navy. If a soldier was caught stealing or committing any other specified offence, he could be sentenced to an extraordinary number of lashes; the maximum could be 2,000 with 200 given each morning for 10 days. The routine was always the same. Soldiers were mustered in a hollow square to see very rough justice done, both as a punishment for the guilty and as a deterrent. Long spears known as halberds were still carried by sergeants in the British army in the 18th century and three or four were tied together to form an elongated cross shape. Offenders had their wrists and ankles secured to the halberds before drummers rolled up their sleeves and began to lash their backs. Buckets of cold water were on hand in case of fainting. As blood spurted and gouts of flesh flew and men screamed in agony, generals maintained that such severity was essential in a modern army. Flogging was only abolished in 1881.

Having established garrisons at a chain of forts along the length of the Great Glen, reaching from what became Fort George near Inverness down to Fort Augustus, Fort William and beyond to Castle Stalker in Appin, he directed his commanders to send raiding parties into the hinterlands on either side. Encountering little or no resistance, they reived all the livestock they could find, driving vast herds of cattle, sheep, horses and goats back to the forts. One captain counted more than 8,000 head of cattle taken in a single raid. It made little difference whether or not their owners had supported Prince Charles or not. Some had papers of indemnity but they were often ignored. An entire people were made to pay for the treason of a few, guilty or not. Around Fort Augustus, the fields were grazed bare by incoming stolen livestock.

Reiving turned out to be profitable work for the occupying army. Lowland Scots and northern English cattle dealers quickly came north in search of bargains and paid the quartermasters rock-bottom prices. During the summer of 1746, when enough grass had grown for long-distance droving, immense herds were seen moving south through the mountain passes. Many turned immediate profits at the Falkirk markets and those who stayed on the move, crossing the hill trails over the Cheviots, sometimes made fortunes in the hungry English cities. Cumberland did not care. His overriding purpose was not profit but to drain the lifeblood out of the Highland economy, a way of life that had been based on stock rearing for many centuries.

The Duke wanted to move more than beasts. In a proposal made to the Prime Minister, the Duke of Newcastle, he advocated mass deportations, an early example of ethnic cleansing. He explained: 'I mean the transporting of particular clans, such as the entire Clan of the Camerons and almost all the tribes of the McDonalds (excepting some of those of the Isles) and several other lesser Clans, of which an exact list may easily be made.'

All that long summer of terror and destruction, Prince Charles remained a fugitive in the Highlands. Many were suspected of harbouring him and the hunt for the leadership of the rebellion, including the likes of Cameron of Lochiel, was used as a pretext for countless acts of savagery. Many murders, rapes and house burnings were reported and doubtless many were not. The hatred of Cumberland and his English officers and men for the High-landers is perhaps explicable. All they knew of Gaelic-speaking culture was that it came racing across the heather, roaring for blood and death, a swarm of half-naked primitives. It seemed that their war bands could materialise out of the mists, they lived in huts made out of sods and stone and spoke to each other in an alien language. Amongst monoglot English-speakers, this last is still a cause of uneasiness but, in 1746, it was yet another sign of backwardness. It was easy to convert babbling, barbarian, often papist Highlanders into subhumans and treat them as such.

What is more surprising is a sustained – and comparatively well-recorded – streak of sadism meted out by Lowland Scots who fought in the government army. The excesses of three officers in particular showed how wide the gulf was between the peoples who lived on either side of the Highland Line. Familiarity bred something much more than contempt.

One Major I. Lockhart of Cholmondley's Regiment led an expedition out of Fort Augustus into the lands of the Grants of Glenmoriston. They lay to the north-west of the Great Glen. Having first shot three clansmen for no other reason than they had met them on the road, Lockhart's men began to round up grazing cattle belonging to Grant of Dundreggan. When the old man appeared with a certificate of immunity signed by the Earl of Loudon and clearly attesting that he had had no involvement whatever with the rebellion, Lockhart ignored it. When Grant persisted, he had the laird stripped naked and prepared to have him hanged next to the corpses of the men killed on the road. At that moment, soldiers dragged Mrs Grant, also stripped naked, next to the tree where the bodies had been strung up and tried to cut off her fingers to get her rings.

It was too much for one young officer in Lockhart's troop. Also by the name of Grant, he was a Highlander who had marched behind Cumberland's standards and he threatened to draw his sword to protect the terrified and patently innocent people. Surprisingly, Lockhart accepted the rebuke and signalled for his men to fall in and move further up Glenmoriston. There, women were raped outside their front doors as children scattered and their houses were fired. Isobel MacDonald suffered dreadfully as she was repeatedly raped by five soldiers as her husband watched, hidden in the heather. And all were left with nothing as their cattle, their only source of sustenance, were driven over the passes to the Great Glen, Fort Augustus and the cattle dealers from the south.

Captain Caroline Scott was an intriguingly named Lowland officer in Guise's Regiment and he had the distinction of holding Fort William against the rebels. But the charm ended emphatically with his unusual Christian name. After Culloden, he embarked on a series of expeditions of terrible vengeance, hanging, raping and burning houses indiscriminately. However, it was a minor act of random malice that made the attitudes behind the routine savagery even starker. On the road near Fort William, Scott's soldiers took hold of an old woman and cut off all her hair. They joked it would make a good wig for a gentleman. Pitifully humiliated, the old lady asked for the return of her handkerchief so that she might cover her bleeding and scalped head. Instead the soldiers kicked her, calling her an old bitch.

An Aberdeen sea captain, John Fergusson, sailed HMS *Furnace* to the Hebrides where it harried the isles in the summer of 1746. His men raped a blind woman on the island of Rona, off Skye, and killed and burned wherever they disembarked. When Fergusson ordered the vicious flogging of a captured officer (who had been commissioned in the French army and was therefore not a rebel but a prisoner of war), a lieutenant in the Royal Scots Fusiliers intervened and stopped it. Brave enough, but there is no record of him or any other more principled soldier attempting to mitigate the appalling treatment of ordinary Highland men and women.

HMS *Furnace* was also a prison ship and, as it nosed around the islands and sea lochs, arrests of suspected and admitted rebels were made. Conditions in the hold were dreadful and some men were held there for eight months, slowly rotting and starving to death. When food was lowered down, it was often fouled. According to Donald Macleod, a survivor, 'The victuals were brought to the prisoners in foul nasty buckets, wherein the fellows [the sailors] used to piss for a piece of ill-natured diversion.'

On 4 June 1746, a strange ceremony took place in Edinburgh, an event emblematic of Lowland attitudes to the Jacobite rebellion and the clansmen who had occupied the city only eight months before. All but two of the standards that flew over the Highland army at Culloden had been captured and brought south to Edinburgh Castle. On the appointed day, the Prince's personal standard was carried out on to Castlehill by the city hangman, John Dalgleish. In procession behind him down to the Lawnmarket and the Mercat Cross came an extraordinary sight. Carrying the colours of Clan Cameron, the Atholl Brigade and the MacDonald regiments and other clans were the chimney sweeps of Edinburgh. With blackened faces and sooty hands, they cavorted around, dragging the silk standards through the dust and rubbish of the streets. A huge crowd jeered and spat on the emblems of the hated Highlanders, rejoicing in their complete defeat. Captured colours were usually kept and treasured by victorious armies as physical evidence of battle honours, of pride and prestige. But these were the flags, the rags of savages, tribesmen, people scarcely human – they had no value and they deserved no respect.

At the Mercat Cross, a fire had been lit and the rebel standards were trailed on the ground around it and probably stamped on by the crowds. From the narrow parapet, a herald proclaimed that these symbols of rebellion were to be burned by the public hangman. Then, to thunderous cheering, each was held over the flames and the clan it belonged to was named – and the crowd howled derision.

The Duke of Cumberland had further ordered that a campaign medal be struck for Culloden, one of the earliest ever made. On one side was the portly duke's profile and on the other the figure of Apollo pointing at a wounded dragon, an inscription, 'ACTUM EST ILICET PERIIT', and the date 'AP XVI MDCCXLVI'. The Latin inscription translates as 'The deed is done, it is all over'. And it was. By the end of that summer of terror, thousands of Highlanders had been killed, the economy ruined and its culture fatally wounded.

Those who visit the country beyond the Highland Line now often sense a great weight of sadness, of emptiness. It is more than that. Beyond the line, beyond the sentinel mountains, lies the landscape of defeat.

Two Scotlands collided at Culloden and, in its vicious aftermath, one was determined upon the destruction of the other. Up on Drumossie Moor, on the edges of the Highland Line, there stand cairns and headstones marking the mass graves of the dead, the burial place of a culture. Melancholic and windswept, the battlefield is not the only monument to the passing of the clans.

Eight miles to the north, at Ardersier, on a spit of low-lying land reaching into the Moray Firth, stands Fort George. It was the most extensive, mightiest and most expensive artillery fortification ever built in Britain and one of the largest in Europe. Completed in 1769, its cost soared over budget and, at more than £200,000, it was greater than the gross domestic product for the whole of Scotland in 1750.

Built to withstand a heavy artillery assault, the fort is laid out in an extended star shape. The stone-faced walls are many metres thick and their wide and flat tops are grassed over. Bastions project in such a way as to allow defending gunners to rake their fire along the face of the walls and discourage assailants with siege ladders. Under the massive walls are heavily fortified vaults where the garrison could seek shelter from bombardment. The immense defences are concentrated to the southern, landward side of the fort while the sea walls are noticeably less substantial. So that the garrison could withstand a long siege, there is a harbour below the coastal defences to allow supply by sea.

All of which is puzzling. The Jacobite army so recently routed at Culloden had little effective artillery and even less skill at using it. As an army, they were incapable of laying down the sort of heavy bombardment that would chase Fort George's defenders into the vaults below the walls. For all of their military success, the clans depended absolutely on the fury and power of the charge and they had neither the knowledge nor the inclination to conduct siege warfare. The design of Fort George seems entirely inappropriate, an enormously expensive deterrent aimed at the wrong enemy. An essentially medieval army that fought with bladed weapons, the clans would never have contemplated attacking it.

It may be that the London government and its military planners had the Stuarts' European supporters, the likes of the fickle French, in mind when they decided to build massive artillery bastions at Ardersier. But, if that were so, then why did the fort's defences concentrate on the landward side, facing the mountains, rather than the seaward?

The 80 guns mounted along the walls were never once fired in anger but they were effective in another way. As a blunt statement of power, of the absolute determination of the London government to crush any future sedition in the Highlands, Fort George was eloquent. Its barracks could accommodate two field battalions, 2,000 men and officers, and, at 42 acres, it was a large military town. Gaelic speakers called it simply *An Gearasdan*, 'The Garrison'.

Fort George was also a focus for another, perhaps more effective, facet of government policy. In the early 18th century, independent companies of soldiers raised from clans loyal to the new dynasty of Hanoverian kings had been deployed to keep order in the Highlands. Their policing duties conferred an enduring name. By 1729, there were six companies and, in Gaelic, they were known as *Am Freiceadan Dubh*, 'The Black Watch'. As an excellent night camouflage, they adopted a navy blue, black and dark green sett for their kilts, what was called the government tartan. In 1740, the Black Watch became the 43rd Regiment of the line and in 1745, when Prince Charles was raising the clans in rebellion, they were fighting under the command of the Duke of Cumberland. At the Battle of Fontenoy against the French, near Tournai in the modern-day Belgium close to the border with France, the Black Watch made an impression. When he saw them charge, the commander of the Brigade du Dauphin was shocked at the 'Highland furies who rushed upon us with more violence than the sea when driven by a tempest'.

As Britain began to see and actively seek opportunities to compile an overseas empire, in the aftermath of Fontenoy and the Seven Years War, the young Prime Minister, William Pitt, believed the army to be desperately short of men. He wrote to the king, seeking to justify the recruitment of men whose chiefs had led them into the charge at Culloden only ten years before: 'I sought for merit wherever it was to be found. It is my boast that I was the first minister who looked for it and found it in the mountains of the north. I called it forth and drew into your service a hardy and intrepid race of men . . . They served with fidelity as they fought with valour and conquered for you in every part of the world.'

One of the first Highland regiments to fight in North America was the Fraser Highlanders. Raised from his estates by the Master of Lovat, Simon Fraser, whose father of the same name had been executed for treason after the Jacobite Rebellion, they fought under the command of General James Wolfe, another veteran of Culloden. On the Heights of Abraham, near the French town of Quebec, they charged Montcalm's army and defeated it. But Wolfe's view of these brave men was cynical:

'The Highlanders are hardy, intrepid, accustomed to rough country, and it is no great mischief if they fall. How can you better employ a secret enemy than by making his end conducive to the common good?'

Recruitment gathered pace and, as the Highlands emptied of young men, the guns at Fort George looked ever more forlorn, an overblown legacy of fear and suspicion. But the parade ground and the barrack blocks were well used. Between 1756 and 1815 at least 40,000 clansmen, perhaps as many as 75,000, were called to the colours and a large proportion drilled at Fort George. It became the depot of the Seaforth Highlanders and later a base for the Lovat Scouts. After 2007, history came full circle when the very first of many distinguished Highland regiments, the Black Watch, marched through the massive gateway as the new garrison.

Less a symbol of military control, or even a powerful discouragement to rebellion, Fort George became something darker, more sinister. As the glens were emptied and farmsteads abandoned, it was a conduit through which Highlanders passed on their way to win an empire and, in so doing, pay a blood price for rebellion.

2

Land of Mountain and Flood

✻

N O OTHER COUNTRY ON the planet has geology more varied than Scotland's. Hundreds of millions of years ago, when the Earth was very young and its crust was moving, forming, splintering and reforming vast primordial continents, pieces sometimes broke off. Known as terranes, they drifted across the ancient oceans, pushed on by tectonic forces, and were bulldozed into other landmasses. What became Scotland was welded together from four terranes of very different kinds and ages and their remains and the places where they joined can still be clearly seen.

The oldest of the terranes formed the Western Isles, Coll, Tiree, Iona, the western peninsula of Islay, the Rhinns, and the Atlantic edges of the north-west Highlands, from Cape Wrath to the Kyles of Lochalsh. More than three billion years old, the rocks of these islands and coastlines are made from Lewisian gneiss. Tremendously hard, gneiss was forged deep in the molten crust of the Earth and gradually forced upwards and cooled. Wind, water and ice erosion wore away the rocks that covered it and now outcrops of this beautiful and very ancient stone can be seen all over the Hebrides and the north-west Highlands.

The singular mountain of Suilven is a monument to how dynamic the movement of the surface of the forming continents could be. Along with the glens and mountains of Applecross and

Torridon, it is made from thick layers of red sandstone shunted over the Lewisian gneiss by tectonic movement. Geologists believe that these sedimentary rocks were laid down by rivers flowing down from the mountains of a huge palaeocontinent known as Laurentia. Now long fragmented, this vast landmass helped weld together the striking landscape of the Scottish Highlands. Many millions of years ago, other layers were deposited. Durness limestone is thought to be the residue of beach deposits on the coasts of Laurentia.

The line of the Great Glen marks the divide between two terranes and shows the angle at which they collided. To the south lie Dalriadan rocks, mostly strata of sandstone, shale and limestone. They were subjected to violent geological change as volcanoes and Ice Ages moved and moulded them.

The abrupt nature of the Highland Boundary Fault, the Highland Line, makes the collision of two very different terranes abundantly clear. In a remarkable aerial photograph taken by Patricia MacDonald as she flew over Loch Lomond, the fault is obvious. A corrugated, buckled ridge can be seen climbing out of the waters of the loch and up Conic Hill before carrying on through the high moorland to the east. Four small islands lying across the foot of the loch also carry the marks of the ancient drama. North of the buckled ridge is mountainous and immediately to the south green farmland stretches out. Seen from the air, the contrast is startling, abrupt.

When the two terranes were first joined, the mountains to the north-west were very high, as high as the Himalayas are now. The sunken Midland Valley, what Scots call the Central Belt, was originally formed in tropical latitudes. Vast and dense forests grew in swamps and, as they died and fell, layers of organic carbon accumulated. As more trees grew and eventually collapsed into the boggy ground, they compressed the original layers to make seams of coal. In historic times, these would become extremely important. The earliest recorded digging of coal was in the outcrops known as heughs and it was organised by medieval monks at draughty abbeys such as Newbattle near Edinburgh.

And, from the 18th century onwards, industrial-scale extraction fuelled the growth of manufacturing in Central Scotland.

Running at approximately the same angle as the Highland Boundary Fault and the Great Glen, the Southern Upland Fault follows a line from Ballantrae in Ayrshire across to Dunbar in East Lothian. The rolling hills of Galloway and the Borders were originally the bed of an ancient ocean and they were planed and smoothed by millions of years of wind, rain and ice.

The final divide between the four terranes that make up Scotland is perhaps the least dramatic but the most informative. On the rocky western coast of the Isle of Man, near the hamlet of Niarbyl, the cliffs of a secluded cove have preserved something unique, the key to a fundamental understanding of the geology and landscape of all Scotland. A thin, greyish-white seam of rock runs diagonally down to the shore before disappearing below the waves of the Irish Sea. It marks exactly the point at which two gigantic continents collided an unimaginably long time ago and it is the only place on Earth where what is known as the Iapetus Suture can be clearly seen.

Approximately 410 million years ago, a vast prehistoric sea called the Iapetus Ocean was shrinking. It lay between three palaeocontinents – Laurentia, Baltica and Avalonia. The combined terranes of Scotland had been driven towards Laurentia and attached to its southern edge while what was to become England, Wales and southern Ireland lay on the northern shores of Avalonia. As the Iapetus Ocean narrowed and tectonic movement drove Scotland and England inexorably towards each other, they slid together at a particular angle, corrugating the crust of the Earth into high mountains and deep valleys. The north-east to south-west lines of all of the faults, from the Great Glen to the Iapetus Suture, run in the same direction because of the angle of that ancient collision.

The basic shape of Scotland was made when Laurentia was bulldozed into Avalonia and its internal boundaries were defined when the four very different terranes came together. But, 65 million years ago, the Atlantic Ocean did not exist and Scotland

and England were attached to North America. And then fire and ice began to move mountains and continents.

A tear appeared in the Earth's crust and it had the effect of stretching it and making it thinner. As Scotland and England became detached and shifted eastwards, the Atlantic began to fill. Volcanoes erupted, bursting through the surface and a line of them ran from St Kilda to Ailsa Craig in the Firth of Clyde. There exists a very obvious caldera of a huge volcano on the Ardnamurchan peninsula but Skye is the most spectacular example of how fire formed the Highlands. Trotternish was made from old lava fields and the magma formed the jagged ranges of the Black Cuillin on one side and the Red Cuillin on the other.

The ice came much later. A long 2.4-million-year period of Ice Ages has just ended or perhaps only paused. At its maximum extent, the last Ice Age covered Scotland and the north of England completely. Only 15,000 years ago a pitiless white landscape buried and crushed the mountains and glens. In places it could be more than a kilometre thick and nothing and no one could survive in what was a sub-polar climate. Hurricanes roared almost incessantly around the base of vast spherical mountains known as ice-domes and all living things were erased from Scotland.

Ice Ages were probably caused by slight variations in the Earth's orbit around the Sun. When, at last, it moved back into kilter, some time around 11,000 BC, the weather began to warm and the ice started to melt. This probably happened quickly, over only a few decades. Glaciers moved, cracked and sheared and their massive weight rumbled and scarted over the landscape. Carrying all sorts of rocky debris inside them, the great frozen rivers acted like gigantic earth movers, breaking open water courses, scooping out high corries and deepening valley floors. Because of higher rain- and snowfall, the glaciers were thicker over the Highlands and steeper gradients meant they moved faster and were formidably powerful. Meltwater rivers rushed with such tremendous force that they sometimes flowed uphill and over watershed ridges. For these reasons, the melting ice had more dramatic effects north of the Highland Line, reshaping the landscape and turning many of the river systems so that they ran westwards into the Atlantic.

In the south and east of Scotland and very noticeably in the North-east, the Moray coastlands and the Buchan, the ice had much less impact. In fact, the glaciers delivered benefits as they deposited gravels and mixtures of clay that formed the bedrock of the more fertile soils found in the broadening valleys of what became the Lowlands.

As the land warmed and the ice retreated, vegetation began to flourish. At first, this probably took the form of the sort of summer grazing seen for a few short months in the Arctic tundras of North America and Siberia. Then as now, the lush, sweet forage drew herds of browsing animals northwards, deer, reindeer and wild horses, and behind them came predators. One of the most resourceful of these was the human being and evidence of a summer hunting expedition has been found on Islay. Dating to around 10,000 BC, a very particular style of flint arrowhead was picked up on a ploughed field in the Rhinns, the island's western peninsula. But it was to be a fleeting reoccupation.

Far to the west, across the Atlantic, a cataclysmic event was about to engulf the world. As the ice melted in northern Canada, it drained into a huge lake, much larger than the North Sea. Hemmed in by ice dams, it began to trickle over its southern ramparts to form the Mississippi river system. But, some time around 9,400 BC, the dams to the north suddenly collapsed. Vast volumes of very cold freshwater broke into the Mackenzie River basin and, within 36 hours, a tsunami was racing into the Arctic and Atlantic oceans.

The Earth's sea levels rose by three metres, no doubt drowning many coastal communities. The effect on Scotland was much more long lasting, more devastating. Such a large volume of freshwater had the catastrophic effect of turning aside the Gulf Stream. Instead of warming the coasts of Scotland and maintaining a temperate climate, it could not reach them and, as a direct and immediate result, the cold returned. Ice and snow lay all year round and, over the mountain spine of Drumalban, from Ben Lomond to Assynt, a huge ice dome reformed. The small bands of pioneers who had returned north quickly retreated and, for more than a thousand years, no one lived in Scotland.

After the Atlantic had diluted the vast volume of freshwater and regained its salinity and the Gulf Stream flowed north once more, the land began to assume its modern appearance. The most profound and perhaps least noticeable recovery was what is known as isostatic uplift. When the great weight of the ice was removed, the crust of the Earth bounced back. It rose most at Rannoch Moor. And, as the huge volumes of water locked up in the ice were released, sea levels also rose. Sometimes these outpaced the rising land and around 5,000 BC northern Scotland almost became an island when the Firth of Clyde broke into Loch Lomond and came close to linking with the Forth. It reached inland as far as Aberfoyle, leaving only a ten-mile wide land bridge connecting the south with the north. When the Forth shrank back to its present levels, it left a wide expanse of boggy and treacherous marshland in its wake. Known as Flanders Moss it divided Scotland more emphatically than any stretch of clear and navigable water and, as late as the 12th century, mapmakers marked the north as 'Scotland Beyond the Sea'.

Out in the Atlantic, more drama waited – an event that would change the climate and the economy of the Highlands. Precisely dated by a study of ancient tree rings, an Icelandic volcano called Hekla erupted in 1159 BC. When the mountain blew itself apart, thunder boomed out across the ocean, a roar that could be heard on the western coasts of Scotland. At a devastating 500 kilometres an hour, a tsunami raced towards coastal communities but, even more destructive, millions of tonnes of ash and debris rocketed into the atmosphere. Perhaps only hours after the tsunami had smashed onshore, the prehistoric peoples of the western Highlands and islands will have seen the sky darken and thunder and lightning crackle and flash. Over the dark mountains, a foul, acidic rain will have fallen.

The eruption of Hekla created a volcanic winter that lasted a generation. Tree ring analysis shows little or no growth for 18 years after 1159 BC. That meant famine and animals and people will have died in their thousands. The Hebrides and the western glens emptied as the land withered into a cold, wet, toxic desert. And many of those who survived are likely to have moved east over the mountain passes to the sanctuary of the Lowlands.

By the beginning of the second millennium BC, peat had begun to cover parts of the Highlands and Islands. Using archaeological remains found under the layers of peat to date the beginning of the process, researchers have estimated its early stages at Rosinish on Benbecula to around 2,300 BC and it seems that, after Hekla, peat began to form at the feet of the sacred complex of standing stones at Callanish on the Isle of Lewis. The great eruption seems to have accelerated the blanketing of the landscape with these soggy, acidic deposits of vegetation and, as more rain fell, more people were driven to move eastwards.

Because of the deteriorating weather and the dwindling population, agriculture became increasingly focused on stock rearing. A lack of suitable, well-drained, peat-free land restricted arable farming and the labour to manage it was also no longer available. Hardy cattle, sheep and goats needed many fewer people to look after them and they could survive in a rain-soaked landscape so long as sufficient grass grew amongst the bracken and the heather. In this way climate, geography and culture combined to make a clear distinction. Those who lived north of the Highland Line were usually herdsmen who tended their beasts on open winter and summer grazing, and who counted their wealth in head of cattle, while in the Lowlands mixed farming, both arable and stock-rearing, was developed on the more fertile soils. And these men measured their wealth in the amount of land they owned or controlled. This fundamental difference between the lives of ploughmen and shepherds would further drive these communities apart and the men who faced each other across the heather at Culloden had much more than language, allegiance and dress to divide them.

These ancient geological and meteorological dramas are not mere footnotes or academic titbits for the curious – they were absolutely determinant for all of our history. Geology moulded the land and the land moulded the people.

3

Moray

❋

I N T H E D A R K D E P T H S of the Cave of the Child-Dead, torches flickered in the draughts as priests laid out the bodies of the little ones. Watched by distraught and grieving parents, the ceremonies began, perhaps with chanting and music, certainly with an atmosphere of solemnity. And then, the extraordinary climax came. Raising a heavy axe above his head, a priest decapitated the child and spitted the severed head on a sharpened pole. This was taken out of the darkness, to the entrance to the cave and planted in the sand and shingle. There the child's dead eyes could look out over the grey sea while its body was defleshed and eventually laid beside the white bones of other children deep in the chill of the sacred cave.

These things happened. Excavations over a long period at what is known as The Sculptor's Cave at Covesea, near Lossiemouth on the coast of the Moray Firth, have uncovered evidence of remarkable prehistoric rituals. Only accessible at low tide and, according to one archaeologist, 'never touched by the sun', the cave opens through two entrance passages at the foot of a sheer sandstone cliff. In prehistoric times, it may have been surrounded by the sea – perhaps it became the Isle of the Dead – and even more difficult to reach.

It was a liminal place and in many senses. In the absence of texts and with little more than the stones and bones of archaeology as an uncertain guide, the beliefs of the early peoples of Scotland can only be surmised. But it seems that caves were places of great spirituality, portals to another world. Three thousand years ago, when the children at Covesea were decapitated, the cosmos had at least three clear spheres – this was the familiar system of an underworld, the Earth and the heavens above. Many Christians still visualise the dark and fiery pits of Hell below us, the temporal and temporary world we live in and a paradise floating somewhere overhead.

These labels and the characteristics attached to them are, of course, recent and are unlikely to have been shared by the people who made the difficult journey to the Covesea cave. If they committed the souls of their dead children in that place by choice, it is unlikely that it will have had hellish connotations. More probable is the sense of Earth gods and goddesses, deities or spiritual forces that might somehow receive their young ones, dead before their time. And perhaps it was significant that the sun never shone into the entrances of the cave.

What certainly mattered in the ancient belief system of the people of Covesea was something atmospheric, even mysterious. In the shadowy depths of the cave, there is a pool of water. Still and shimmering, it was sacred, perhaps the focus of the shrine. Valuable bronze and iron objects were found in or near it – and that was by no means unusual. All over Britain and much of Europe, prehistoric peoples cast metal objects, their most precious portable possessions, into pools, lochs, rivers and other watery places. Clearly they believed the gods to reside below the dark lustre of the water. At Covesea and elsewhere, it was not a pool but a bridge to another world.

In 1929 and 1930, Sylvia Benton and a team of local workmen found more than 1,800 human bones. It appeared that the cave had been used as an ossuary and, as in communal chambered tombs in Orkney and elsewhere, the skeletons had been disarticulated. Metal objects uncovered amongst the debris dated the earliest use of what seemed to be a shrine to some time around 1,000 BC. Many bones belonged to children and a close examination of the cervical vertebrae showed that they had been decapitated, almost certainly when they were already dead.

After two centuries or so, it seems that beliefs shifted elsewhere and the bones in the cave lay undisturbed for many years. Working through the strata, Sylvia Benton's team came across clear evidence of a later revival, a time when people began to come back to Covesea with their dead. Roman coins, pins, beads and bracelets were discovered and the excavators were able to date the second period to the 2nd, 3rd and 4th centuries AD.

When archaeologists again took an interest in this fascinating site in the late 1970s, new techniques allowed a great deal more precision. Near the entrances to the cave shrine, Ian and Alexandra Shepherd made an arresting find. They came across the lower jawbones of several children. It appeared that once they had been decapitated, their severed heads had been displayed on poles. And, as the flesh and hair fell away in the winds and rain that blew in off the Moray Firth and the little skulls were exposed, the lower jaws became detached and dropped to the ground. But, strangely, no skulls were found.

When the Shepherds looked more closely at the cervical vertebrae under powerful microscopes, they could see that one had been cut clean through by a single chopping stroke. Smiths working in bronze around 1,000 BC could not have produced a blade hard and sharp enough to cut through bone in that way. Other vertebrae showed signs of marks made by equally sharp and heavy blades. Were there two distinct periods in the life of the cave shrine when severed heads were set up for veneration of some kind? Radiocarbon dating was conclusive. One of the vertebrae was cut some time between 231 AD and 395 AD. This incontrovertibly placed the second occupation of Covesea in what is often called the Iron Age, a time when heavy and fearsomely sharp weapons were forged.

What also intrigued the Shepherds was a clear change in emphasis. The later severed heads, from the 3rd and 4th centuries AD, were almost all adults and only one of the cervical vertebrae came from the skeleton of a child. Once more, beliefs were shifting.

There was, however, one constant, something shared by the

prehistoric peoples of the Moray Firth with many Celtic societies across Western Europe. In his history of the Roman conquest of what became France, *De Bello Gallico*, Julius Caesar was struck by the importance of the human head in the beliefs of his enemies. Because they believed absolutely in an afterlife, the warriors he faced could be recklessly brave and very difficult to subdue. Moreover, some even fought naked in battle, certain of the protection of their gods. Not only did they believe their soul to be indestructible in death, they also thought that it resided in their heads. And if you cut off the head of an adversary, you could capture his soul. Plutarch described the actions of a Celtic nation known as the Senones when they defeated a Roman legion at Clusium in Northern Italy:

> They cut off the heads of enemies slain in battle and attach them to the necks of their horses. The bloodstained spoils they hand over to their attendants and carry off as booty, while striking up a paean and singing a song of victory; and they nail up these first fruits on their houses . . . They embalm in cedar oil the heads of the most distinguished enemies, and preserve them carefully in a chest and display them with pride to strangers, saying that for this head one of their ancestors, or his father, or the man himself, refused the offer of a large sum of money. They say that some of them boast that they refused the weight of the head in gold.

Across France and elsewhere, sacred sites have been excavated where heads were displayed in niches or in some other way. Dating mainly to the late first millennium BC, hundreds of heads carved in wood and stone have been found.

When Rome marched into the north of Britain after AD 70 and the legions moved against the Brigantes, a federation of kindreds straddling the Pennines, a pitched battle was fought at Stanwick, the site of a fort near Scotch Corner in Yorkshire. Amongst the debris at the foot of the ramparts, archaeologists were surprised to find skulls without associated skeletons and that they appeared to be older than the date of the battle. They had come across the remains of what became known as a ghost fence. When the legions attacked the Brigantian stronghold, their priests had set up a ring of skulls, certain that their immense power would turn back the Roman attack. But the gods and the souls of the dead failed them and Stanwick was overrun.

Off with their Heads

With more than 400 deities noted in one source or another, Celtic religious beliefs are far from clear or consistent but one theme recurs. It revolved around the importance of the head, apparently the locus of the soul for many Celts in Europe and in Britain and Ireland. As Julius Caesar noted in De Bello Gallico, *severed heads were displayed in sacred places and much sought after as trophies. In Scotland, at Lochend near Edinburgh, a multiple burial dating to the 1st or 2nd centuries AD has been found. The skeletons of at least twenty adults and one child were recovered. But seven skulls were missing, and the neck vertebrae showed that they had been removed by a deep sword cut to the neck at the time of death. Archaeologists made another telltale discovery. In the loose earth near the burial, they found six skulls. It appears that they had been placed there for display. Was another ghost fence built at Lochend? Much closer to Covesea, Sueno's Stone in Moray was carved in the 9th century AD. It carries a very graphic representation of a battle. One of the sequences on this famous Pictish stone is particularly gory – a row of headless bodies, presumably the defeated whose heads had become trophies.*

It may well be that, at Covesea, similar beliefs were at work. When the priests decapitated the children and the older corpses, they may have set up their skulls on poles at the entrances to the cave as a ghost fence, a means of deterring any who might defile the sanctity of the shrine within. The souls of the dead may have been the guardians of an Otherworld, the realm of the ancestors, and perhaps the skulls of children were thought to possess a special, pristine power.

Twenty-first-century scientists have recently been able to add something more forensic to these fascinating mysteries and specifically to say more about the origins of the ancestors of the early peoples of Moray. As the decapitations in the cave show so vividly, these people did not think like us – but they did look like modern human beings. Apart from clothes, haircuts and other obvious accoutrements of 21st-century life, the major difference in the early population was demographic. Compared to modern society, they were young. Often because of complications in childbirth (in an era before contraception), women died earlier and, if they survived the years of fertility, they aged faster in a society without dentistry or antibiotics. For men, their life expectancy depended very much on what they did. As now, aristocrats and royalty lived longer than ordinary people. The one major difference was an assumption that men of noble birth would be warriors and such records as exist for early Scotland are littered with the bloody corpses of noblemen who fell in battle.

The people who entered the cave at Covesea were like us in another, very important way. Many modern Scots share their DNA. At the height of the last Ice Age, small communities outwintered the snows and storms in steep-sided valleys in southwest France and northern Spain. Known as the Ice Age refuges, these places sheltered a remarkable people. On the walls of dark, secret and sometimes precipitous caves they painted their world. At Lascaux, Chauvet, Altamira and in hundreds of other hidden places, herds of wild horses, deer, wild cattle and other animals thunder across the cave walls. Sometimes the paintings bear an eerie signature. After filling their mouths with pigment, artists placed a hand flat on the cave wall, sprayed over it and left a stencil.

The DNA marker (a variant specific to south-west France and northern Spain) of the male cave painters was M284. And, when the weather warmed and the ice began to retreat, men carrying this marker moved northwards. In a matter of only a few generations, many reached the furthest end of Europe, what would become Scotland. M284 became a founding lineage and now 4 per cent of all men living in Scotland, about 100,000, are their direct descendants. In the millennia immediately after the Ice Age this proportion will have been much higher and many of the people of Covesea will have been the direct descendants of the cave painters. But to infer any accompanying cultural transmission or a continuity of belief would be stretching the evidence to breaking point.

Until approximately 4,000 BC, there were large islands in the North Sea and, before then, much of the southern basin had been dry land, a lost subcontinent now known to scientists as Doggerland. Its 5,000-year history was an effect of the last Ice Age. Over Scandinavia, a huge ice dome pressed down on the crust of the Earth and, in turn, pushed up the land to the south in what is known by geologists as a forebulge. This extraordinary phenomenon, a lost world to the east of Britain, was very significant for our early history for it meant that the pioneers who populated Scotland after the ice could walk there.

While the cave painters came from the south, other founding lineages approached from the east, having crossed Doggerland, and yet more came from the west, approaching Scotland up the Irish Sea corridor. In Moray, the legacy of these ancient population movements is very striking. More than 27 per cent of all men in the coastlands (and down as far south as Stonehaven the proportion is 30 per cent) carry S21, a DNA marker that originated in northern Europe. By contrast, only 7 per cent of men in the Hebrides have it. There the pattern is reversed and most men carry S145, a marker that took a western route to Scotland and is rare in the east. The statistics do not exactly match the geography but the general pattern is clear. Allowing for a degree of modern population movement, the Y chromosome DNA of the eastern Lowlands of Scotland is different from that of the Highlands and the west. In a meaningful way, the Highland Line was, from early times, a frontier between peoples whose ancient origins differed significantly.

In England, Y chromosome DNA sampling has exposed a similar east–west divide despite a lack of dramatic geography. There is a simple but not immediately obvious reason for this. As a land-based culture used to travelling in vehicles of various sorts, we easily forget the historical role of seas, lochs and navigable rivers as highways. For all but the last 150 years, travel on water was faster and more reliable than any overland route. Ancient colonisation hugged the coastline as communities expanded or moved on into virgin or sparsely populated territory by boat, often in short-range hops. Britain's eastern and western coastlines are very much longer than its southern or northern and, once settlers had turned one way or the other, either into the Irish Sea or, after 4,000 BC, the North Sea, they moved north, using the sea as a highway. Early seaborne trading contacts further encouraged this east–west population split. Travel overland was only undertaken when absolutely necessary or where navigable rivers and lochs (such as in the Great Glen) made journeys manageable.

The greatest revolution in world history is also the most mysterious. Farming changed lives utterly but the processes and people who drove this revolution remain unknown. Only DNA research offers a sense of how ideas moved from one community to another and across continents. The domestication of animals and the cultivation of crops began in what used to be called the Fertile Crescent or Mesopotamia. Now Iraq and parts of Syria, it had a benign climate and was watered by two great rivers, the Tigris and Euphrates. Some time around 9,000 BC, the new techniques of food production began to spread and it appears that women were in the vanguard of this slowly evolving revolution.

Until the beginnings of mechanisation in the early 20th century, most of the routine drudgery of farm labour – jobs like weeding, mucking, milking, singling, shawing and sickle work – was done by women. In Scotland, they were latterly known as bondagers after the nature of their contracts with farmers. Over an enormous span of time, 11,000 years, it seems that little changed. Moving in step with the archaeology of the spread of farming across Europe, two mitochondrial DNA markers (the sort of DNA passed on by mothers to their daughters) can be detected approaching Scotland from both the east and the southwest. Around 4,000 BC, a new marker, mtDNAJ1b1, arrived in western Britain and Ireland. Approximately 3 per cent of Scottish women, or 75,000, still have it in their genes. Simultaneously, a second new marker made landfall in the east. This was mtDNA-J2a1 and it had made a long journey up the great river valleys of Europe, the Danube and the Rhine.

These women were not alone. Over a lengthy period after 4,000 BC, a new Y chromosome marker arrived and began to replicate very quickly indeed. Now R1b is carried by between 60 per cent and 70 per cent of all Scottish men, around 1.75 million. The reason for this explosion in the proportion of a particular marker must be associated with the success of farming. More food was produced, it fed more people and more people were needed to bring in bigger harvests and increase the size of herds and flocks. It appears that farming ignited a population explosion in prehistoric Scotland.

Language often follows population movement and new techniques demanded new vocabulary. It seems very likely that the spread of farming from Mesopotamia – east as well as west – also spread the large family of languages known as the Indo-European group. Although it may seem like a puzzling claim to many British people, most European languages have a great deal in common, both in structure and vocabulary. Certainly French speakers are much more likely to understand Spaniards or Italians than, say, Japanese or Koreans.

Against that linguistic background, economics began to exert a powerful influence. Because it can produce surpluses in good years and its seasonal cycle allows other work such as basic manufacturing, farming encouraged trade. Archaeologists have turned up an increasing range of ancient commodities. In the second and first millennia BC, northern Europe developed a thirst for Mediterranean wine and the bronze smiths of the south needed British tin to make their lustrous, gold-like alloy. Pelts, textiles, dye, amber, gold and silver all made long journeys, probably passing through several pairs of hands on the way. Historians now believe that these busy commercial contacts, mostly seaborne, also carried a cargo of language. Up and down the Atlantic coastlines of Europe and Britain, merchants needed to understand producers for both of them to profit and it seems that a family of Celtic languages developed into a trading lingua franca.

From inscriptions, place-names, proper names and occasional scraps of transcription and translation, the distribution of these Celtic languages can be reasonably mapped across Western Europe. In what is now Portugal and Spain, Lusitanian and Celtiberian were certainly spoken in the first millennium BC, while in France and Northern Italy, Gaulish and Lepontic were heard. Up and down the length of Britain dialects of Old Welsh (a clear ancestor of the modern language and related to Gaulish) became common and, in Ireland, an early form of Gaelic was spoken. Over time, these languages followed different paths, some to extinction, others developing marked differences. By the time the bodies of the dead children were first brought into the cave at Covesea, around 1,000 BC, it is likely that their parents and their priests spoke a northern dialect of Old Welsh. By the time the cave was reoccupied, the language had acquired a distinctive name and its speakers had become a famous historical enigma.

The Sculptor's Cave is so called because of a series of symbols carved on the walls near the entrances. Only one can be read as a naturalistic representation – what looks like a fish with fins and a tail. Even the descriptions of the others are obscure – a triple vesica, a pentacle, a crescent and v-rod, a step and a mirror case. But they are not unique. All of them and several others form part of a mysterious visual vocabulary that appears on more than 350 symbol stones carved by a people known to history as the Picts. Some of these are monumental – one standing near Covesea is 6.5 metres high – and they are also intricate, sometimes stunning works of art, while others are clearly more primitive. The earliest stones were set up at the beginning of the 5th century AD, at the end of the life of the cave shrine at Covesea. Clearly its sanctity had endured and it remained a place to be revered by the Picts.

The name first comes on record in AD 296, when Roman commentators reported that Pictish war bands had broken through Hadrian's Wall and raided as far south as the city of Chester. Sounding very much like a soldiers' nickname for an unfamiliar enemy, the first Picts or the Painted Warriors may not have originated in the north of Scotland, may not have been Picts at all. Their habit of wearing warpaint – almost certainly tattoos – may have seemed unusual, perhaps even quaint to the garrison of Hadrian's Wall, something no longer done in the south, something they had not seen before and what prompted the Latin tag. In any event, the name stuck and, over the 4th and 5th centuries, the Picts became a feared and far-ranging threat to the province of Britannia. After a raid that reached London, they were described as *transmarini* and, while this is an obvious reference to their ability to attack from the sea, it may also mean that the Romans realised that they originated from Scotland Beyond the Sea, north of the Forth, the warriors who crossed the sea.

Pictish symbol stones carry beautiful representations of several animals and these hint at the names the Picts gave themselves. At Covesea the fish is probably a salmon and elsewhere there are eagles, wolves, horses, stags, bulls, boar and a creature that looks like a stylised dolphin. Some of these could be found on an early map of Scotland and one has survived on modern versions.

The Greek geographer Ptolemy never visited Britain but he did plot the territories of the peoples who lived there and the names of some of their places. In the 2nd century AD, probably working in distant Alexandria, he used the accounts of others. One of these was almost certainly the log of a voyage around the coasts of Scotland kept by the captain of a Roman fleet. After the inconclusive battle at Mons Graupius in AD 83 and the withdrawal of the legions from the Highlands, their general sent his supporting fleet to circumnavigate the island. Propaganda may have been the motive and Agricola probably wanted to give the impression of conquest and mighty Rome's ability to strike anywhere, even as far as the farthest reaches of the known world, to the edges of the limitless ocean.

Ptolemy's use of the log of the Agricolan reconnaissance (no other circumnavigation is on record before he set to work and very suggestive is his omission of both Hadrian's and the Antonine Wall even though both existed when the map was made) means that his map is of a Scotland seen from the sea. Mostly it is coastal settlements that are identified and the interior left largely blank. Many of the names of the kindreds and their territories also seem to hug the shores but it is those names that intrigue. Ptolemy noted the Epidii, 'the Horse People', in Argyll, the Caereni, 'the Sheep Folk', in Wester Ross and Sutherland, the Lugi, 'the Raven People', in Easter Ross, the Venicones, 'the Kindred Hounds', in Fife, and, on a later map, the Orcades, 'the Boar People', appear – a name that has endured.

Moray was the land of the Vacomagi and it meant something like 'the People of the Plain', possibly a reference to the fertile Laigh of Moray. Down the North Sea coast, from the Buchan to Tayside, were the Taexali, a name that has so far resisted interpretation. In any event, a simple observation may be safely made and it is that the early people of the north of Scotland admired the attributes of animals, often took them as totems and kindred names and made beautiful sculpture from their forms. Perhaps more than DNA links the cave painters of Lascaux and elsewhere in France and Spain with the Picts. Artists working in both cultures represented animals and their movement very much better than most.

Historians have traditionally been perplexed by the Picts and their anxieties are deepened by the mysteries of the symbol stones, their unfathomable language and its lack of any written record. No one now can say anything meaningful in Pictish apart from a few personal names and place-names. No verbs, no syntax and no obvious links with other languages have survived. Pictish was once thought to be non-Indo-European – some sort of throwback to prehistory. And, to make matters worse, the Picts appear to have suddenly disappeared in the first half of the 9th century. In a blood-soaked battle fought in Strathearn in 839, the Pictish nobility was said to have been slaughtered by a Viking army and, from that moment, their culture withered and no more symbol stones were raised after c. 850. After an exotic and puzzling flowering in the north and east of Scotland, this enigmatic society seemed to vanish into the darkness of the past.

Given their prominence in contemporary British society, this is all very surprising. The first really great British scholar whose work has survived was Bede of Jarrow. A monk born in the shadow of Hadrian's Wall, he spent his cloistered life in the twin monastery of Jarrow and Monkwearmouth (near Sunderland) and wrote a magnificent history of Britain. Here is the opening:

At the present time there are in Britain, in harmony with the five books of the divine law, five languages and four nations – English, British, Irish and Picts. Each of these have their own language; but all are united in their study of God's truth by the fifth – Latin – which has become a common medium through the study of the scriptures. At first the only inhabitants of the island were the Britons, from whom it takes its name, and who, according to tradition, crossed into Britain from Armorica, and occupied the southern parts. When they had spread northwards and possessed the greater part of the island, it is said that some Picts from Scythia put to sea in a few longships, and were driven by storms around the coasts of Britain, arriving at length on the north coast of Ireland. Here they found the nation of the Irish, from whom they asked permission to settle; but their request was refused . . . The Irish replied that there was not room for them both, but said: 'We can give you good advice. We know that there is another island not far to the east, which we often see in the distance on clear days. If you choose to go there, you can make it fit to live in; should you meet resistance, we will come to your aid.' So the Picts crossed into Britain, and began to settle in the north of the island, since the Britons were in possession of the south. Having no women with them, these Picts asked wives of the Irish, who consented on condition that, when any dispute arose, they should choose a king from the female royal line rather than the male. This custom continues among the Picts to this day. As time went on, Britain received a third nation, that of the

Irish; they migrated from Ireland under their chieftain Reuda and by a combination of force and treaty, obtained from the Picts the settlements they still hold. From the name of this chieftain, they are still known as the Dalreudans [sic], for in their tongue 'dal' means a division.

Worth quoting at length, this passage mixes forensic and myth-history and it gave rise to more Pictish exotica such as the discredited view that their monarchy operated a matrilineal succession. But what is clear from the outset of Bede's history is that he and his contemporaries saw these northern peoples as having a highly significant, clear and separate identity in a British context. And new research has shown that their origins in Scotland were far from mysterious and can set a much more precise context in which the Picts should be seen. Once that is understood the mystery melts away like morning mist over the Moray Firth.

Geneticists have discovered a distinctive DNA marker and given it the clumsy label of R1b, str47-Pict. It not only demonstrates that far from disappearing, the direct male descendants of the Picts live in modern Scotland – and in significant numbers. More than 7 per cent of Scottish men, 175,000 in all, carry what should be called R1b-Pict. As the label suggests they are descended from the great influx of farmers with the R1b marker who came to Scotland after 4,000 BC and multiplied so quickly. Far from being latecomers allowed to settle in the sparsely populated Scotland described by Bede, the Picts were part of one of the oldest and most successful lineages in the north.

Before they carved the designs on the cave walls at Covesea or raised their great symbol stones, these remarkable people had farmed the fertile fields of Moray, Aberdeenshire, Tayside and Fife for many generations. Pictish culture can be understood against a background of continuity. Ptolemy's kindreds bearing animal names were nations of Picts even though the Roman circumnavigation of Scotland predated their first documentary mention by two centuries. And the distribution of R1b-Pict, based on a robust sample of 3,000 DNA tests, is very obviously concentrated north of the Forth, in Scotland Beyond the Sea. There are high percentages of this Y chromosome marker in Moray and Tayside, as would be expected, but also many men in Skye and Argyll carry it. These latter statistics more than suggest a society that spoke Pictish before the advent of Gaels from Ireland – they insist on it. But that is to anticipate events in both a chronological and geographical sense.

From the 5th century to the 9th, Pictish culture flourished in the north and east until the fateful defeat by the Vikings in Strathearn in 839. But it appears that it did not die and that the Pictish nobility did not disappear.

Clan Gregor's motto is defiant. *'S Rioghall Mo Dhream* means 'Royal is my Race' and most MacGregors believe it to be a reference to kinship with Kenneth MacAlpin, the 9th-century king from whom all Scottish kings are numbered. DNA offers an ironic gloss. It confirms a legendary association with royalty in that many members of Clan Gregor are descended from a single individual, almost certainly a king. But not King Kenneth MacAlpin. Out of a sample of 144 MacGregors to be tested, 53 carry a royal lineage. It is a variant of R1b-Pict and it almost certainly means that they are the descendants of Pictish kings.

These men and their aristocracy were patrons of the sculptors who made the symbol stones. Some show representations of the nobility at play. At Hilton of Cadboll, near Tain on the Dornoch Firth, stands a very beautiful stone and a wonderfully vigorous hunting scene careers across one face of it. With her hounds and huntsmen in pursuit of a stag, an elegant lady rides side-saddle. Above the hue and cry are carved symbols much less easily understood but, like the hunting scene, they represent continuity.

Some of the repertoire of symbols seen on hundreds of stones may well be stylised forms of domestic objects such as combs or mirrors. But above the elegant lady and her men is a vesica with a V-rod. A vesica is a crescent on its side with the pointed ends turned downwards and a V-rod is a line broken into a wide V-shape with decoration on both ends. The same design, more simply rendered, can be seen at Covesea. These are designs of objects with a direct connection with the pool inside the cave shrine and the metalwork found in or near it.

Before metal objects were cast into the water, they were usually slighted, ritually damaged, so that their power changed in some way. Archaeologists talk of swords, shields and other things being 'killed'. The V-rod is a broken arrow. Clearly obvious at Covesea, one end has a stylised point and, at the other, is a design that closely resembles fletching. Elsewhere Z-rods can be seen and these were probably broken spears. The vesica is more problematic but it may represent a bent shield or more likely a shield boss, usually the only metal component. Two circular prehistoric shields made entirely of metal (and therefore ceremonial because they were too heavy to be practical) were recently pulled out of the boggy ground by a loch near Yetholm in the Borders.

These symbols are exactly that – symbolic of the objects deposited in the water and an upstanding stone testament to the piety of wealthy individuals. As Christianity was adopted by the Picts, crosses were often carved on one side of the stones and symbols and secular scenes on the others – another example of continuity and gradual transition.

Moreb is almost certainly a Pictish version of 'Moray', perhaps deriving from an early Celtic form, *more-treb*, meaning 'sea settlement'. It described a much larger ancient territory that included Inverness and the lands around the Beauly and Cromarty Firths while, eastwards, it stretched to the Buchan and was bounded in the south by the Mounth, where the Grampian massif almost reaches the sea at Stonehaven. But it was a remarkable moment in Roman imperial decline that brought the warriors of Moreb on to the pages of history. In 367, what was known as the Barbarian Conspiracy erupted in the province of Britannia. After a period of diplomacy and military planning, an alliance of Gaelic war bands from Ireland, Franks and Saxons from across the North Sea, a previously unknown people called the Attacotti (a strange name meaning something like the 'Old

Ones') perhaps from the Hebrides, and the kings of the Picts attacked the province simultaneously and probably from several directions. They defeated a defending army and killed its commander, Nectaridus, as well as capturing a barbarian general, Fullofaudes. He led what were probably mercenary forces hired by Rome.

For three years, between 367 and 370, the war bands trailed destruction, looting, death and ruin in their wake. Unable to respond quickly to the chaos engulfing Britannia, Rome seemed paralysed. Perhaps there were tremendous and competing pressures along the Rhine and Danube frontier. When a relief force finally disembarked with Count Theodosius, a tough and experienced general, in charge, the raiders were driven out and security restored.

Ammianus Marcellinus, the historian who recorded the anarchy of the Barbarian Conspiracy, noted two sorts of Picts – the DiCaledonii and the Verturiones. Caledonians had already appeared in Roman chronicles and the so-called Double-Caledonians of 367 may refer to two allied kindreds, perhaps neighbours. Their kings ruled south of the Mounth, in Tayside and Angus. Place names remember them. Dunkeld means the 'Dun or Fort of the Caledonians' and Schiehallion is the enigmatic 'Magic Mountain of the Caledonians'. Places named after peoples in this way often denote the proximity of frontiers and perhaps the mountain country beyond Dunkeld was held by another kindred. This may be a very early shadow of the Highland Line.

The warriors and kings of the Verturiones, later known as the people of Fortriu, ruled Moreb, the Moray coastlands, the territory north of the Mounth, what became the centre of Pictland. That these kings could maintain war bands fighting in the south for three consecutive campaigning seasons at a tremendous distance from their base insists on the existence of forces of professional soldiers. And, in turn, it speaks of a society sufficiently wealthy and well organised to sustain ambitious kings and their far-travelled military. What also fired these men was the promise of plunder and the rich Roman province of Britannia had plenty that was portable.

The patchwork of political power in Pictland was likely more complex and dynamic than such records as exist allow. A document of the 12th century, *De Situ Albanie*, that draws on much earlier material, listed seven Pictish provinces and, within those, a further seven sub-kings. While clearly a formula, the names are informative and sometimes attested elsewhere – *Fib* was an old name for 'Fife', *Cat* is linked to 'Caithness' and *Fotla* was 'Atholl and Gowrie'. *Fortriu* was long believed to be a reference to 'Strathearn and Menteith' but convincing recent research has relocated it to 'Moray'.

Academic argument aside, the list in *De Situ Albanie* reflects a political reality, a group of smaller Pictish kingdoms that shared a common culture (especially obvious in the style of the symbol stones) and a common language. In Ireland a similar pattern was given some degree of unity by the institution of High Kingship, an honour usually associated with the kingship of Tara. Pictland too seems to have had High Kings, with the title of Kings of Fortriu, and these men almost certainly ruled over the kindreds north of the Mounth by the time of the Barbarian Conspiracy of 367. And in time their reach would extend southwards, down as far as the shores of the Firth of Forth.

Picts on the Make

Lossio Veda is a shadowy but fascinating figure, a man who probably lived in the 3rd century AD and who was almost certainly a merchant. A bronze plaque found at Colchester explains. It is dedicated to 'Mars Medocius of the Campeses and the Victory of Our Emperor Severus Alexander' by Lossio Veda's uncle, a man described as a 'Caledo' or Caledonian and whose name is given as Vepogenus. It means 'born in Fife'. Being able to pay for this dedication and having it set up a long way south of his origins probably means that, as a merchant, he had established a family firm in the province of Britannia.

Like their medieval counterparts, the early kings, their households and their war bands moved around their realms in order to consume the food rents owed by their subjects. Moray kings must have been sea kings, sailing around the shores of the firth from one stronghold to another. Their greatest coastal power centre has all but disappeared even though it could still be clearly seen until 1805 and now its mighty aspect can only be imagined. This place, the principal fortress of the High Kings of Fortriu, was three times larger than any other in Dark Ages Scotland. Known locally as The Broch, a name that poignantly recalls ancient architecture, Burghead was built as a planned town after 1805 to act as Moray's central herring fishing station and a major outlet for the export of the region's grain and, in the process, the old Pictish fortress was all but destroyed.

A headland that may once have been an island, like the caves at nearby Covesea, Burghead was a perfect base for sea kings and their ships. On three sides of a roughly rectangular shape, there were rocky cliffs but immediately to the south-west lay a sandy beach where boats could be dragged up above the high-tide mark and easily refloated when needed. At 80 feet above sea level, the headland is high with long views over the Moray Firth to the Black Isle and the mouth of the Cromarty Firth. The landward approach was defended by three huge ditches and high timber-laced stone walls tied together with long iron pins and arranged in an arrowhead formation. These ditches and walls may have had ancient origins for, on Ptolemy's map of Scotland, Burghead is plotted as *Pinnata Castra*, 'the Winged Fort'. Here is a description of the old Pictish stronghold from Charles Cordiner's *Antiquaries and Scenery of the North of Scotland*, written in 1780, on the eve of its destruction: '[It was] one of the most celebrated places of rendezvous of the buccaneers from Norway [the Vikings]. The vast ramparts still remaining bear the weightiest testimony to its great strength ... The triple ditch and rampart are yet neat and entire. The top had been defended by logs of oak piled on one another. Many pieces are still to be seen half-burnt.'

As the houses and streets of the planned town were laid out

and built, more than thirty Pictish relief sculptures of bulls came to light. Only six survive and they are thought to be unique to Burghead. They allow speculation on a name – perhaps this immense fortification, the greatest in Scotland, was known to those who made it as 'the Bull Fort'.

The events of the Barbarian Conspiracy of the late 4th century make evident the wealth and reach of the sea kings of Moray. As they sailed out of the Bull Fort with their war bands, the succeeding centuries saw their formidable power expand over much of Scotland north of the Forth. To the west, the shared DNA marker of R1b-Pict suggests at least cultural if not political links with Skye and the Atlantic coast. When St Columba came from Ireland to take possession of Iona so that he could establish a community of monks there in 565, Bede noted that it had belonged to 'the Picts living in that part of Britain [and they] gave it to the Irish monks long ago because they received the Faith of Christ through their preaching'. Perhaps a high king at Burghead had given his assent.

Columba's biographer, Adomnan, wrote of the saint's missionary journeys up the Great Glen to Moray and the heart of Pictland. He famously met King Bridei, probably at his fortress at Craig Phadraig, two miles west of Inverness. Despite several miracles and his besting of Bridei's pagan priest, Adomnan did not report much success for Columba. More immediate impact was made by soldiers from Ireland than by saints. Some time around AD 500, Gaelic-speaking warriors began to cross the North Channel in significant numbers. At least three kindreds settled on the Argyll coast, what had been the land of the Epidii on the Ptolemy map, and the new name announced their arrival. Argyll means 'the Coastlands of the Gael'. At the conclusion of the introduction to Bede's great history quoted above, he set down a version of this process, 'a combination of treaty and force', whereby the new Irish kindreds 'obtained from the Picts the settlements they still hold'.

Such were the beginnings of Dalriada, the Gaelic-speaking kingdom that would eventually impose its language and its dynasties over much of Scotland. DNA studies not only track the coming of the Irish Gaels, they also offer a revealing gloss on the early development of power politics.

In 2008, researchers began to notice an Irish marker that appeared to come up again and again in many Y chromosome tests. Known as M222, it is carried by no fewer than 20 per cent of all Irish men and its frequency in the north rises as high as 40 per cent. What astonished analysts was the incontrovertible fact that all of these men were descended from one lineage, from a single individual. DNA markers can be dated, and it became clear that this man lived in the north of Ireland some time in the 5th century. The overwhelming likelihood is that he was the first High King, Niall Noigiallach. Tremendously powerful, his second name reflected the extent of his reach for Noigiallach means 'of the Nine Hostages'. Sub-kings were compelled to send hostages, usually their children, to the household of the High King as guarantors of compliance and continuing support. Niall ruled over nine kingdoms and their nine sub-kings.

As well as political, this man's influence was also genetic. Like most powerful men at that time, Niall had sex with many women and, as a consequence, fathered many sons. And they in turn, as scions of a royal house, repeated what in essence was an evolutionary process. A much later Irish example illustrates. A descendant of Niall, Lord Turlough O'Donnell died in 1423, perhaps from exhaustion. He fathered 14 legitimate sons and likely many more bastards. The 14 produced 59 grandsons and, if the same rate of enthusiasm had been maintained, Turlough would have had 248 great-grandsons and 1,040 great-great-grandsons. Within four generations, the old man could have bred an army.

This ancient process explains much. Repeated in almost every society, what researchers call social selection allowed kings and aristocrats to father war bands and household retinues. Chroniclers of Dark Ages history usually wrote in Latin and they attached suggestive labels – *comitatus* had an earlier meaning of 'a court or retinue' but came to signify 'a war band'; *cohors* was similar and eventually used for 'a unit in the Roman army' as well as 'a war band'; while *familia* could mean 'a household (including slaves)' or even 'a troop of cavalry warriors'. Bands of blood brothers fought side by side for many centuries and it was a form of military organisation that endured for a simple reason. Cousins, uncles, brothers, nephews, sons and grandsons would fight harder for each other than an army of strangers would because bonds of kinship were strong. When the clansmen mustered at Culloden in 1746, many of their leaders were also their relatives and all fought for their blood brothers who charged across the moor at their shoulders.

What is striking about the M222 marker is that it clearly moved and in considerable numbers. In the 5th and 6th centuries, bands of men directly descended from Niall Noigiallach sailed the North Channel to carve out the kingdoms of Dalriada. Bede's version of events turns out to be far from fanciful but backed by modern science. In 21st-century Scotland, 6 per cent of all men carry the M222 marker, around 150,000 are the direct descendants of the Irish High King, and there is a heavy concentration of these individuals in the west of Scotland. If not an invasion, there was certainly an incursion of Irish Gaelic speakers from the 4th to the 6th centuries, probably people of substance, almost certainly warriors.

As the fortunes of the Dalriadan kings fluctuated with the prowess or otherwise of their war bands, the dynamics of language offer an interesting historical twist. In the 7th and 8th centuries, the name that the Irish gave to their own language was changing. The use of *Erainn* was giving way to *Goidel*, the precursor of Gael. This, in turn, was a loan word from Old Welsh, the family of languages spoken on mainland Britain that included Pictish. To them *Gwydd* meant 'wild' or 'savage' (the modern Welsh for an Irishman is *Gwyddel*). The precise processes involved in this exchange can never be clearly tracked but it appears that the Gaels adopted a description of themselves by Old Welsh speakers, the sort of nickname warriors might have liked, even gloried in. It may have been conferred in the 5th century when Irish war bands from Leinster colonised the Lleyn Peninsula in North Wales. The names are cognate. The invaders were expelled but the ruins of their settlements were known as *cytian yr Gwyddelod*, 'the huts of the Irish'.

As well as terrifying the British, the wild Gaels fought amongst themselves. Principal rivals in Dalriada were the Cenel Loairn, the Kindred of Lorne, and the Cenel nGabrain, the ancestors of King Kenneth MacAlpin. They contended for the High Kingship of Dalriada but mostly it remained the preserve of the Cenel nGabrain. Paradoxically it was Pictish aggression that ultimately drove the Cenel Loairn out of northern Argyll and forced their kings and their war bands to seek new territory. Meanwhile the Cenel nGabrain, having been spared the worst of the Pictish attacks, flourished in southern Argyll and eventually moved east into Perthshire and the heart of Scotland to establish themselves as High Kings of Scotland. By contrast, it seems that the Cenel Loairn faded from history and after 736 no mention of them is made in Argyll. Their kings and their warriors appeared to vanish.

It was thought for many years that a few place-names were all the old kindred had left behind but recent scholarship has radically altered that view. In fact, the Cenel Loairn has been rediscovered – and found in Moray. A careful analysis of royal genealogies has identified a series of Gaelic names and, by the 11th century, these men were claiming the High Kingship of Scotland, using the ancient rights of the Cenel Loairn in Dalriada as support for their pretension. On their side, the MacAlpin kings used their descent from the Cenel nGabrain to legitimise their position in a similar way. But it seems that the Loairn had left their homelands in northern Argyll, trekked up the Great Glen to Moray and somehow made themselves kings there, constituting a direct threat to the MacAlpin hold on the High Kingship.

By 943 to 949, matters had escalated into war when 'Malcolm went with his army into Moray and slew Cellach'. In this brief passage, the chroniclers were recounting the deeds of Malcolm I MacAlpin – the beginnings of a repeating pattern and what would amount to a long and bloody dynastic conflict. Cellach was not the only King of Moray to be killed by the armies of the High King – or by rivals from the Cenel Loairn. Around 1020, Findlaech was assassinated by the sons of his brother, Maelbrigte.

By 1032, Malcolm II of Scotland had subdued Moray, burning Gillacomgain 'along with 50 of his men'. This unfortunate was one of the sons of Maelbrigte but the chroniclers, normally very precise about titles, did not style him as a king. Instead, Gillacomgain was Mormaer, or Great Steward, of Moray, an office that implies a previous subjection to Malcolm. But Gillacomgain's death would be avenged as the kings of Moray and the Cenel Loairn began to blaze a bloody path to fame, both historical and literary.

In a chronicle compiled in Mainz by an exiled Scottish cleric known as Marianus Scotus, the entry for 1040 is blunt: 'Duncan, the king of Scotland, was killed in the autumn, by his Dux Macbethad, Findlaech's son, who succeeded to the kingship for seventeen years.' When Cnut, the king of England, Denmark and Norway, came to Scotland to receive the submission of its kings, King Macbeth was counted amongst them.

Sources are scant but it seems that Scotland was relatively peaceful after 1040. Macbeth appears to have been secure enough to go on pilgrimage to Rome in 1050 where 'he scattered money like seed to the poor'. Two years later, the king began an enduring historical process when he invited two Norman knights to come north from England: 'Osbert and Hugh surrendered their castles . . . went into Scotland and were kindly received by Macbeth, King of Scots.' Their stay was short. Here is entry in the *Anglo-Saxon Chronicle* for the year 1054: 'At this time the Earl Siward went with a great army into Scotland with both fleet and land-force; and brought thence much war-spoil, such as no man had gained before; but his son, Osbert and his sister's son, Siward, and numbers of his housecarls as well as those of the king were slain there on the Day of the Seven Sleepers.'

This forgotten Christian festival was held on 27 July, a day that lived on in history in unexpected disguises. William Shakespeare unwittingly absorbed its significance for it planted in his imagination the notion that Malcolm III was placed on the throne of Scotland with English help. The battle on the Day of the Seven Sleepers and all the attendant drama of the Scottish play were also emblematic of attitudes with an ancient provenance. It was written between 1603 and 1607, just after James VI of Scotland had become the James I of Great Britain and Ireland. The opening decade of the 17th century saw a renewed onslaught by the king and his advisors on what he saw as the lawless Highlands of Scotland. Culminating in the suppressions of the Statutes of Iona in 1610, the royal campaign attempted to bring the clans and the great magnates of the north firmly under control. For these entirely political reasons, Macbeth is portrayed by Shakespeare as a wild Gael, a blood-soaked regicide and a threat to order, civilisation and progress. But, while the historical realities of 11th-century Scotland may have been very different from Shakespeare's propagandist fiction, the tensions in the play were not entirely a work of imagination.

Later Scottish chroniclers wrote that Siward's fleet sailed into the Firth of Tay and penetrated the southern Pictish heartlands. Andrew Wyntoun's *Orygynale Cronykil of Scotland* was compiled in the early 15th century and some of what he wrote found its way into Shakespeare's great tragedy. Siward's fleet 'passed over Forth, down straight to Tay, up that water the high way, to Birnam to gather whole'. The chronicler went on to locate the Battle of the Seven Sleepers at Dunsinane, clearly Dunsinnan Hill, where the ramparts of an ancient hill fort can still be seen. Whether or not the battle was, in fact, a siege is not known – nor is it clear if Birnam Wood was used as cover – but it was certainly ferocious as between three and four thousand were said to have died at Dunsinane. But, despite the carnage, Macbeth survived and reigned for a further three years.

The Day of the Seven Sleepers may have slid into obscurity but it maintained a curious linguistic presence in modern Gaelic. The festival originally recalled the 3rd-century martyrdom of the Seven Sleepers of Ephesus, now in modern Turkey. To escape the persecutions of the reign of the Roman Emperor Decius, seven young men sought refuge in a cave. They fell asleep and did not wake for two hundred years. When they were seen in what had become a Christian city as old men, they were somehow recognised and, on their deaths, celebrated as martyrs. When Gaelic speakers of the 21st century complain of being very tired, some say, *'Tha mise seachd sean sgith'* – 'I am as tired as seven old men'.

After 1054, Macbeth may have lost control of southern territories and been forced to retreat into Moray but the pressure did not subside. In 1057, armies clashed at Lumphanan. It seems that Macbeth had been raiding or campaigning south of the Mounth and that the future Malcolm III had overtaken his war band. Lumphanan lies immediately to the north of the mouth of a pass through the mountains known as the Cairn o' Mount. Macbeth was mortally wounded but able to ride south to Scone, the ceremonial centre of southern Pictland, where its kings were traditionally anointed. There 'he spewed blood on the evening of a night after a duel', according to a bardic prophet known as Berchan, and his stepson Lulach was confirmed as his successor, the new High King of Scotland. The son of Gruoch, Macbeth's queen, he reigned for only seven months and, during a battle in 1058, 'Lulach, king of Scotland, was treacherously slain by Malcolm, son of Duncan', ran the entry in the Irish *Annals of Tigernach*. This pivotal battle, an event that would shift the centre of Scotland's historical gravity, was fought at Essie in Strathbogie, south of Huntly.

The destruction of the dynasty of the Cenel Loairn did not, however, lead to the suppression of the kingdom of Moray. In 1085 a man with the fascinating name of Maelschnetai (it means something like 'the Follower of the Snows' so perhaps he campaigned from a mountain base) was calling himself King of Moray. And, by 1130, his successor, Angus, the grandson of Lulach, believed himself sufficiently powerful to challenge David I for the High Kingship of Scotland. Having led his war bands south of the Mounth, he was decisively defeated at Stracathro near Brechin.

The Emperor of the North Sea

A great but little recognised king of England was Cnut or Canute, the man ridiculed for trying to send back the waves. In reality, he was one of the most powerful men ever to rule in England. The association with the sea is apposite for Cnut created a sea empire. He controlled almost every shore of the North Sea as king of Denmark, Norway and England and as overlord of Scotland. In 1031, the Emperor of the North Sea visited Scotland and, according to the Anglo-Saxon Chronicle, *King Malcolm and King Maelbeth submitted to his power – that is, Malcolm II and Macbeth, King of Moray. The latter was probably known to Cnut and the Norse earls of Orkney as Karl Hundason and he was said by the composers of the sagas to have lost a great battle to Earl Thorfinn, the Skull-splitter. Thorfinn's father, Torf-Einar, was so called because he cut turf at Tarbat Ness on the coast of Easter Ross. The significance of this was that his action marked the southern boundary of his earldom with Macbeth's kingdom of Moray.*

As he did in the Borders and elsewhere in Scotland, David I sought a simple and effective solution to unrest in the further reaches of his kingdom. He imported outsiders who would owe their position entirely to him to act as royal representatives in Moray and also as a catalyst for change and improvement. And an unintended consequence of this radical policy was to divide the old kingdom more clearly into Highland and Lowland zones.

When a man called Flemming Freskin arrived in the north, he immediately began to distribute some of the best land (presumably the forfeited royal estates of the dead King Angus and also those of his supporters) to more incomers. Freskin adopted the name of *de Moravia*, 'of Moray', which eventually became the name Murray and, under his rule, much of the best land in the Laigh passed into new ownership. Sheriffdoms at Inverness, Nairn, Forres and Elgin supplied a judicial and administrative framework for royal control and the spiritual focus of a new and grand cathedral at Elgin completed a familiar feudal picture.

David I's colonisation of the lowlands of Moray created an audible cultural boundary. As the fertile farms of the Gaelic-speaking descendants of the Cenel Loairn were taken over by newcomers, their language began to fade and die. Gaelic had replaced Pictish around the 9th century and now it was itself being supplanted by Scots English. The towns of Nairn, Elgin, Forres and Huntly and their rich hinterlands were peopled from the south and Gaelic began to retreat into the mountains and more remote glens. From Strathbogie right across to Lochaber and Lochalsh, it became the language of shepherds and stocksmen while the ploughmen of the Laigh of Moray and as far east as the Buchan spoke a dialect of English that came to be known as Doric.

Around Nairn there is an invisible line. Travellers going west hear a sudden shift from Doric to a version of English once thought to be the purest, least accented and most clearly enunciated in Britain. Around Inverness, Gaelic was still widely spoken until the late 19th century and the supposedly pure English adopted after that time was, at first, a second language for many and, as such, it had no accent.

Allegiances also shrank back into Highland fastnesses. After King Angus's defeat in 1130, resistance to MacMalcolm rule persisted for another century. William, the son of Duncan, David I's half-brother, appeared to be loyal and fought alongside his king at his defeat in the Battle of the Standard in 1138. But his son, Donald MacWilliam, styled himself as a Gaelic magnate and, through his marriage into the ancient Cenel Loairn House of Moray, asserted a fresh claim for the High Kingship of Scotland. Matters came to a head in 1187. Here is the informative entry from the chronicle of Roger of Howden: 'William, king of Scotland, assembled a great army and set out for Moray to subdue a certain enemy of his, who was named MacWilliam; who also said he was born of royal stock, and by right of his parents, so he affirmed, claimed the kingdom of Scotland, through consent and council of the earls and the barons of the kingdom . . . The king William, therefore, considering that he must either lose the kingdom of Scotland or slay MacWilliam, or else drive him from the confines of his kingdom, set out to go into Moray.'

To meet the royal host, the MacWilliam, King Donald, had raised an army in the mountains and glens and it must have been formidable. William the Lion did not live up to his soubriquet and chose to stay behind the walls of Inverness Castle while his magnates fought the rebels. Somewhere in the moorland near Garve, in Easter Ross, the MacWilliam was defeated, decapitated and his head brought as a grisly trophy to Inverness. No doubt it was set on a spike for all to bear witness. But still the unrest would not die down and rebellion flared again in the north in the early 13th century. After a battle in 1228 or 1229 when Gillescop, a new leader of the MacWilliam faction, was killed, it was determined to exterminate the line of the Cenel Loairn and Moray utterly. Presumably acting on intelligence, knights were sent to Forfar to capture and kill the last living claimant. This is the entry in the *Chronicle of Lanercost* in North Cumbria and, over eight centuries later, the disapproval is still palpable: 'After the enemy had been successfully overcome, a somewhat too cruel vengeance was taken for the blood of the slain, the same [Gillescop] MacWilliam's daughter who had not long left her mother's womb, innocent as she was, was put to death in the burgh of Forfar, in view of the market place, after a proclamation by the public crier: her head was struck against the column of the [market] cross, and her brains dashed out.'

The horrific killing of a baby girl, publicly executed, was the last sad act in the long history of the kingdom of Moray and a brutal testimony to the power of the men who ruled over it. The blood on the cross shaft meant that the coastlands of the firth had passed into the realm of Scotland but the destiny of those who lived in the mountains was less certain.

4

The Fire of the Dram

✹

T HE ROLE OF Islington Borough Council in the development of Scotch whisky is sometimes overlooked. In the central matter of definition, it took the lead. For reasons now lost in the mists of local authority bureaucracy, the officials of the north London borough had summonses served on two local landlords for selling whisky 'not of the nature, quality and substance demanded'. The cases went to court in 1906 and, under the provisions of the Merchandise Marks Act, the judge upheld the complaints.

There was uproar in Scotland – and a great deal at stake. In effect, the London judge's ruling defined malt whisky, the sort made by traditional methods in a pot still, usually in a Highland distillery, as the only alcoholic drink that could claim to be Scotch whisky. Nothing else could carry that label. And that was the problem. In 1832, Aeneas Coffey had patented a new type of still that could function continuously to produce vast quantities of whisky made from grain of any kind. Twenty years later, in Edinburgh, Andrew Usher began to blend these new grain whiskies with the malts produced in the Highlands and elsewhere. These blends gave the cheaper spirit character and colour and made Scotch whisky more plentiful and affordable. But it might never have become popular outside of Scotland, in London, or indeed Islington.

Soon after Usher's blend went on sale in Edinburgh, a calamity delivered a tremendous opportunity. French vineyards were devastated by a plague of insects known as Phylloxera vastatrix. Between 1858 and 1865, French winemakers had hoped to rejuvenate their rootstock by importing grafts from California but instead they killed them and, all over Bordeaux and other great wine regions of France, row upon row of vines rotted and died. The roots and leaves of the American grafts were immune to Phylloxera but when these deadly but hardy insects arrived, having survived winter journeys across the Atlantic, they fell upon the French vineyards and devoured them. Once the blight had become widespread, around 1865, French wine and brandy production declined steeply and many vineyards were eventually forced to cease production entirely as they realised they would have to replant. In turn, Phylloxera changed English drinking habits. As cellars emptied, wine and brandy and soda were soon replaced by whisky and soda. As the French vines withered, business boomed in Scotland. Having been formed in 1877, the Distillers Company used its scale to increase production and many independent blended brands became famous – John Haig, Johnnie Walker, Whyte & Mackay and James Buchanan. And, as demand from the blenders for malt also rose, new distilleries were built not only in Speyside but all over Scotland. Big business was quickly made out of what had been a cottage industry for centuries.

The switch from French brandy to Scotch whisky was also driven by fashion. After Walter Scott had woven his wizardry with tales like 'The Lay of the Last Minstrel', *Waverley*, *Rob Roy* and other fictional forays into the Highlands, the mists of romance had begun to swirl around the bens and the glens. And, when Queen Victoria and Prince Albert fell in love with all things tartan, bought Balmoral and even declared themselves to be Jacobites at heart, the marketing campaign was complete and London society followed them north. Hunting lodges were built, some on a grand scale, shooting estates created and, as ranks of kilted courtiers and aspiring courtiers jigged, reeled, strathspeyed, puffed and sweated through interminable Highland balls, many gratefully turned to Scotch whisky for relief and refreshment. Scott, Phylloxera and Victoria combined to put the dram on the map.

Eyeliner for Men

Alcohol was discovered by a culture that does not allow its adherents to drink it. First distilled in the 10th century by the Persian chemist Al-Razi, ethyl alcohol was used medically in Islamic society. The derivation of the English word is surprising. It is cognate with kohl, a slightly outdated term for eyeliner or eye shadow. In Arabic, kuhl *originally referred to a fine powder used as eye makeup for men when mixed with water. It was also used as an antiseptic. Alcohol comes from* al-kuhl, *literally 'the kohl' and, as late as the 16th century, the word meant a fine powder in English. It eventually came to be applied to any fluid obtained by distillation and the term was recently reintroduced to Arabic as* al-kuhul.

The origins of distilling are uncertain but very ancient. It was brought from the Near East to Europe by the Arabs and medieval treatises were written by Albertus Magnus and Ramon Lull, men who were much influenced by the scholars of the Caliphate of Cordoba in particular. At first, it was used to make perfumes and essences for medicine. Alcohol is an Arab word but, for religious reasons, not necessarily an Arab drink. It was certainly made in Ireland in the early Middle Ages and, like many other items of Irish iconography, was traditionally understood to have been introduced by St Patrick. However that may be, the first documentary record of production in Scotland crops up in 1494 when malted barley was sent to 'Friar John Cor, by order of the King, to make *acquavitae*'. This Latin phrase for 'water of life' is directly translated into Gaelic as *uisge beatha* and whisky is simply an anglicised rendering of *uisge*, 'water'. It seems that King James IV enjoyed a dram for, in 1498, his Treasury recorded a payment to 'the barbour that brocht acqua vite to the King'.

As in continental monasteries, many of them famous for their wine and recipes for fortifying spirits such as Benedictine and Chartreuse, whisky was probably made by Scottish monks in the Middle Ages. Pluscarden Abbey, near Elgin, had a tremendous reputation for beer that, as David Daiches writes in his book *Scotch Whisky: Its Past and Present*, 'made the hearts of all rejoice and filled the abbey with unutterable bliss, raising the devotions to the pitch that the surrounding hills echoed to their hallelujahs' and, since distillation is only one step beyond brewing, the monks may have made whisky as well. If they did, the hallelujahs will have been redoubled. And as the Treasury entry of 1498 suggests, it was also distilled by the barber-surgeons of Edinburgh who were granted rights of manufacture in 1505. Then as now, whisky was thought to have medicinal qualities. No doubt for those and other reasons, it was popular and quickly attracted the attentions of the taxman. To the eternal chagrin of many Scots, the first government licence to make whisky was granted to the Bushmills Distillery in 1609 – in County Antrim in Northern Ireland.

Techniques have changed very little since then. In essence, the process of making malt whisky is brewing followed by distilling. First, barley is soaked to encourage the dry seeds to germinate and begin to convert their starch into sugar. Before it becomes too advanced, germination is halted by heating and it is at that point that the barley is said to be malted. Sometimes peat reek is allowed to suffuse the grain and impart its intense aroma. Then the barley is ground into grist and boiled or 'mashed' in large copper vessels so that all the sugars are extracted. When allowed to cool, this 'wort' is poured into tanks known as 'wash backs' where yeast is mixed in and fermentation begins.

This strong-smelling, beer-like liquid is then transferred to copper stills. All of these are onion-shaped and when the wort is heated, the alcohol distils – that is, it rises as vapour before condensing into a liquid. This process is repeated and what has become raw whisky is decanted into oak barrels. These usually had a previous life for sherry or bourbon and they impart a great deal of a malt whisky's character. Racked in a secure warehouse, the barrels are stored for a minimum of three years. Most of a distillery's output goes to the blenders but the mounting popularity of single malt – a malt made in a single distillery – has meant more being stored for longer, at least ten years, sometimes longer. Twenty-one years is the usual maximum.

Domestic production did not last anything like as long as thousands of stills bubbled in thousands of farmhouses and cottages all over Scotland. It was probably consumed very quickly, like most wine. What made Speyside particularly suitable was geology and weather. The pure, soft water needed for distilling good whisky tumbled down the damp mountainsides of the Highland massif. Peat to heat the stills could be cut from many high moorlands and, down in the Laigh of Moray, the fields of barley needed to make the malt waved in the summer breezes of the firth. Whisky is one of the very few cultural phenomena that crosses the Highland Line and, indeed, it is made possible by the line's existence. It is a glorious union of Lowland and Highland.

Water matters. As David Daiches says in his book, *Scotch Whisky*, 'soft water flowing through peat over granite' is said to matter very much in the making of good whisky. It must be pure, clear and soft as well as available in reliable quantities. In reality, most distilleries do not have access to soft water but most of those that do are to be found in Speyside. Running parallel to the Great Glen and the Highland Line faults, the Spey and its tributaries are home to more than 30 distilleries, many of them world-famous names. All malt whisky should be drunk with added water for it releases the full flavour and it is best, if possible, to use water from the same source as the whisky. During the reign of Queen Victoria, Glen Grant used to keep samples near the distillery dam so that discerning customers could taste their drams with the perfect accompaniment. Nowadays bottled still water from the Highlands is a more feasible alternative.

The Scotch Malt Whisky Society

Now headquartered at The Vaults in Leith and with branches in Edinburgh and London, the SMWS has become an institution and an international mail order business. It began in a much more humble manner. A small group of malt whisky enthusiasts clubbed together to buy and bottle a modest quantity of Glenfarclas, a lovely Speyside whisky. Thereafter, they kept buying small, uncommercial amounts and, as the joys of Scotland's national drink in its unblended state waxed ever more popular, membership grew. Bottled from single casks, SMWS whisky has extraordinary character but perhaps its greatest achievement was the purchase of a 31-year-old Springbank some years ago. Very dark, intense and unfathomably complex, its quality has never been bettered. Not that it was possible to tell it was a Springbank. SMWS tradition dictates that all whiskies are numbered and not named. A glossary has to be consulted by those who only buy occasionally. Tremendously flowery and imaginative tasting notes are offered as a substitute for brand names and sometimes drinkers have marvelled at the unlikely comparisons. In the latest list of bottlings, tasting notes have included 'church pews and hymn books', 'ladies' handbags' and 'suede shoes walking through clover'. No matter how inventive, nothing will match the 31-year-old Springbank.

Wherever rain falls and snow melts in the Highlands and the gathered water begins to trickle and flow, it affects the character of whisky. Granite-based streams run clear but where rain and snow seep through fissures and small fractures to collect underground, it becomes mineralised. This can impart a quite different quality but some distilleries located in the Lowlands in areas of intensive farming have had to cease production because their water supplies had become polluted with nitrates from fertilisers. But these difficulties are recent and the early distillers had other, quite different problems.

The Westminster governments of the 18th century and early 19th century had no taste for whisky unless it could be taxed. But, in the more remote glens, the excisemen – also known as 'the gaugers' (pronounced gougers) – had the impossible endless task of finding and closing down thousands of illicit stills. Often they scanned the horizon for the telltale column of peat reek that would give away the location of an operating still but lookouts usually ensured its rapid dismantling and immediate disappearance. One ingenious crofter hid his illicit still near his cottage and dug an underground flue so that the peat smoke was conducted into his cottage chimney and became impossible to detect. Production of illegal whisky was undertaken on an industrial scale in Speyside and indeed was a vital part of the rural economy. Without regular income from distilling, many upland farmers would have been unable to pay their rents. Landlords knew that and colluded in the trade.

Distribution is generally a difficulty for small producers, legal or otherwise, but the farmer distillers of Speyside had developed a reliable network. Thomas Guthrie, the founder of the Ragged School network and one of the leaders of the Free Church of Scotland, was born in 1803. Here is a passage from the *Autobiography of Thomas Guthrie*:

When a boy in Brechin, I was quite familiar with the appearance and on-goings of the Highland smugglers. They rode on Highland ponies, carrying on each side of their small, shaggy, but brave and hardy steeds, a small cask or 'keg' as it was called, of illicit whisky, manufactured amid the wilds of Aberdeenshire or the glens of the Grampians. They took up a position on some commanding eminence during the day, where they could, as from a watchtower, descry the distant approach of the enemy, the exciseman or gauger: then, when night fell, every man to horse, descending the mountains only six miles from Brechin, they scoured the plains, rattled into the villages and towns, disposing of their whisky to agents they had everywhere; and, now safe, returned at their leisure, or often in a triumphal procession. They were often caught, no doubt, with the contraband whisky in their possession. Then they were subjected to heavy fines besides the loss of their goods. But – daring, stout, active fellows – they often broke through the nets, and were not slack, if it offered them a chance of escape, to break the heads of the gaugers. I have seen a troop of thirty of them riding in Indian file, and in broad day, through the streets of Brechin, after they had succeeded in disposing of their whisky, and, as they rode leisurely along, beating time with their formidable codgels on the empty barrels to the great amusement of the public and mortification of the excisemen, who had nothing for it but to bite their nails and stand, as best they could, the raillery of the smugglers and the laughter of the people . . . Everybody, with a few exceptions, drank what was in reality illicit whisky – far superior to that made under the eye of the Excise – lord and lairds, members of Parliament and ministers of the Gospel, and everybody else.

Against a background of near-universal collusion, the whisky trade was impossible to police. Alexander Gordon, the 4th Duke of Gordon, understood this. As the owner of vast tracts of Inverness-shire, Morayshire and Banffshire, he found himself in the centre of the world of illicit distilling. The core problem was that the rates of duty and the costs of licensing a legal still were far too high and on an inappropriate scale. In 1823, Gordon promoted a new act of parliament that set distilling on a new and sensible footing. Having promised his best efforts to help legalise whisky production amongst the tenantry of his own estates, the Duke helped George Smith, a farmer in Glenlivet, to go into legitimate business in 1824. Glenlivet malt already had a reputation (one that has endured) and, when King George IV arrived in Scotland on a state visit in 1822, the portly monarch demanded to be served nothing but. Doubtless no butler or courtier dared point out to the king that he was consuming contraband his government's gaugers had pursued around the countryside.

At first, George Smith found it difficult to establish the new licensed still but, when he ran out of cash, the Duke of Gordon came to the rescue with a loan of £600. George's unlicensed neighbours were none too pleased either and, for years, he never left Glenlivet without a pair of pistols. Elsewhere illicit distillers had burned down licensed premises, seeing them as deadly rivals in what was, as Thomas Guthrie attests, a well-established trade in the early 19th century. A solution more drastic than a posse of damp and beleaguered excisemen was required and, in 1827, a troop of cavalry soldiers garrisoned Corgarff Castle. Lying in the shadow of the highest of the Cairngorms, above Glenlivet, and commanding the glens of west Aberdeenshire, the castle was well placed to scour the more remote uplands. In three years, the troopers suppressed hundreds of illicit stills and, by 1834, George Smith was the only distiller in Scotland's most famous whisky glen. It was a monopoly that could not last.

The logistics of the Smiths' business were pleasingly simple. All the ingredients to make superb malt whisky were at hand and, even in the age of horse-drawn transport, could readily be brought together in quantity. Once whisky had been made and aged, the barrels were trundled 35 miles down through the glens and on across the Laigh of Moray to Burghead. Anchored in the new harbour carved out of the ancient Pictish fortress, ships waited to load their precious cargo and deliver it to thirsty customers in Edinburgh, London and elsewhere. This happy combination of circumstances was obvious to others – and so was the prestige of the name of Glenlivet. Dozens of new licensed distilleries were set up (almost certainly by those who had learned their craft illicitly) and they printed the name of their labels. After all, Glenlivet was a place-name, it did not belong to anyone.

George Smith's son and heir, Col. J. G. Smith, thought otherwise. In 1880, he petitioned the Court of Session and asserted that his local rivals were passing themselves off to unsuspecting customers as somehow connected to the original Glenlivet distillery. The ruling represented a partial success. Others could continue to use the name but only if it was hyphenated with the distillery that made the whisky behind the label – Glenlossie-Glenlivet, Glenfarclas-Glenlivet and so on. Only one, however, that belonging to George & J. G. Smith, was entitled to call itself 'The Glenlivet'.

In Islington, no one was sure about the identity of any sort of whisky. After the initial ruling against blended Scotch whisky, the Distillers Company and others encouraged the landlords to appeal. Eventually a Royal Commission was set up to deliberate on what might be labelled as whisky and what might not. A programme of intensive research was launched. Government officials walked through the doors of 39 pubs in England and 23 in Scotland, ordered a dram and then, to the amazement of the landlords, did not drink it. Instead it was poured into a bottle and sent away for analysis.

Finally reporting in July 1909 (and spelling whisky with an 'e'), the Royal Commission came to momentous conclusions. First, it stated the obvious – at least what would have been obvious to anyone who enjoyed whisky: 'On reference to the analyses, it will be seen that there is a very wide variation between whiskies from different distilleries; and that there is a very wide variation between different whiskies from the same distilleries in different years.'

And then their findings moved quickly to the point – the issue of malt whisky made in a pot still and grain whisky from a patent still: '[W]e have received no evidence to show that the form of the still has any necessary relation to the wholesomeness of the spirit produced . . . we are unable to recommend that the use of the word "whiskey" should be restricted to spirit manufactured by the pot-still process.'

The Commission added a final paragraph that defined whisky even more closely and made it forever Scotch: 'Our general conclusion, therefore, on this part of our enquiry is that "whiskey" is a spirit obtained by distillation from a mash of cereal grains saccharified [turned into sugar] by a diastase [an enzyme] of malt; that "Scotch whiskey" is whiskey, as above defined, distilled in Scotland; and that "Irish whiskey" is whiskey, as above defined, distilled in Ireland.'

Brand protection has been a continuous process. In May 2011, the Scotch Whisky Association secured a binding legal agreement that echoed J. G. Smith's efforts on behalf of Glenlivet. Manufacturers who used the phrase 'Scottish spirits' on their labels while promoting 'whisky' on their websites were forced to desist because the courts believed that consumers might be misled into thinking that they were buying Scotch whisky.

The Ferintosh Exemption

As much as artillery, whisky won the battle of Culloden. Such is the considered opinion of an eminent Scottish scholar and it is not an extravagant claim. In 1688, when the Stuarts were replaced by William of Orange, loyal Jacobites burned the distilleries of Mr Forbes of Culloden at Ferintosh in Ross-shire. He was a supporter of the new king. In compensation the Scottish government granted him exemption from excise payments in return for a modest annual fee. In 1715, during the Jacobite Rising, Forbes of Culloden raised troops to support the government and the Hanoverian succession. Thirty years later, Duncan Forbes of Culloden was Lord President of the Court of Session and again he demonstrated his family's loyalty by persuading several clan chiefs to stay at home. By 1786, the exemption was rescinded for a generous payment of £21,000. In the meantime, Ferintosh whisky had acquired a tremendous reputation, relished for its peaty flavour. Duncan Forbes's heirs were happy with the settlement but a young Robert Burns was not:

> *Thee, Ferintosh! O sadly lost!*
> *Scotland lament frae coast to coast!*
> *Now colic grips, an' barkin hoast*
> *May kill us a'*
> *For loyal Forbes' chartered boast*
> *Is taen awa!*

In the United States, there was a strange period in its modern history when consumers were banned entirely from buying alcohol of any description. Despite a veto from President Woodrow Wilson, the Volstead Act began the notorious era of Prohibition in late 1919. For 14 years, organised crime grew and thrived on the illegal import of alcohol, a good deal of which came from Scotland by sea. The reputation of one smuggler, Capt. McCoy, was such that his name entered the language as a synonym for authenticity, 'the real McCoy'. Evidently, his supply of whisky and other drinks was not adulterated or of low quality. Paradoxically, the effect of Prohibition was to establish a taste for Scotch whisky in the USA, a market that has expanded steadily. All over the world, in the fast-developing economies of India, China and Brazil, this unique product is now enjoyed, even treated with reverence – as it should be. In his excellent *Scotch Whisky: Its Past and Present*, David Daiches wrote a characteristically elegant conclusion: 'The proper drinking of Scotch whisky is more than indulgence: it is a toast to civilisation, a manifesto of man's determination to use the resources of nature to refresh mind and body and enjoy to the full the senses with which he has been endowed.'

5

The Battle of the Graupian Mountain

❖

I N THE SHADOW OF THE MOUNTAINS, standards were planted around the stone circle, their pennants fluttering in the breeze, their totem animals watching over the great muster. To the Prayer Field below Bennachie, a mighty host was marching. In the summer of 83, the kings of the Caledonian kindreds had ridden to the sacred places at the edges of their realms, made sacrifices to sanctify their alliances and talked of the great battle that would surely come. Perhaps they sealed their pact in blood. The ancient ceremony endured long enough to be recorded in the self-consciously Celtic atmosphere of 13th-century Galloway when one of its leading magnates made a bond with a mercenary captain called Gilleruth: 'They made an unheard of covenant, inventing a kind of sorcery, in accord with certain abominable customs of their ancient forefathers. For all those barbarians and their leaders . . . shed blood from the pre-cordial vein into a large vessel . . . and they stirred and mixed the blood after it was drawn: and afterwards they offered it mixed to one another in turn and drank it as a sign that they were henceforward bound in an indissoluble, and as it were, consanguineal covenant, united in good fortune and ill, even to the sacrifice of their lives.'

All of the Caledonian kings knew that a huge Roman army was marching north. A year before, under the command of their general Agricola, large detachments from three legions, several regiments of auxiliaries and squadrons of cavalry had crossed the

River Forth and invaded the north. It seemed that Rome had decided to conquer the whole island for their empire but the campaign began with a near-disaster. Acting on intelligence, Agricola changed his strategy. The campaign is very well recorded in Tacitus's biography of his father-in-law:

> To avoid encirclement by superior forces familiar with the country, he himself divided his army into three divisions and advanced.
>
> When the enemy discovered this, with a rapid change of plan they massed for a night attack on the Ninth Legion, as being by far the weakest in numbers. They cut down the sentries and burst into the sleeping camp, creating panic. Fighting was already going on inside the camp itself when Agricola, who had learned of the enemy's route from his scouts and was following close on their tracks, ordered the most mobile of his cavalry and infantry to charge the combatants from the rear and then the whole army was to raise the battle-cry. At first light the standards gleamed.

In order to mask what looks very like the basic military blunder of dividing his forces, Tacitus makes Agricola seem more alert to the danger than he was in reality. Much more likely is that somehow, in the melee of fighting inside the camp, the commander of the IX Legion got gallopers away to summon help. When they found Agricola's division, presumably asleep in their own camp, they roused them and they buckled on their armour, rushed to the rescue and prevented what would have been annihilation. After this close-run rescue, the Romans retreated southwards to overwinter and to plan a great campaign in the north, the last push needed to bring all of the island of Britannia into the Empire.

Having left garrisons in the forts of southern Scotland, Agricola almost certainly set up his headquarters at the legionary fortress at Carlisle. As the winter winds whistled off the Solway Firth and sentries shivered on the ramparts, staff officers gathered in the Principia, sited somewhere inside the walls of the medieval castle. Stiff vellum maps were rolled out and preparations made. Messengers were sent south to the Prefect of the *Classis Britannica*, the British Fleet. Based at Boulogne, with depots at Dover and Chester, the fleet had originally been built to ferry the legions across the English Channel in AD 43 when the Emperor Claudius ordered an invasion. It both serviced the needs of the army in Britain and kept the Channel clear of pirates and other hostile ships.

By the close of the 1st century AD, the British Fleet had 7,000 sailors and marines under the command of its *trierarchs*, the sea captains, and around 40 ships were in active service. Aside from the more bulky and functional transports that plied regularly between Boulogne, Dover and the other Channel ports, the fleet was mostly made up of biremes. Called *liburnae* after Liburnia, an area of the north-east Adriatic whose pirates first built and developed them, they were fast and sleek with a single square sail and two banks of oarsmen. The prow of each was formed into a ramming beak with a large eye painted on either side and, running before the wind, with the oarsmen pulling hard, the *liburnae* of the *Classis Britannica* could slice quickly through the waves. To those watching from the shore, the Roman fleet looked like a school of giant sharks.

Agricola's *mandata*, his orders to the Prefect of the fleet, were to set sail for the north. A rendezvous with the land army may have been arranged in the Firth of Forth but other duties were specified by the general. Tacitus takes up the narrative:

> Accordingly, he sent the fleet ahead to plunder at various points in order to spread panic and uncertainty. The army was marching light, reinforced by the bravest of the Britons and those whose loyalty had been tested in a long period of peace. So he came to the Graupian Mountain. It had already been occupied by the enemy.
>
> The Britons were, in fact, in no way broken by the outcome of the previous battle: they were awaiting either revenge or enslavement. They had at last learned the lesson that a common

74

danger could only be warded off by a united front. By means of embassies and alliances they had rallied the forces of all their states. Already more than 30,000 armed men could be observed and still all the young men and famous warriors, whose 'old age was still fresh and green', each man wearing the decorations he had won, were flowing in.

So that each king and his war band knew where to muster, the signal mountain ridge of Bennachie was probably chosen and, close by, there lay a famous and sacred place. The stone circle at East Aquhorthies stands in the shadow of what Tacitus called the Graupian Mountain. The name translates as 'the Prayer Field' and it may be that a blood brotherhood of Caledonian kings gathered there in the late summer of 83.

An army of 30,000, even allowing for Roman exaggeration, meant an alliance of many kindreds in the north and they must have come from the names and territories discovered by the fleet on their circumnavigation. These were later plotted on Ptolemy's map. Perhaps the Raven King of the Lugi crossed the Moray Firth with his war band, and the blood-smeared warriors of the Smertae rode east from the Beauly and Dornoch Firths. For strength in numbers, they may have made a rendezvous with their neighbours, the Decantae, 'the Noble Kindred'. Beyond them, on the Atlantic coast of the west, the Carnonacae, 'the People of the Cairns', might have crossed the mountain passes to join the muster. From the south the war bands of the kings of the Venicones, 'the Kindred Hounds', surely came to the Prayer Field below the Graupian Mountain.

As elsewhere in Europe, the Celtic culture of the north of Britain was geared to war and eminence was measured by military prowess. A century before the great muster at Bennachie, Julius Caesar recorded what he saw amongst the leaders of the kindreds of Gaul during his wars of conquest: 'Whenever war breaks out and their services are required . . . they all take the field, surrounded by their retainers and dependants of whom each noble has a greater or smaller number according to his birth and fortune. The possession of such a following is the only criterion of influence and power they recognise.'

While retainers, clients and farmers could afford only the most basic weaponry – a spear, a small round shield and perhaps a long knife – kings and aristocrats wore and carried beautifully made war gear. Bronze and iron helmets have been uncovered by archaeologists and occasionally their animal crests have survived. These tiny metal sculptures of boars, horses, stags, ravens and bulls were both powerful totems and badges of identity.

Although probably first used as a form of protection for the neck and collarbone, torcs may also have been indicators of rank. Found in gold, silver and bronze, some were thick and heavy, perhaps chafing in the urgent movement of battle. Celtic smiths could also make chain mail but only the wealthiest could afford it. Made up from hundreds of small iron rings linked and forged together, a mail shirt takes a modern blacksmith more than 800 hours to complete. But they were much prized because of the freedom of movement they allowed.

Swords were carried only by aristocrats, their tempered steel edges razor sharp and their scabbards gorgeously decorated. These were long slashing swords, like cavalry sabres, and much less suited for stabbing and thrusting in close-quarter conflict. This was to prove a decisive factor in the Battle of the Graupian Mountain.

To protect all of that finery and metalwork, warriors carried shields and again they were sometimes decorated with animal totems. Very beautiful and elaborate shields probably not intended for war (but nevertheless closely resembling practical shields) have been pulled out of watery places. From the deep, anaerobic silt of the River Thames came the famous Battersea Shield and a shield carrying a representation of a boar made from leather was lifted out of the River Witham in Lincolnshire.

Warpaint in the form of tattoos was much cheaper and therefore enjoyed far more widespread use amongst the mass of the huge army mustering at Mons Graupius. Even though no miraculous example of preservation exists, it is likely that the marks made by the tattooist meant something. Other cultures used them as a means of affirming membership of kindreds or military brotherhoods. Historians record such warrior bands in classical Greece and elsewhere in the Mediterranean but the closest parallels are to be found in Ireland. These were the *Fianna*, brotherhoods of young warriors who often terrorised the countryside like bandits or hired themselves out as mercenaries. Later commentators called them 'the sons of death' who bound themselves with evil and pagan oaths and could be identified by *diabolo instinctu*, the tattooed marks of the Devil. Similar devilish marks were almost certainly seen everywhere in the Caledonian army at Bennachie.

Roman Crowns

Only two officers who fought at the Battle of the Graupian Mountain are known by name. Aulus Julius Atticus was killed when, as Tacitus states, 'his youthful eagerness and his spirited horse carried him into the enemy's ranks'. Like Agricola, he was probably fighting far from his native place, the Roman province simply called Province, now Provence. The other officer, Gaius Julius Karus, was probably also a Provencal and an inscription notes that he was decorated for bravery 'in bello Britannico*', the British war. Roman military decorations were formal, awarded at a ceremony and not worn on daily duties. Karus received a Mural Crown, a gold circlet cast to resemble a battlement, and it was given to the first soldier who climbed the wall of a besieged city and planted the standard of the attacking force on it. In his British war, Agricola's army besieged no cities or towns. The only time Tacitus wrote of the Romans attacking a battlement, it was their own in the relief of the camp of the IX Legion. Perhaps Karus led a cohort that retook the rampart held by the insurgent Caledonians. The greatest award a soldier could receive was a Grass Crown and it was reserved for commanders who broke through a blockade to rescue a surrounded Roman army. Made from oak leaves, the Civic Crown was one rung down and it was appropriated by emperors. Its humble motif found its way into the nomenclature of modern military decorations. Interestingly, the intrinsic value of a crown increased as the achievement it rewarded decreased in scale. Gold crowns were given for minor acts of bravery, grass and oak leaves for major acts of heroism.*

In order to make themselves seem bigger and more fearsome, warriors stiffened and spiked up their hair with limewash. This made it a ghostly greyish-white colour and, together with a body covered with tattoos, the effect must indeed have been terrifying. Many men were said by Roman and Greek writers to have fought naked. While there is some evidence that this could mean completely naked, the sense of nudity in Latin and Greek was not quite so absolute, and it could mean that they wore a torc and a helmet. At any rate, compared to the well-protected legionaries and auxiliaries, the mass of the Celtic army at Mons Graupius wore no armour and may have fought bare-chested. Their tattoos were likely to have been seen as magical and powerful – and they should be visible to the gods and their comrades in arms.

The kings of the Caledonian kindreds had reasons other than its prominence for choosing a battleground at Bennachie. At the foot of the mountain, on either side of where the Gadie Burn runs and on the banks of the River Urie, the terrain was reasonably flat. When war bands came to the muster, many kings and aristocrats arrived with their chariots and they would need good ground to manoeuvre in battle. Pulled by two ponies (their tails would have been docked so that they did not foul the wheels or the beam and their manes will have been plaited to make sure the reins and harness did not snag), these small wooden carts were driven by a charioteer who crouched low at the front. Behind him stood a warrior, bracing himself on the flexible wicker floor as the solid wheels bounced over rough ground. The Romans were mightily impressed by the skills and agility of charioteers and when Julius Caesar faced British armies on his expeditions of 55 BC and 54 BC, this was what he saw, and wrote about in his *De Bello Gallico*:

This is their method of fighting from chariots. First they drive around in all directions and throw missiles and cause confusion in the ranks through fear of their horses and the din of their wheels; and when they have worked their way in between the cavalry squadrons, they jump down from the chariots and fight on foot. Meanwhile, the charioteers gradually withdraw from the fighting and position their chariots so that, if they are hard pressed by a host of enemies, they have an escape route to their own side. Thus they provide the mobility of cavalry and the stability of infantry in battle; and by daily practice and training they accomplish so much that, even on the steepest slopes, they can easily continue at full gallop, control and turn swiftly, and run along the beam, stand on the yoke, and from there quickly get back in the chariot.

Agricola and his men saw many chariots at Mons Graupius but they had an added refinement. Tacitus described them as '*covini*'. Fixed to the ends of their axles were scythes which spun viciously when the ponies galloped. Deadly and terrifying to infantry the covini may have been but, on rough, tussocky and boggy ground, they could easily foul and capsize, sending their occupants flying.

At Deskford, near the Moray Firth coast, a carnyx was found. A long J-shaped war trumpet with a boar's open-mouthed head at one end and a mouthpiece at the other, it could be played to imitate animal noises and in particular the snorts and squeals of a charging boar. Others may have been used to mimic the cawing of ravens, the whinnying of horses, the roar of bulls or whatever calls and snorts the totem animal of a kindred might have made. Roman commentators thought carnyxes terrifying in battle. Perhaps they were used at the muster below Bennachie to announce the arrival of different kindreds.

The choice of a sacred site such as East Aquhorthies was not only based on its fame. Such a vast army must have expected victory and the booty that came with it. Caesar explains:

> [T]hey vow to Mars the booty that they hope to take and after a victory they sacrifice the captives, both animal and human, and collect the rest of the spoils in one place. Among many of the tribes great piles can be seen on consecrated ground. It is almost unknown for anyone, in defiance of religious law, to conceal his booty at home or to remove anything placed there. Such a crime is punishable by a terrible death under torture.

As the Caledonian kindreds converged on the Graupian Mountain, they were being watched. Mounted Roman scouts, known as '*exploratores*', skirted their columns, perhaps even captured stragglers, and relayed what information they had gleaned back to Agricola and his commanders. How big was the Caledonian army? Did they have cavalry, archers, chariots? Whatever the nature of the opposing forces, it seemed that they and not the Romans had chosen their ground. Tacitus noted that the Graupian Mountain 'had already been occupied by the enemy'. And, even though the warriors of the kindreds had stationed themselves on the slopes at the foot of the great amphitheatre that is Bennachie, it seemed that, at last, Agricola had his chance – a pitched battle where determination and discipline would triumph.

The sequence of events is implied rather than documented by Tacitus and archaeological finds suggest that the Roman army approached the battlefield from the south-east, marching up the valley of the meandering River Don. At Kintore, the remains of a camp have been found, one large enough to enclose Agricola's vast army. When modern engineers planned a new dual carriageway in 2000 that would drive through part of the site, rescue archaeologists worked quickly. To their surprise, they found the stone bases of 120 field ovens. These strongly suggested something more substantial than an overnight marching camp so perhaps the fortifications were dug as a base where Agricola could wait for the Caledonian muster that his scouts had been reporting. If the Classis Britannica was lying off the mouth of the Dee in what is now Aberdeen harbour, then barges packed with supplies could have been towed up the river to feed the camp at Kintore.

In fact, the army of the kindreds massed further north and Agricola was forced to break camp and march eight miles to battle. The Caledonians who had stormed the camp of the IX Legion the year before had seen a Roman army moving through the countryside but, for the war bands from the north, it was a new and awesome sight.

Rome and the Woods

In the Dark Ages, the Great Wood of Caledon occasionally turned up in sources. The historical Merlin was said to have gone mad after defeat in a particularly gory battle and fled into the Great Wood where he lived a hermitical life. Something like it appears to have existed when Agricola's legions marched north in the 80s AD. After the attack on the camp of the IX Legion, Tacitus wrote that the Caledonians retreated and disappeared into the forest. Impenetrable, dangerous and dark, the forest was an image full of menace in a Roman imagination. Terrible things had happened to legions in forests. In 391 BC, Celtic war bands had crossed the Apennines and destroyed a Roman army in the Ciminian Forest on the southern borders of Tuscany. Afterwards the Senate forbad consuls or generals from leading soldiers into the woods. In AD 9, much worse befell the young Empire. A huge Roman army, comprised of the XVII, XVIII and XIX legions, marched into the Teutoburg Forest. Attacked by the hordes of the barbarian general, Arminius (the original Herman the German), the Romans were annihilated and Varus, their hapless commander, was forced to commit suicide. His corpse was decapitated and his head much prized as a trophy. So great was the humiliation that the Emperor Augustus tore his clothes, refused to cut his hair and went about in rags for months. And the three lost legions were never reformed. Agricola only just managed to avoid a similar disaster on the fringes of the Highland Line.

Following standard military practice, Agricola will have set squadrons of cavalry in front of the column, sweeping the intended line of advance, watching for ambush. There may have been as many as 2,000 troopers riding in the vanguard and on the flanks of the main body of infantry. Then came the battle-hardened Batavians and Tungrians, the regiments of auxiliaries from the lands of the Rhine delta led by their own tribal aristocrats. Behind them rode Agricola and his tribunes, surrounded by a mounted bodyguard. They led the crack troops, the legionaries – detachments of the XX Valeria Victrix, the IX Hispana and the II Augusta. Their burnished armour glinting in the sun, their standard bearers lifting the insignia high, their hobnailed sandals making the low, rumbling thunder of thousands of men on the march, the Roman army was a belly-hollowing sight.

As the kindreds watched their enemy approach, perhaps clashing their weapons in defiance, the legionaries then did something remarkable. When they halted and began to dig a marching camp at Durno, near the handy water supply from the River Urie, it was, in the words of the historian Josephus, as though 'a town was produced in a moment'. In the Jewish War of AD 66–74, Josephus had been amazed by Roman military efficiency. After surveyors had selected and pegged out a site, it was cleared of scrub and roughly levelled and then the ditch and rampart more precisely marked out. Defended by an armed screen of infantry and cavalry, soldiers took a *dolabra* from their packs and began to dig a ditch. Working very quickly – for this was a moment of weakness and the enemy will have been in plain sight – they used these axe-shaped mattocks to cut turf which was placed on the inside of an ever-deepening ditch to form a foundation for a rampart. When the V-shaped ditch had reached a regulation depth and the upcast had been tamped down on the turf base, stakes were driven in and, as Josephus says again, 'quicker than thought, thanks to the great number and skill of the workers', a marching camp rose magically out of the landscape.

At Durno, the long perimeter was adapted to the fall of the ground and shaped into a kinked rectangle. Straight rows of leather tents were pitched, defended gateways made and, in the centre, Agricola's headquarters was set up. Now, the armies faced each other, no more than a mile or two apart. Battle would have to be joined without delay. At least 40,000 men and horses simply could not subsist for long in such a small area. But was there contact between the generals, an agreement to fight, an offer of terms? It seems very likely but impossible to know for certain.

Following classical convention, Tacitus put speeches in the mouths of each commander before battle. Naturally they say a great deal more about the attitudes of a Roman aristocrat, albeit a relative liberal, than they could about the host massed at the foot of Bennachie. In any case, there are several passages clearly borrowed from other sources, most of them histories of campaigns in other parts of the empire. Calgacus was the name of the Caledonian general, described by Tacitus as 'one outstanding among their many leaders for his valour and nobility', and means, simply, the Swordsman. Most likely a soldiers' nickname, something like 'skilled with a sword', the name is not particularly helpful. In any event how many of the host of 30,000 warriors could have heard such a speech? Perhaps Calgacus rode back and forth along the ranks in a chariot, exhorting his countrymen to victory.

Meanwhile, Agricola probably addressed his troops behind the ramparts of the camp at Durno, perhaps exhorting them from an elevated position on horseback. In his retirement the old general may have reminisced with his son-in-law, Tacitus, about what he said on that fateful day but it cannot have resembled what appeared in the account of the battle. As written, Agricola's speech is an elegantly constructed example of classical rhetoric designed to be read rather than said. At the moment of greatest tension and apprehension, with adrenalin flowing, few generals wax lyrical. As the Roman historian Plutarch acidly remarked, '[N]o one talks such nonsense when there is steel at hand.' But the speech is important in another sense – for what it has to say about geography. Several phrases allude to the location of the battle being in the far north of Scotland and the long march through forests and across estuaries to reach what would be the climax and turning point of years of campaigning. 'The furthest point of Britain is no longer a matter of report or rumour,' claimed Agricola, 'for we hold it with camps and with arms. Britain has been discovered and subjugated.'

The 30,000 warriors mustered on the slopes of the great bowl of Bennachie will have considered such an assertion presumptuous – at best. The few hours that were to follow would be more eloquent than any general's speech. Once Agricola had concluded his exhortations, history began to move and events unfold. Tacitus takes up the story:

Even while Agricola was still speaking, the eagerness of the soldiers was apparent and a tremendous outburst of enthusiasm greeted the end of his speech. At once they ran to take up their arms. While they were inspired and eager to charge, he deployed them in battle-line. Of the auxiliaries, he put the infantry, which numbered eight thousand, in the centre, with the three thousand cavalry spread out on the flanks. The legions were stationed in front of the rampart: victory in a battle where no Roman blood was shed would be a tremendous honour; if the auxiliaries were driven back, the legions were a reserve.

The Britons' line was posted on the heights, both to make a show and to intimidate: their front ranks were on the flat ground, the remainder were packed together on the slopes of the hill, rising up as it were in tiers. The charioteers filled the middle of the plain, making a din as they rode back and forth.

Historians have wondered at Tacitus's notion that it was a matter of honour to avoid the shedding of Roman legionary blood in battle. Certainly it was prudent to be careful with the lives of expensively trained and armed soldiers but most of the triumphs of the Republic and the Empire had been achieved by the legions. If this was indeed Agricola's motive for placing the regiments of auxiliaries in the front rank, then it was unique. No other Roman general is recorded as having adopted a similar strategy.

A much more likely reason was a sensible response to what Agricola could see on the flat ground below Bennachie. Hundreds of chariots with scythed wheels were racing back and forth. And chariots had caused problems in Gaul for Roman legionary infantry. Agricola placed his Batavians, Tungrians and his new Southern British recruits in the front rank because they knew how to deal with chariots. While legionary training focused on close-order fighting in tight formations, where men ground forward, stabbing, pushing, thrusting their shields in the faces of their enemies, the auxiliaries were more flexible. The best way of dealing with chariots was to open up the ranks, allow them to be driven through and then surround them. These warriors from the Rhine delta and Southern Britain had stood against the scything charge of chariots before and they knew how to neutralise them.

More than that, the auxiliaries would have been unfazed by the din made by a Celtic host, the blaring of carnyxes, the clashing of swords and spears on shields and the calling out of challenges. As the Caledonian warriors worked themselves up into what was called the rage fit, the fury needed to drive a man to charge into his enemies, the Batavians, Tungrians and Britons will have stood their ground. They had seen and heard it before. And no man will have been tempted to break ranks and respond to the taunting of the charioteers. Single combat in the no-man's-land between battle lines was not uncommon – an ancient tradition, it had endured long enough to pit King Robert the Bruce against Henry de Bohun at Bannockburn in 1314 – but it was not something Roman commanders would allow. Tacitus again: 'At this point, Agricola was anxious, in view of the enemy's superior numbers, that they might attack his front and flanks simultaneously, so he opened out his ranks. Although the line was going to be rather extended and many were urging him to bring up the legions, he was always ready to hope for the best and resolute in the face of difficulties. So he sent away his horse and took up his position on foot in front of the colours.'

The last sentence sounds more like a literary flourish than the record of a real event. Roman generals rarely made the mistake of allowing themselves to sucked into the thick of the fighting. In an infantry battle, especially one fought at close quarters with bladed weapons, all that any soldier can usually see is what is directly in front of him – and that is someone who wanted to kill him. And above the shouting, the deafening noise of screaming war cries and screaming agonies, very little else can be heard. Communicating orders was a formidable problem. So that they could see how the battle was moving and could direct his forces to plug gaps, advance or retreat, generals had, literally, to be above the fray. Perhaps Agricola dismounted to make himself less of a target for missiles but the hint that he took his place in the van, in front of the colours so that he could defend them, is only at attempt by Tacitus to add physical courage to the list of his father-in-law's many other virtues.

From whatever vantage point he chose, the general realised immediately that he had an overriding difficulty, something he had to overcome if Rome was to triumph. The mass of the Caledonians had planted themselves on the slopes of Bennachie and were, therefore, in a very strong position. Infantry charging downhill will always have much greater momentum. And, even if many in the front ranks fall, the sheer impetus of those running behind them will almost always carry all before them. Not for no reason is the phrase 'fighting an uphill battle' used to describe adversity. In order to achieve a decisive victory, Agricola needed to bring the Caledonians down off Bennachie – and it seems that he disposed his forces in order to achieve that.

Watching from the higher ground, Calgacus will have counted only 8,000 or so in the Batavian, Tungrian and British regiments and squadrons of around 3,000 cavalry close at hand. With 30,000 at his disposal, he must have felt that the odds were in his favour, even though he could not have failed to see the reserve of legionaries drawn up in front of the ramparts of the temporary camp at Durno. What he did not realise was that Agricola's disposition of so few men at the battle front was an attempt to tempt Calgacus to charge downhill to secure a quick victory – but, crucially, also abandon his powerful position on the slopes and allow the Romans to do what they did best, to fight a pitched battle.

Meanwhile, the front lines closed on each other so that both sides were now able to see clearly the enemy they had to kill. Under their metal helmets and with their shields up to deflect missiles, the auxiliaries glared at the half-naked, tattooed warriors with the spiked lime-washed hair. And then the first orders were roared across the battlefield and trumpets sounded. Volleys of javelins flew into the air and the Caledonians responded with spears. In order for javelins to be effective, men needed to be within 30 metres of their targets. Tacitus's excellent narrative continues:

> The battle opened with fighting at long range: the Britons not only stood firm but displayed skill in parrying the javelins of our men with their massive swords or catching them on their short shields, while hurling a great rain of spears themselves. Then Agricola exhorted the four Batavian and two Tungrian cohorts to fight hand to hand at sword's point. This was what they had been trained for in their long service, whereas it was awkward for the enemy with their small shields and enormous swords – for the swords of the Britons, having no points, were unsuited for a cut and thrust struggle and close-quarters battle. So the Batavians rained blows indiscriminately, struck with their shield-bosses, and stabbed in the face. When they had cut down those posted on the plain, they started to push their battle-line up the hillsides. The other cohorts, in eager competition, pressed forward to attack, and cut down the nearest of the enemy. In the haste of victory a good many were left half-dead or untouched.

Agricola had ordered the Batavians, Tungrians and British regiments to open out their ranks not only to extend their line but also so that the scythed chariots could be neutralised. But in the tussocky, rough and perhaps boggy ground, the Roman advance appeared to stall and falter. It may be that it was then Calgacus saw his chance. Tacitus again: 'The Britons stationed on the hilltops had as yet taken no part in the battle, and, not being involved, were regarding our small numbers with contempt. Now they began gradually to descend and to work their way round the rear of the winning side. But Agricola, who had feared this very move, sent four regiments of cavalry, which had been reserved for the emergencies of battle, to block them as they came on. The more ferociously they charged, the more vigorously he drove them back and scattered them in flight.'

This was the turning point of the battle. Having lured Calgacus off the hillside, Agricola had then to defeat him decisively on the plains, not only prevent a fatal encirclement of his army but also drive the Caledonians from the field. With only his cavalry, without the intervention of the legions, he succeeded. 'Thus the Britons' tactics recoiled on themselves. The cavalry regiments, on the general's command, wheeled round from the front of the battle and charged the enemy in the rear. Now indeed a vast and grim spectacle unfolded on the open plains: the cavalry pursued, inflicted wounds, took captives, and, as fresh foes appeared, butchered their prisoners.'

According to Tacitus, the Battle of the Graupian Mountain turned into a rout and 10,000 Caledonians were killed, no doubt most of them falling as they fled. Only 360 Romans died. One of these numbers seems suspiciously rounded and can only be an estimate while the other is surprisingly small. While Tacitus may have risked exaggeration, he was nevertheless right to report an emphatic Roman victory. At the very ends of the Earth, against overwhelming odds, in difficult and unfamiliar territory and in the shadow of the mountains, Roman soldiers had crushed a barbarian army. 'At dawn the next day,' wrote Tacitus, 'the scale of the victory was more apparent: the silence of desolation on all sides, the hills lonely, homesteads smouldering in the distance, not a man to encounter the scouts.'

Emphatic though it was – and, in the long story of the Highland Line, no greater battle was fought – the victory at the Graupian Mountain had no lasting political impact. With the summer already over, Agricola turned his army southwards and led them to winter quarters. Meanwhile the British Fleet sailed as far north as Shetland and circumnavigated what its captains must have thought of as the conquered island of Britain. But it was a fleeting moment of triumph. In the angry, concise phrase, 'Britain was completely conquered – and straight away let go', Tacitus expressed his disgust at the actions of the Emperor Domitian. Trouble was bubbling up elsewhere in the Empire and he ordered the transfer of troops from Britain. Rome retreated south and, by AD 90, the Caledonian kings were once again masters of Scotland north of the Forth.

The battle itself may have had little long-term significance but the transmission of its story did. In a fascinating footnote, it named – wrongly – some of Scotland's most impressive geography. When Tacitus's manuscript was first printed in Italy between 1475 and 1480 by Francesco dal Pozzo, a mistake was made. Instead of 'the Graupian Mountain', the Italian editors rendered it as 'the Grampian Mountain' and the mistaken name has stuck.

6

The History of the Sun

✴

A BRILLIANT AMERICAN scientist, Jack Eddy, understood how delicate was the balance between the history of the Sun and the history and health of the Earth. By gathering historical data reaching back to Galileo and even beyond and by using new, unexpected sources in an enormously influential paper published in 1976, he offered a much clearer picture of a prime cause of climate change.

Eddy studied the period known as the Little Ice Age. This prolonged sequence of bad weather lasted many centuries, from the early 14th to the mid 19th. There were intervals of relative relief but records showed that there were especially severe winters and poor summers from 1460–1550, 1645–1715 and 1790–1820. Using the pioneering work of Victorian scientists, Edward Maunder and Gustav Spörer, Eddy realised that these long cold and wet periods coincided with changes on the surface of the Sun.

Since the earliest records were kept in China in 324 BC, observers have been able to see with the naked eye black spots on the Sun, usually when it is weak, at sunrise and sunset, and can be looked at directly. Later, astronomers could avoid the blinding dazzle by looking through glass, darkly. By the time Galileo had revolutionised techniques and understandings of the heavens, regular records of what was known as sunspot activity were being kept. From an analysis of these, Jack Eddy realised that the three sequences of prolonged bad weather during the Little Ice Age corresponded closely with low or no counts of sunspots.

At first reading, this may seem counter-intuitive. These black areas can be huge, sometimes 80,000 kilometres in circumference, larger than the Earth itself. Surely fewer black spots on the surface of the Sun should make it shine more brightly and send out even more warmth into the solar system. What Eddy explained in 1976 was that the opposite was true. The margins of sunspots turn out to be much hotter than the rest of the surface of the Sun and the more there are, the greater the brightness and heat, what is called the Solar Constant.

During the second half of the 17th century, astronomers saw very few sunspots. In what Jack Eddy called the Maunder Minimum (after the 19th-century scientist who first noticed it), there was a series of short and wet summers followed by very cold winters. This particularly affected tree growth and, in a fascinating aside, music-loving scientists believe that the birth of the great violin maker, Antonio Stradivari, a year before the onset of the Maunder Minimum, was very significant. His famous instruments are thought to have unrivalled tone because of the slow-growing, very dense wood he used.

In his paper of 1976, Eddy showed that, as a direct result of a very small variation, as little as 0.1 per cent, in the Solar Constant caused by the absence of sunspots, the Earth's weather changed dramatically. Across a wide swathe of Northern Europe, the summer of 1695 saw weeks of heavy rain and flooding and then a sudden autumn frost blackened ripening crops over a huge area. From Estonia in the eastern Baltic, through Scandinavia and in Scotland, there was wholesale crop failure and a meagre or non-existent harvest. A bitter winter followed the autumn frost and people slowly began to starve. 1696 was little better as rain fell throughout the summer. Children and old people were the first to die as the snows came early, falling in October. And, by the time of the thaws and the snowmelt of the following spring, many corpses were revealed.

In Aberdeenshire, the effects of what was counted as a famine on a biblical scale were recalled by a minister, the Rev. Alexander Johnson. In the central, normally fertile parishes of Mar and the Garioch, there was devastation:

> Of 16 families that resided at the farm of Littertie, 13 were extinguished. On the estate of Greens, which presently accommodates 169 individuals, 3 families (the proprietor's included) only survived. The extensive farms of Touchar, Greeness, Overhill and Burnshide of Idoch, now containing more than 100 souls, together with some farms of the parish of Turriff, being entirely desolated, were converted into a sheep-walk by the Errol Family, to whom they belonged. The inhabitants of the parish in general were diminished by death to one half, or as some affirm, to one fourth of the preceding number.

It is likely that, over the whole of Aberdeenshire, a fifth of the population of the county perished in the years after 1695 and, in the Highlands, the death rate was just as severe. Many emigrated, often to Ulster, and deserted landscapes such as those described by Alexander Johnson were seen everywhere in the north.

Perhaps on humanitarian grounds, certainly for economic reasons, landowners in the generation following the famine were determined to improve agricultural methods. Sir Archibald Grant's father bought the Monymusk Estate in 1713, never having seen it for himself. It lay to the south of Bennachie and, when the young Grant arrived, he wrote a depressing description of what he found – essentially the aftermath of the famine:

> The house was an old castle with battlements and six different roofs of varying heights and directions, confusedly and inconveniently combined, and all rotten, with two wings more modern, of two stories [sic] only, the half of windows of the higher rising above the roofs, with granaries, stables and houses for all cattle, and of the vermin attending them, close adjoining, and with the heath and muir reaching in angles or gushets to the gate, and

The Parish State

By the 18th century, Scotland was a nation of parishes, more than 900 in all, and such was the grip of the Kirk on local life that this system amounted to a state within a state. Kirk elders were elected for life to act as boards of governors. They selected the minister each time there was a vacancy and were ultimately more powerful. Parishes were the lowest, most local rung of government and they had three key functions. The collection and distribution of funds for the poor was the framework of a very elementary welfare state. Schools were paid for and supervised by the parish and the Kirk Session supervised the morals of the parishioners. While more serious offences were referred to higher authority, parish courts dealt with assault, theft, wife-beating and sexual behaviour. If anyone wished to move from one parish to another, they required a passport known as a testificat, a certificate of good behaviour that required to be agreed and signed by the minister. In 1712, the Toleration Act allowed the Episcopalian Church to hold services and the legislation was much resented for it broke the monopoly hold of the Kirk. By the 1750s, the judicial powers of the parish courts were on the wane and they increasingly focused on sexual offences. A deliberately humiliating tariff of punishments was devised. Offenders had to appear before the congregation wearing sackcloth each Sunday. Three appearances were demanded for fornicators, six for a second offence and twenty-six for adulterers, and those who committed incest were forced to appear every Sunday for a year.

much heath near, and what land near the farms was in culture [cultivation], by which their cattle and dung were always at the door. The whole land raised and uneven, and full of stones, many of them very large, of a hard iron quality, and all the rigs crooked in the shape of an S, and very high and full of noxious weeds and poor, being worn out by culture, without proper manure or tillage. Much of the land and muir near the house, poor and boggy; the rivulet that runs before the house in pits and shallow streams, often varying channel with banks, always ragged and broken. The people poor, ignorant and slothful: and ingrained enemies to planting, enclosing or any improvements or cleanness; no keeping of sheep or cattle or roads but four months when oats and barley, which was the only sorts of their grain, was on ground. The farm houses, and even corn mills and mains and school, all poor dirty huts, pulled in pieces for manure or fell of themselves almost each alternate year.

In essence, Grant was describing the landscape of medieval Scotland, a rural landscape that had lain unchanged for many centuries. It was open, windswept, without fences or hedges, and there were few trees to provide shelter. Land was let in small parcels to cottars who tilled the inbye fields and grazed animals on what was called the muir or moorland. A scatter of farm cottages patterned the countryside and the holdings attached to each were not laid out in the tidy pattern of modern fields. Instead, open rigs were ploughed and planted usually only with oats or barley (the S-shape Grant complained about was caused by the need for a cumbersome plough team of oxen to begin their turn early at the end of each furrow). In the ditches between the rigs, thistles, corncockle and other weeds were allowed to grow tall so that the cottars could cut them in the late autumn for winter forage for their beasts. Over centuries of tillage, stones had been tumbled into the ditches, something Grant remarked upon.

There were no machines to help with heavy labour. Cottars depended exclusively on muscle power – their own and that of oxen and horses – to do all the work of farming and the landscape reflected those limitations. It was certainly not picturesque, and only occasionally beautiful, but it was very quiet. In an age before the clank of machinery or, much later, the hum of engines, rural Scotland heard only the bleating ewes and lambs, the trumpeting of cattle and the cry and shriek of birds. And, on moonless nights, the hushed countryside could be a dangerous place, black-dark with no roads or outside lights. It is little wonder that people stayed indoors, huddled around the fire, talking of ghosts, ghouls and the fell creatures of the silent night.

The tumbledown houses noted by Archibald Grant may well have been snug enough. Most will have been built in the common long-house shape with living quarters at one end and a byre at the other. Dividing humans and beasts was a passageway called a through-gang and it led directly from the front door to the back. Often there was a midden near a door, against the wall of the house, a rubbish tip of organic matter (there was no other sort until the modern era) that would rot down and be used to muck the inbye fields after the harvest. Abutting the back door was usually a yard, somewhere beasts could be led out and tethered for milking or some other purpose. Because cottages were dark and often smoky, most domestic work was done outside if the weather allowed. Surprisingly, at least for delicate modern nostrils, much was done by the midden.

Inside a cottage a constant fire burned or smouldered. As many did, the cottars at Monymusk had access to peat. Some cottages acquired chimneys and a fireplace but others persisted with the traditional down-hearth. This was a central fire whose smoke drifted upwards and seeped through the thatch. Made safe by a circle of large, flat and blackened stones, it was used for cooking as well as heat and light, and cooking pots sat on those stones that projected a little into the embers. Families sat around the fire on low stools or on the floor of brackens or straw over beaten earth to eat and talk and they slept in its glow.

These simple little houses may seem primitive, leaky, shared with mice, rats and fleas, but they were usually warm. Nowadays, people rarely arrive home utterly exhausted, soaked to the bone, or numbed by the intense cold of the winter. We are not often so tired and hungry that our bodies shake because of a lack of calories. In the relatively recent past, Scots who worked on the land regularly suffered all of these extremes and their dark little cottages were a welcome place of warmth, shelter from the elements and somewhere they could fill their hollow bellies with hot food and enjoy the firelit company of their families.

What Archibald Grant saw at Monymusk was a pressing need to change that ancient way of life. In order to avoid the appalling privations of the late 1690s and to make the most of his decaying estate, he began to take action. His immediate priority was trees.

By indulgence of a very worthy father, I was allowed in 1716, though very young, to begin to enclose and plant and provide and prepare nurseries. At the time there was not one acre on the whole estate enclosed, nor any timber upon it, but a few elms, sycamore and ash about a small kitchen garden adjoining the house, and some straggling trees at some of the farm yards, with a small copse wood, not enclosed and dwarfish and browsed by sheep and cattle.

Grant was only 20 years old when he began to have trees planted but even he could not hope to see them mature. What his saplings in their shelter belts and avenues would eventually achieve was the clear enclosure of land into fields of a workable size. Throughout the 17th and 18th centuries, landowners pushed hard and sometimes ruthlessly to change the ancient pattern of farming and there was an undoubted and heavy human cost. Improvement was forced through but at a price that is sometimes ignored amidst the general approval of progress.

By definition, enclosure ended ancient customary rights whereby small farmers and cottars could make use of what had been seen as common land. When powerful landowners claimed ownership of commons and also consolidated estates, they evicted cottars and incorporated their smallholdings into much larger, more commercial farms. This process became known as 'the Lowland Clearances', a time of brutal, enforced social change much less recognised than the later Highland Clearances. Mirroring the later fate of crofters, cottars were swept off land their families had farmed for many generations, their snug little houses were often levelled and the old arrangement of inbye, outbye and the common muir consigned to history.

At Monymusk, Archibald Grant not only began the planting of trees – it is estimated that he had 50 million put in the ground in his lifetime – he also had the land drained and cleared of stones. These were used to build drystane dykes around the new fields and this simple, obvious but very arduous process probably doubled the number of acres that could be cultivated on his estate. Equally important was good drainage. New techniques were imported from the Netherlands and hidden under many of Scotland's quiet and green fields are many thousands of miles of drains. These supplied another use for the stones picked up from the rigs. Old stane-drains were constructed at first (and many were still working until modern deep ploughing destroyed them) and later augmented or replaced by tiled conduits made from fired clay.

In 1722, Archibald Grant was elected MP for Aberdeenshire. His visits to Westminster brought him into contact with famous agricultural improvers, notably Jethro Tull and 'Turnip' Townshend, the English aristocrat nicknamed for the vegetable he introduced. Tull's seed drill replaced the old method of sowing by broadcast, the rhythmic scattering of seeds from side to side by hand while walking up and down the rigs. Instead of this more random and wasteful method, the seed drill planted in neat and regular rows. This, in turn, helped greatly with the grinding job of summer weeding. Between the straight rows of seedlings, Tull's new horse-drawn hoe could root out weeds quickly and repeatedly and prevent the young plants from being choked.

Crop rotation rather than the introduction of turnips (admirable vegetable though it is) was the real innovation imported by Viscount Townshend. In the old agriculture, rigs were rotated on a three-field system with two bearing crops while the third was left fallow. In Flanders, Townshend saw the benefits of four-field rotation because it left nothing fallow. Instead, nutrient-restoring root crops such as turnips and clover (classed as a legume) were planted. The particular advantage of turnips was that they supplemented winter feed for cattle and avoided the need for the traditional cull in late autumn. Some varieties were imported from Sweden and were, of course, called swedes. In Scotland the Swedish word for them was imported as well and *rotabagga* quickly adapted into Scots as 'bagies'.

Bagies were grown first in Scotland at Monymusk. While he was at Westminster, Archibald Grant ran his estate through his factor, Alexander Jaffrey, and sent streams of instruction north by letter. These served as a handy chronicle of some of the most radical changes. It is clear that the effects of new rotations, new crops, new machinery, all of the labour of land improvement and the intensive programme of tree planting took a generation or more to become obvious – but, despite initial hostility amongst the people of Monymusk, they were dramatic. With improved crop yields, milker cows kept alive through the winter and the general rise in the quality of the food produced, people were healthier and the spectre of famine dimmed and eventually disappeared. By the time of *The First Statistical Account of Scotland* in 1792, the population of Monymusk Parish has risen to 1,127.

All over 18th-century Scotland, improving landlords and farmers created a new landscape, the homely geometry of fields, fences and hedges, drystane dykes snaking up hillsides, dense shelter belts and woods of deciduous and evergreen trees and busy farm steadings clustered together with the cottage rows – everywhere there was the overwhelming sense of the hand of man. Tull's seed drill and Townshend's innovations played vital roles but perhaps the most influential of all was a Scotsman whose name is now almost entirely forgotten. A Berwickshire blacksmith, James Small, invented the swing plough and it revolutionised agriculture.

Working in smiddies in Berwickshire and in Yorkshire and in contact with the Carron Ironworks near Falkirk, Small made and remade dozens of prototypes of his new design. He wanted to replace the auld Scotch ploo. It was heavy and needed a team of oxen to pull it through the ground. Mostly made of wood, it often broke down and was unable to turn the furrow slice over completely. It also needed plough followers to bash down big clods and pull out weeds. By contrast, Small invented a plough-share cast entirely from iron. Its slightly screwed shape enabled it to plough deeper and to turn over the furrow slice completely. And, because it could cut cleanly through the ground and created less friction, a pair of horses or even a single strong horse could pull it. No plough followers were needed and both horse and plough could be guided by one skilled man.

Small did not patent his invention (and he died in poverty) and therefore it was copied and adapted all over Britain and abroad. Because it was designed to plough deeper than the auld ploo, it improved drainage and brought more land into cultivation. More than any other Scot, more than Grant or the other improvers in the south, James Small changed the landscape and made life better and easier for those who worked on it. And, by his gifts, he also greatly accentuated the economic and cultural differences between Highland and Lowland.

As one-man ploughing and other sorts of horse working developed and the use of machinery spread in the Lowlands, 18th-century farming became less and less labour intensive. Emigration abroad and to towns and cities took many away from the land their families had worked on for generations but others stayed and adapted. Horse working needed blacksmiths and not just for shoeing. Smiddies turned out cartwheels and made and repaired iron ploughs, harrows and all sorts of other gear. Masons and labourers built the new farmhouses and steadings and laid down better roads. There was a tremendous surge in textile production as it became, literally, a cottage industry. Not only was wool off the backs of the flocks woven into cloth, the increasing amount of flax grown on Scottish farms was made into linen. The Scots word for flax is lint and it can still be seen as an element in rural place-names all over the Lowlands.

All of these seismic shifts in agriculture certainly changed life on the land radically but they also exerted a profound influence on those who were not directly affected – those who lived on the other side of the Highland Line.

As the new techniques were progressively adopted and more land came under the plough, stock rearing became less attractive to Lowland farmers. High-yield cereal production was, in any case, more immediately profitable than waiting for cattle to mature. It was different in the glens. As the depredations inflicted by the Duke of Cumberland and his troops in the aftermath of Culloden demonstrated, Highland pastures could sustain many herds and flocks. In fact, the Union of the Parliaments of 1707 had opened up lucrative, large and hungry markets in England. Scotch beef was popular – even if its producers were not. Before the events of 1745 and 1746, cattle droving had begun to develop and, by the middle of the 19th century, the business of supplying the south with beef had become an enormously important sector of the Scottish economy.

Here is a description of the main destination of droving out of the Highlands – the series of cattle markets known as the Falkirk Trysts. In 1849, they made a deep impression on an English essayist, Thomas Gisborne:

[At Falkirk people] will there witness a scene to which certainly Great Britain, perhaps even the whole world, does not afford a parallel . . . There are three trysts every year – the first in August, the second in September, and the last and largest in October. The cattle stand in a field in the parish of Larbert at a distance of nearly three miles from Falkirk, at a place called Stenhousemuir. The field on which they assemble contains above 200 acres, well-fenced and in every way adapted for the purpose. The scene, seen from horseback, from a cart, or some erection, is particularly imposing. All is animation, bustle, business and activity; servants running about shouting to the cattle, keeping them together in their particular lots and ever and anon cudgels are at work upon the horns and rumps of the restless animals that attempt to wander in search of grass or water.

The cattle dealers of all descriptions chiefly on horseback, are scouring the field in search of the lots they require. The Scottish drovers are for the most part mounted on small, shaggy, spirited ponies that are obviously quite at home among the cattle; and they carry their riders through the throngest groups [of cattle] with astonishing alacrity. The English dealers have in general, large, stout horses, and they pace the ground with more caution, surveying every lot carefully as they go along. When they discover the cattle they want, they enquire the price. A good deal of riggling takes place, and when the parties come to an agreement, the purchaser claps a penny of arles [a deposit] into the hand of the stockholder, observing at the same time 'It's a bargain'. Tar dishes are then got, and the purchaser's mark being put upon the cattle, they are driven from the field. Besides numbers of shows, from 60 to 70 tents are erected along the field for selling spirits and provisions . . . What an indescribable clamour prevails in most of these party-coloured abodes!

Far in the afternoon, when frequent calls have elevated the spirits and stimulated the colloquial powers of the visitors, a person hears the uncouth Cumberland jargon and the prevailing Gaelic, along with innumerable provincial dialects, in their genuine purity, mingled in one astounding roar. All seem inclined to speak: and raising their voices to command attention, the whole of the orators are obliged to bellow as loudly as they can possibly roar. When the cattle dealers are in the way of their business, their conversation is full of animation, and their technical phrases are generally appropriate and highly amusing.

The trysts were the – usually – joyful culmination of immense journeys, a great deal of effort, some danger and no little skill. Droving developed in the Highlands as more than a complement or a reaction to the agricultural revolution in the Lowlands. The Union of 1707 opened a huge market for beef (and lamb and mutton) while improving farmers were cultivating more and more arable land and, for Highland stocksmen, their beasts became more valuable, in fact their sole cash crop. More than that, the market for salt beef expanded greatly in the later 18th century as Britain sought to be Great and embarked on a series of imperial wars, both in Europe and North America. Not only did the glens and the islands supply many of the soldiers who fought and died to create the Empire, those they left at home reared the beef the armies marched on. But, by the time Thomas Gisborne wrote his entertaining account of the Falkirk Trysts in 1849, droving was beginning to wane. Built at tremendous speed, railways were reaching across the country and, by the 1860s, cattle dealers could buy their beasts 'off the hill' and transport them quickly to southern markets by train. The tracks could not reach everywhere, particularly through the awkward and pre-cipitous geography of the Highlands, and the trysts lingered on until the end of the 19th century. But their great days had passed and the remarkable phenomenon of droving became little more than a memory.

It left few accounting records but historians have pieced together some colourful sources that show that the organisation of the trade was simple yet impressive in its scale. Highland chiefs and landowners were generally paid rents in kind rather than cash and cattle was the main currency. Landowners also acted as agents for tenant farmers who had surplus to sell or they bought from them directly. Many crofter–farmers had to sell their beasts on before the winter in any case since they did not have easy access to the new sources of fodder being grown in the Lowlands. And cattle supplied their own transport. They walked to market.

After the first herds were collected up in localities, the cattle were driven on to a larger, more central market. Aikey Fair at Old Deer in the Buchan was one such. The largest in the north of Scotland, it was always very busy at the end of July. After one fair day in 1839, a drove of 6,000 beasts moved south through Tarves in a continuous line, a mile long.

Lairds and their tacksmen, the men on the shaggy ponies who so impressed Thomas Gisborne, drove their herds to Lowland markets or trysts but most men walked and had dogs with them to keep the herds together. It was thought that one man and a good dog could manage 50–60 head. And, when drovers stopped for the night, the first thing they did was to find food for their faithful dogs. Often these men were farmers who could afford to be away between sowing time and harvest time. All were armed. Moving large herds of valuable animals through countryside that was not very friendly could be problematic and men carried dirks, pistols, swords and even muskets. In the Disarming Acts after the Jacobite Rebellions of 1715 and 1745, drovers were ex-empted. The trade was so important to England that it could not be jeopardised and, in the Highlands, cattle stealing was almost an honourable tradition and very widespread.

At the likes of Aikey Fair in the Buchan and St Lawrence Fair in the Garioch, cattlemen who assembled droves as large as that of 1839 may have done so for security but such scale did present problems. As thousands of beasts moved through the countryside, especially in late July, they could be a danger to crops and stampeding or panicked animals would break down fences in moments. Eventually, droving paths were made, corridors 50–100 feet wide enclosed by dykes or turf banks on either side. Some are still visible in the Border hills. However many there were in a drove, the beasts were not to be hurried. So that they kept their condition and could graze and drink along the way, dogs did not snap at their heels and men tried only to keep the herd moving forward as one. If a drove covered ten or twelve miles a day, that was a good day.

In the late summer of 1723, a large drove was collected at Broadford on the Isle of Skye and then moved eastwards to the shore at Kylerhea, where there is a narrow strait. An account of 1813 tells what happened next:

All the cattle reared in the Isle of Skye which are sent to the southern markets pass from that island to the mainland by the ferry of Kylerhea. Their numbers are very considerable, by some supposed to be 5,000 but by others 8,000 annually, and the method of ferrying them is not in boats . . . but they are forced to swim over Kylerhea. For this purpose the drovers purchase ropes which are cut at the length of three feet having a noose at one end. This noose is put round the under-jaw of every cow, taking care to have the tongue free. The reason given for leaving the tongue loose that the animal may be able to keep the salt water from going down its throat in such a quantity as to fill all the cavities in the body which would prevent the action of the lungs; for every beast is found dead and said to be drowned at the landing place to which this mark of attention has not been paid. Whenever the noose is put under the jaw, all the beasts destined to be ferried together are led by the ferryman into the water until they are afloat, which puts an end to their resistance. Then every cow is tied to the tail of the cow before [in front] until a string of six or eight be joined. A man in the stern of the boat holds the rope of the foremost cow. The rowers then play [sic] their oars immediately. During the time of high water or soon before or after full tide is the most favourable passage because the current is then least violent. The ferrymen are so dextrous that very few beasts are lost.

Once the cattle had shaken off the seawater and been untied, the drovers moved them inland from Glenelg to Glen Shiel before reaching the Great Glen at Fort Augustus. From there, they pushed on into the mountains and over the difficult Pass of Corrieyairack and thence to Dalwhinnie. There, in the late summer of 1723, they met a travelling clergyman, Bishop Forbes, and he was also impressed by the drovers' skill, organisation and resourcefulness:

They had four or five horses with provisions for themselves by the way, particularly blankets to wrap themselves in when sleeping in the open air, as they rest on the bleak mountains, the heathy moors, or the verdant glens, just as it happens, towards the evening. They tend their flocks [he means herds] by night and never move till about eight in the morning and then march the cattle at leisure that they may feed a little as they go along. They rest awhile at midday to take some dinner and so let the cattle feed and rest as they please. The proprietor does not travel with the cattle but has one [man] for his deputy to command the whole and he goes to the place appointed against the day fixed for the fair. When the flock is very large, as the present, they divide it, though belonging to one, into several droves that they may not hurt one another in narrow passes, particularly on bridges many of which they go along. Each drove has a particular number of men with some boys to look after the cattle.

What kept the herds together was mostly instinct. Compared with modern bullocks that spend winters in huge cattle courts and are fed on silage, Highland cattle of the 18th century were wild and often difficult to manage. Having spent all their lives, winter and summer, out in unfenced, open pasture, conforming to their own hierarchies, deferring to king bulls, they could be a handful for the herd laddies and their dogs. Not shaggy like the familiar picture-postcard Highland cattle, they were in reality small and most of them black. But they did have horns and, in the narrow places mentioned by Bishop Forbes or in potentially panicky situations like river crossings where they might at best spook or at worst stampede, they could be difficult and dangerous.

Armed, kilted, weather beaten and used to living outside, Highlanders also presented a vivid spectacle as the herds moved through the Lowlands at the end of their journeys. Observers thought them bearlike, swathed in thick plaids that smelled of heather and peat smoke, and some believed the drovers to be wild, shaggy like their ponies and uncultured. What helped convert the unfamiliar into a threat was, of course, language. The herdsmen shouted at their cattle and their dogs in Gaelic and many will not have had much English.

But the drovers were much respected for their skill and hardihood. Here is Edmund Burt, writing in the 1720s, watching a difficult moment in a drove:

> It was a time of rain by a wide river where there was a boat to ferry over the drovers. The cows were about 50 in number and took the water like spaniels, and when they were in, their drivers made a hideous cry to urge them forwards: this, they told me, they did to keep the foremost of them from turning about, for in that case, the rest would do the like and then they would be in danger, especially the weakest of them, to be swept away and drowned by the torrent.

Even now, long after the end of droving, their routes can still be made out, especially in the more remote glens. At their habitual overnight stopping places, what were known as 'stances', the beasts' droppings mucked the ground over many summers. Consequently the grass in those places still looks significantly greener in the springtime and the ewes and their lambs graze there because it is the most succulent. It is a surprising but appropriate elegy for a remarkable age, a period when many peaceful journeys were made across the Highland Line.

7

Swordland

❋

O N 8 APRIL 1940, Colonel Birger Eriksen must have reflected that, in life, timing was everything. The commander of the Oscarsborg Fortress, an artillery battery built on islands in the Oslofjord, was 64 and had only one year's service left until retirement. When Hitler had ordered the invasion of Poland in September 1939, Eriksen and his fellow officers suspected that there would be war in other parts of Europe and that Norway's neutrality was unlikely to be respected. What made matters even worse was an immediate lack of manpower for the Norwegian army. Conscription was quickly introduced. Almost the entire 450-strong garrison of the Oscarsborg Fortress was made up of raw recruits and, as if that was not bad enough, the commander of their most deadly armament, a secret land-based torpedo battery was on sick leave.

Desperate measures were required. There were rumours of a German army mobilising on the Danish frontier. Eriksen sent an urgent message to an old comrade who had retired to the town of Drøbak, just across the fjord from the fortress. Would the 78-year-old Andreas Anderssen take his uniform out of the wardrobe, dust it and himself down and rejoin the Norwegian army? A boat was sent and the old man, who had retired in 1927, landed on the island and immediately ordered a thorough inspection of the torpedo battery. It was then made ready for action. Having first served at the secret installation in 1909, he knew its workings intimately.

On the late evening of 8 April, Col. Eriksen received a series of disturbing reports. A flotilla of unidentified warships had entered the Oslofjord. The fortress at the mouth of the fjord had fired warning shots but, in the gloaming, the dark outlines of at least six ships were able to force their way into the fjord and they were steaming northwards to Oscarsborg and beyond it to Oslo. From King Haakon, his government and the Norwegian Parliament, there had been no clear direction, no orders on how to deal with the momentous events that were unfolding as darkness fell. Col. Eriksen had very little reliable intelligence of any sort and no confirmation that the flotilla closing in on his fortress were German or Allied. And Norway was formally neutral.

After a hurried conference with Lt Col. (retd) Anderssen, Eriksen gave orders to make ready. The artillery crews would stand to. All men with even the slightest experience were pressed into service on the ramparts. Cooks were woken and, with the young recruits helping, they and others manned the great guns.

Just after 4 a.m. on 9 April, Col. Eriksen was told that his lookouts could make out the looming shape of a large battleship leading a flotilla of smaller vessels, at least one of which was heavily armed. All batteries were alerted, the breaches of their huge guns were loaded and Andreas Anderssen had torpedoes forward, ready to fire. As the unidentified ships steamed into range and Eriksen prepared to give the order to attack, he said, 'Either I will be decorated or I will be court-martialled. Fire!'

The cooks, the raw recruits and the few experienced NCOs and artillery officers did their job fearlessly and clinically. Shells slammed into the leading ship and it immediately caught fire. Anderssen's deadly torpedoes slid silently under the dark waters of the fjord and scored direct hits. The large battleship blazed, doomed, and it passed close to the walls of the Oscarsborg Fortress. Bizarrely, the defenders thought they could hear men on the stricken ship singing. It was 'Deutschland, Deutschland über alles'. A few minutes later Col. Eriksen received a delayed message that the flotilla had at last been identified as German. The leading ship was the battleship *Blücher* and it sank with all hands in the Oslofjord a little way to the north of Andreas Anderssen's torpedo battery. Believing the waters to be mined, the rest of the flotilla turned about and fled south.

This extraordinary episode was the first action of the war in Western Europe, the end of the eight-month hiatus popularly known as 'the Phoney War'. Eriksen and Anderssen's heroics allowed King Haakon, his government and his gold reserves to escape from Oslo and carry on resistance until June 1940 before Norway was forced to surrender. All the Dad's Army of the Oscarsborg could do was delay the inevitable but, in that context, their conduct is even more admirable – because they knew that. Hitler's empire expanded to include Denmark and Norway for brutal but sound strategic reasons. Occupation allowed direct access to Sweden's iron ore reserves but, in the words of the directive authorising the invasion, there was another specific purpose: 'to give our navy and air force a wider start-line against Britain'.

Even the wildest optimists in the German High Command could never have anticipated the overrunning of the Netherlands and Belgium and the fall of France in a matter of a few days in the summer of 1940. The evacuation of the bulk of the British Expeditionary Force (BEF) from the beaches around Dunkirk may have been hailed as a miracle but, in terms of the loss of vital equipment, it was nothing less than a disaster. Most of the British army's heavy artillery was abandoned – more than 1,000 field guns, 850 anti-tank guns and 600 tanks. Those divisions left at home had been compelled to hand over much of their heavy weaponry to the BEF and, when Denmark, Norway, the Netherlands, Belgium and France collapsed with frightening speed, torn apart by Blitzkrieg and lightning-fast panzer division strikes, Britain was suddenly left defenceless. The eastern shores of the North Sea bristled with danger and, when the Battle of Britain began in July 1940, it was widely seen as a prelude to invasion.

Stripped of most of their tanks and heavy guns, the army in Britain was not only weak and sparse, it lacked the German mobility that had defeated the French and encircled the BEF. In Scotland, such troops as were available were concentrated around the naval bases at Rosyth on the Forth, Invergordon on the Moray Firth and Scapa Flow in Orkney. A tiny garrison of between 5,000 and 10,000 men was all that was available to repel any landings along a 600 km coastline, from Alness, north of Inverness, all the way down to Grangemouth on the Forth. And, after the battalions assigned to protect naval bases were subtracted from this pitiful total, it meant that, in a cold reality, there were no soldiers to fight on the beaches as Churchill had exhorted them to do. In 1940, the Germans could have walked into Scotland unopposed.

Strategists believed that, while an invasion would almost certainly target Southern England, a significant diversionary attack could be launched across the North Sea against Scotland, perhaps from bases in Norway. Ports such as Peterhead and Aberdeen could quickly funnel German troops into the east of the country and Moray and Aberdeenshire had several aerodromes and flat terrain suitable for glider and paratrooper assault. It was vital to contain an invasion in the north and prevent the Germans from reaching the cities and heavy industry of the Central Belt. But there were no soldiers and no guns to put up an effective resistance. Geography and history came to the rescue. Here is an extract from War Office records: 'There is a bottleneck at Stonehaven. To make defence in this locality fully effective, there would have to be subsidiary posts on the road, Braemar–Devil's Elbow and in the area Kingussie–Dalwhinnie to prevent an enemy turning movement to the west.'

Deep in the dark green shade of Fetteresso Forest, overgrown on the sides of minor roads or scattered on remote mountainsides are the remains of Scotland's response to the real and imminent threat of invasion. In the second half of 1940, what was known as 'the Cowie Stop Line' was hurriedly constructed and its story and its resonances are fascinating.

At Stonehaven, the Highland massif almost reaches the North Sea. Only a narrow land corridor, much of it boggy and difficult until the drainage schemes of the 18th and 19th centuries, allows access between Aberdeenshire, the Moray coastlands to the north and Angus, the Mearns and Tayside to the south. In addition, there are high passes in the west through which an army might move – the Cairn o' Mount road and the pass from Braemar down to Glenshee and Blairgowrie are the most travelled. On the latter route, at the Devil's Elbow, where a notorious series of hairpin bends had to be negotiated on the road to Glenshee, ranks of concrete anti-tank cubes were strung out in long lines.

The Cowie Water was chosen as the most critical and most formidable section of the stop line. It runs eastwards from the foothills of the mountains before falling into the sea at Stonehaven. While it was not deep or wide, the little river flowed in exactly the right place and its bank could be altered to make an effective obstacle for tanks. Men from 217 Pioneer Company, aided by Royal Engineers, cut away the southern bank along much of its length and raised it so that it presented a sheer face of around two metres in height. No tank could use its tracks to climb that or hope to bulldoze its way through the sold earth behind.

Pillboxes designed to house Bren-gun crews were built at possible crossings and bridges and anti-tank cubes placed where the Cowie flowed through flatter terrain. Bridges were to be demolished and substantial steel and concrete roadblocks set up elsewhere. The town of Stonehaven itself was considered to be appropriate for the sort of intensive street fighting that can delay an advancing army. At 18 km in length the Cowie Stop Line is thought to be the most complete of many built in the early years of the Second World War. And, on the night of 7 September 1940, the people of Stonehaven and along the Cowie Water thought that it was about to be put to the test. The code word 'Cromwell' was issued, a warning that a German invasion was imminent. Church bells rang out an alarm in the town and many looked anxiously out to sea, searching the horizon for an enemy fleet.

After 1945, the Cowie Stop Line was gradually forgotten, trees were planted by its steep banks and moss grew over the concrete cubes and the pillboxes. But it was not a unique monument to the strategic importance of this narrow neck of land, where the Highland Line almost reaches the sea.

Malcolm's Mount at Stonehaven was said to be the burial mound of the first king of Scots of that name. When archaeologists uncovered a cist, or stone-lined grave, in 1822, the tradition seemed to be confirmed. In fact, the burial was much older and could not have been that of the 10th-century king. But rare documentary evidence does insist that Malcolm I was killed in 954 by 'the Men of the Mearns at Fetteresso, that is, in the Swordland'. The place-name of Fetteresso survives close to Malcolm's Mount not only in the form Kirktown of Fetteresso but in other adjacent places. Swordland, or *Claideom*, was a wider label and it appears to have been attached to the narrow neck of land between the foothills of the Grampian ranges and the sea at Stonehaven. The name must have denoted, as it did in Ireland, an area of regular dispute, a place of conflict.

The 10th-century chronicle that spoke of warfare in the Swordland also introduced another old place-name. The Mearns approximated to one of Scotland's smaller and more ancient counties. Kincardineshire was swept into oblivion by the reorganisation of local authorities in 1975. Its county town and namesake of Kincardine disappeared much earlier, in the middle ages, and, by the 17th century, the administrative centre had settled on Stonehaven. But through all of these changes, the old name of the Mearns has stuck. Often it is twinned with another, as in Angus and the Mearns, and that hints at its meaning. It derives from the Old Welsh term *maer*, which means 'a steward'. Thus the Mearns means 'the Stewartry', an area governed by an official appointed by someone of higher degree, probably a king. It may be that the Mearns, the Swordland, was a dependency of the kings of Angus, the rulers of the lands between the Tay and the Mounth.

For famously fertile farming country, the major legacy of the

Mearns is perhaps surprising. Two writers, separated by seven centuries, were born and raised within a few miles of each other. Lewis Grassic Gibbon, the pen-name of James Leslie Mitchell, wrote some of the greatest fiction ever published anywhere. *Sunset Song* and its sequels, *Cloud Howe* and *Grey Granite*, appeared between 1932 and 1934. Mitchell's compatriot from the Mearns was John of Fordun, a much less celebrated figure but very influential nonetheless.

Born around 1360 at Fordoun in the rich farming district known as the Howe of the Mearns, John almost certainly went on to become a chaplain at St Machar's Cathedral in Aberdeen. His achievement was singular and innovative. Having gathered material from many sources, perhaps as far afield as Ireland and England, Fordun compiled the first continuous history of Scotland. In what became known as the *Scotichronicon*, he began by establishing a foundation legend of some originality and quickly brought the story up the death of David I in 1153. Fordun also collected research and this was converted into a narrative by the continuator of the *Scotichronicon*, a remarkable man called Walter Bower, the Abbot of the island community of Inchcolm in the middle of the 15th century.

One of Fordun's most fascinating passages concerns an early attempt at defining the distinctions between Highland and Lowland culture. Born close to the Highland Line and spending much of his adult life in Aberdeen, he was in a position to observe these closely: 'The manners and customs of the Scots vary with the diversity of their speech. For two languages are spoken amongst them, the Scottish [Gaelic] and the Teutonic [English]; the latter of which is the language of those who occupy the seaboard and the plains, while the race of Scottish speech inhabits the Highlands and outlying islands. The people of the coast are of domestic and civilised habits . . . The Highlanders and people of the islands, on the other hand, are a savage and untamed race, rude and independent.'

Fordun set an enduring tone. His attitudes were repeated and embroidered by virtually every historian writing in Scots and

Latin in the 15th and 16th centuries, and the apposition of Highland barbarism and Lowland civilisation became the conventional wisdom. By the 1580s, abuse had replaced condescension. Alexander Montgomerie was a poet at the court of the young James VI and he is chiefly remembered for an elaborate, ornamented allegory called *The Cherrie and the Slae*. In high contrast to its delicacies, here is the poet's view of Highlanders:

> How the first Helandman
> Of God was maid,
> Of a horse turd,
> In Argyle,
> It is said.

As a further means of distancing Lowland Scotland from Highland, an exchange of terms took place over the course of the first half of the 15th century. Fordun's labelling of Gaelic as 'Scottish' was replaced by Erse or 'Irish', making a native language appear foreign. The transfer was completed when Teutonic or English came to be called 'Scots', making an imported dialect appear native. Such linguistic shifts are significant as they track swings in the balance of political power and cultural identity.

On the ground, in the detail of everyday life, these changes were, in reality, much less dramatic, the division between Highland and Lowland much less graphic than Fordun would have had readers believe. The likelihood must be that he exaggerated division because he was attempting, as Scotland's first great narrative historian, to give some order to the chaos of all the material he had assembled. But his overstatement of cultural difference is nonetheless surprising, given his upbringing in the Mearns. During Fordun's own lifetime Gaelic was still spoken in the fertile farmlands of the Buchan, the most easterly of the Moray coastlands. Although undoubtedly in retreat, Gaelic was also still heard in the late 14th century in the Carse of Gowrie on the northern shores of the Firth of Tay, in West Fife and Kinross and in Strathearn. These are all areas of prime agricultural land, unquestionably parts of the Lowlands.

Divisions were blurred even closer to Fordun's birthplace. On Cat Law, a prominent hill north of Kirriemuir, there is a spring near the summit. In 1253, it was known as Tubernacoppech, a rendering of *Tobar na Copaich*, 'the Well of the Dockens'. On a map of 1790, it is translated as 'the Docken Well'. What this means is a long-term coexistence of Gaelic and English in one locality, long enough for the Gaelic place-name to be correctly translated rather than replaced with a new name by incomers ignorant of or uninterested in the language.

Elsewhere in the Lowlands of Scotland, place-names confirm a patchy linguistic picture with few stark divisions. Cothill or Cuthil is a version of *comhdhail*, the Gaelic word for 'a formal meeting place', 'an assembly'. These were probably open-air courts where a judge – in Gaelic, a *britheamh* or *brieve* or, in Scots, a 'doomster' or 'dempster' – handed down judgements on cases presented to them. There are more than fifty Cothill or Cuthil place-names and seven of them can be found south of the Forth, in areas where Gaelic was never the dominant language.

A fascinating remnant of the early centuries of Christianity is to be found on the map of Scotland, in the shape of three Dysarts. The largest is the town on the Fife coast and there are two others – one in Perthshire, one in Angus. The name comes from the Gaelic *diseart*, itself a rendering of 'desert'. Early monasticism was much influenced by the teachings of the Desert Fathers, a group of ascetics who sought a solitary life of prayer and contemplation in the harsh deserts of Syria, ancient Palestine and Egypt. Their western admirers adopted the word as *diseart*, for a hermitage, and, having no deserts to surround them, they often chose sites by the sea or on riverbanks.

English arrived in Scotland in two stages but the language it first displaced was not Gaelic but dialects of Old Welsh, the language spoken the length and breadth of Britain during the Roman occupation of the south and long afterwards. With the invasions of the Angles in the 7th and 8th centuries, the south-east of Scotland began to speak their early version of English. As their war bands seized the productive farms and estates of the lower Tweed Valley, Teviotdale, Lauderdale and East Lothian, they forced the adoption of their dominant tongue.

The second incursion of English occurred much later. After 1100, David I, his brothers and successors introduced Norman, Flemish, English and other adventurers who quickly established themselves in Scotland. But, crucially, he and his new people founded towns. In order to create markets to stimulate the economy and generate customs revenue, the likes of Roxburgh, Berwick, Lanark and others were given charters. And business boomed. Roxburgh and Berwick were by far the busiest burghs, expanding quickly on the back of a vigorous trade in the wool of Border sheep. And business was conducted in English. As trading networks proliferated, it spread across Scotland with them. It was the language of commerce while Old Welsh and Gaelic were spoken in country districts by the farmers who produced the animals, the wool, the hides and all the other agricultural products brought into the markets of the new burghs. It was the beginning of an old divide between town and country and, in many areas of Scotland, it was a divide deepened by the use of different languages.

Much later, the coexistence and interaction between the two languages of modern Scotland was recorded – and a facet of the linguistic divide put very succinctly. In 1698, a pious purpose produced what amounted to a record of the geography of Gaelic at the end of the 17th century. The *More Particular List of the Highland Parishes* was compiled to make the distribution of bibles in Irish Gaelic (there was no translation into Scots Gaelic available until 1767) more efficient. It is very informative. Again and again the compilers came across the common phenomenon of many native Gaelic speakers who were able to 'buy and sell in English, [but] who do not understand a sermon in that language'.

These assiduous researches were augmented in 1706 by the beginnings of a fascinating case study in language shift. The ministers of the parishes of the county of Caithness produced a series of accounts of the gradual replacement of Gaelic with English. 'There are seven parishes in Caithness where the Irish [Gaelic] language is used, viz. Thurso, Hallkirk, Reay, Latheron, Farr, Wick, Durness. But the people of Wick understand English also.'

Although there were anomalies on either side, there existed a clear linguistic frontier. It ran in a line from Wick to Thurso on the Pentland Firth. To the east, most people spoke English and to the west most used Gaelic. Increasing trade and the growth of the fishing industry in the towns and larger villages began to encourage rapid change. By the 1720s, the previously bilingual parish of Wick had become monoglot English and, in the 1730s, the number of parishes in Caithness where Gaelic was widely spoken had shrunk to only four.

There were other forces at work. For centuries, the two dominant families of the far north-east had been feuding. On the English-speaking side of the linguistic frontier, the Sinclair Earls of Caithness had pursued an aggressively expansionist policy that affected all areas of life. In the parish of Watten, right on the cultural divide, they imposed a monoglot English speaker as the new minister, the Rev. John Dunbar, in 1659. After a large group of Gaelic speakers, at least 90 men, objected, the elders and heritors (most of them linked to the Sinclairs) simply expelled them from the congregation.

To the west of the frontier, the MacKays of Strathnaver had been active in cattle raiding in the 1650s and the events at Watten very likely reflected heightened tensions between the two speech communities. In any event, local politics polarised the Gaelic–English divide and in Caithness at least there was an emphatic Highland Line by the early 18th century. But, by 1797, English was crossing it, making deep inroads. Here is an extract from *The First Statistical Account* for Hallkirk Parish, an area immediately to the west of the divide: 'Some speak only the Erse [Gaelic], but do not speak or understand the English; some understand the English, but do not speak it; some speak the English but do not speak or understand the Erse; some understand the Erse, but do not speak it; but the greatest number speak and understand both these languages equally well. This is their state with regard to language; but of late years, the English is making great progress at the expense of the Erse.'

All along the length of the Highland Line Gaelic was retreating into the mountains and the glens. In Comrie in Perthshire, *The First Statistical Account* of 1794 offered more detail: 'The common language of the people is Gaelic. All the natives understand it; but many, especially the old, do not understand the English well. All the young people can speak English; but in order to acquire it, they must go to service in the Low Country.'

By 'the Low Country', the minister meant the Lowlands of Scotland. In an account of the Jacobite Rebellion of 1745 published in 1802, clergyman John Home observed incomprehension in Perthshire: 'The same shire, the same parish . . . contains parts of both, so that a Highlander and Lowlander (each of them standing at the door of the cottage where he was born) hear their neighbours speak a language which they do not understand.'

Gaelic only became a literary language in the 19th and 20th centuries. Even now, in the 21st, some older native speakers cannot write it. Beautiful, lyrical, naturally alliterative, mouth-filling, Gaelic's stories lived for centuries in the memories of its bards and seannachies, the tellers of tales. Until the modern era, very little was written down so it is much more difficult to switch perspective and discover a Gaelic perception of the Lowlands and Lowlanders. Nevertheless, in a fascinating essay, the scholar, John MacInnes, marshals much of the scant evidence and looks outwards from the Highlands at his fellow Scots in the south and east. His first sentences are unequivocal:

It would not be difficult to assemble a body of evidence to show that the Gaels of Scotland regarded the people of the Lowlands with something less than love. And it would be just as easy to show that the Lowlanders were perfectly capable of returning the compliment.

The great bard, Alasdair mac Mhaighstir Alasdair wrote memorably in 1751 of *miorun mor nan Gall*, 'the great malice of the Lowlanders'. As much as anything, he was reacting to a series of attacks on the Gaelic language that had begun in earnest in the early 17th century. These had acquired a political edge after the Jacobite Rebellions of 1715 and 1745–46 and, indeed, Alasdair himself had been an officer in one of the MacDonald regiments at Culloden. In 1716, the Society for the Propagation of Christian Knowledge was equally unequivocal: 'Nothing can be more effectual for reducing these countries [the Highlands] to order, and making them useful to the Common-wealth than teaching them their duty to God, their King and Country and rooting out their Irish language, and this has been the case of the Society so far as they could, for all the Scholars are taught in English.'

So much for the battle lines, both cultural and military. But the picture was more nuanced. Edmund Burt was an engineer and building contractor who worked for General Wade on the great road-building schemes for the Highlands in 1724–28. He wrote a series of essays published as *Letters From a Gentleman in the North of Scotland* and these were read and quoted by both Sir Walter Scott and the historian, Thomas Babington Macaulay. Burt's observations of the people he met were perceptive:

> They have an adherence to one another as Highlanders, in opposition to the people of the Low Country, whom they despise as inferior to them in Courage, and believe they have a right to plunder them whenever it is within their Power. This last arises from a Tradition, that the Lowlands, in old Times were the possession of their Ancestors.

Burt came across these attitudes amongst 'the middling and ordinary Highlanders, who are very tenacious of old Customs and opinions'.

Amongst Gaelic bards and seannachies, courage and the heroic were, of course, constant themes. In battle, it was swordplay and the fury of the charge that mattered and marked out a Highland warrior. When Domhnall Cam mac Dubhghaill, a great swordsman of the Clan Macaulay, heard that guns had become the dominant weapon in warfare, he mourned the passing of the heroic age: '*Tha latha a ghaisgich seachad.*' – 'The day of the hero has passed.' And similar sentiments were expressed 150 years later when Iain Ruadh Stiubhart reflected on events at Culloden:

> *Lasair-theine nan Gall,*
> *Frasadh pheilear m'ar ceann,*
> *Mhill sud eireachdas lann 's bu bheud e.*

> The bombardment of the Lowlanders,
> The showering of shot around our heads,
> That destroyed the brilliance of swordplay – more is the pity.

Aonghus mac Alasdair Ruaidh of Glencoe was contemptuous about his enemies, Lowlanders with guns. They could kill warriors at a distance without the need for the courage for hand-to-hand fighting. Aonghus was outraged:

> *Bhith 'gan leagail le luaidhe*
> *Is gun tilgeadh buachaillean bho i.*

> Being felled with lead,
> When even cowherds can throw it.

In the exchange of sword blows, that was where courage could be seen, either among the Lowlanders or:

> *Bodaich Machair a' bhuachair*
> *No siol uasal nan Garbhchrioch.*

> The peasants of the Plain of Cow-dung
> Or the noble seed of the Rough Bounds.

Such contempt for Lowlanders even crossed the Atlantic. At the end of the 18th century, the Kintail bard, Iain mac Mhurchaidh, wrote of the non-Gaels he saw in North Carolina in precisely the same terms used to describe the peasants and farmers of the Low Country of Scotland:

> *Gur beag orm fein na daione seo tha ann*
> *Le an cotaichean dubha, ad mhor air an ceann*
> *Le am briogseanan goirid air an sgoltadh gu an bann*
> *Chan fhaicear an t'osan, is e a' bhochdainn an tha ann.*

> Little do I care for the folk who live here,
> With their black coats and great hats on their heads
> With the short breeches split to the band
> The kilt hose, alas, is not seen.

In Edmund Burt's letters, there is a sense of paradox. While Highlanders felt occasional contempt for Lowlanders – something enthusiastically reciprocated – there were also unmistakeable impulses to unity. Just as the Welsh saw England as *Lloegr*, the lost lands that might one day be regained, so the Gaels believed that all of Scotland might once again be theirs and that Gaelic-speaking kings would reign once more. And, like the Welsh, their poetry and prophesy had a messianic streak. In the oral tradition, the legend of the Sleeping Warrior was powerful and, for the Gaels of the 17th and 18th centuries, this took on a surprising twist.

Thomas the Rhymer became immensely famous as a prophet. In reality, Thomas of Ercildoune, Earlston in the Scottish Borders, began to utter visions of the future at the outset of the Wars of Independence at the end of the 13th century. To Gaelic speakers, he became a heroic figure, his origins grew mythic and he became known as Tomas Reumhair or Thomas the Wanderer (or Rhymer). Associated with horses and the awakening of warriors, the prophecies prompted poetry:

When Thomas comes with his horses,
The day of plunder will be on the Clyde,
Nine thousand good men will be drowned,
And a young king will attain the crown.

Eventually Thomas himself became a messianic figure – a redeemer for the Gaels – and the army at Culloden called themselves *Clann nan Reumhair*, 'the Rhymer's children'.

8

The Furrowed Field

✱

OLD GRANNIE WAS A marvel – admired the length and breadth of rural Scotland but nowhere more so than in the north-east Lowlands where she founded a dynasty. Having given birth 25 times in her long life, she had her photograph taken two days before she died, on 1 July 1859. Tragically, she was struck by lightning while sheltering under a tree. At the request of His Royal Highness Prince Albert, the Prince Consort, a copy was made and sent to Balmoral where it went on display – in the royal collection of cattle photographs.

Old Grannie was the Prima Cow, the no. 1 in the Herd Book, the mother of the world-famous Aberdeen Angus breed, perhaps the most notable creation of the farmers who worked the fertile fields in the shadow of the Grampians. The breed began its illustrious history when Hugh Watson of Keillor in the county of Angus began to cross different types so that he could produce a big, black beef bullock with no horns. These were first known as Angus Doddies or Humlies and their lack of horns made them much easier to handle and less likely to injure each other, especially when bulls were covering their cows.

Watson's favourite bull was Old Jock, Primus Bull and no. 1 in the Herd Book. He was sired by Grey-Breasted Jock who, despite his seniority, was lodged at no. 2 in the Herd Book. Both covered Old Grannie and she had seven calves by them. A canny publicist for his undoubted breeding skills, Hugh Watson often showed his prize cattle and, over a long career, won more than 500 rosettes and trophies at agricultural shows from Perth up to Moray. His hornless, or polled, black cattle consequently became tremendously favoured by farmers and many modern bulls can trace descent through the Herd Books from Old Grannie, Grey-Breasted Jock and Old Jock.

It was William McCombie of Tillyfour, near Alford in Aberdeenshire, who took cattle rearing a stage further and created the Aberdeen Angus breed as it is now known. His career began as the age of droving was waning and, by his death in 1880, Scotch beef cattle were regularly transported by rail to southern markets. And not just any Scotch beef but the much admired Aberdeen Angus.

What McCombie realised was that trains changed breeding. Animals did not any longer have to be suitable for the rigours of droving, long journeys of 200 or 300 miles over sometimes difficult terrain. If they could be transported to market, then they could be bigger, carry more weight and fetch high prices. And crucially, they lost no condition on a short rail journey and were delivered in their glossy prime.

To breed larger beasts McCombie crossed his own Aberdeen-shire polled stock with the progeny of Old Grannie, Old Jock and other show-class beasts produced by Hugh Watson and other Angus cattle farmers. And then he set about marketing the new breed, which was quickly branded as Aberdeen Angus – without a hyphen.

Knowing that Queen Victoria and Prince Albert had fallen in love with Scotland and Deeside in particular, McCombie executed a brilliant publicity coup. In 1867, he entered his prime bullock, Black Prince, for the Birmingham and Smithfield shows, which he duly won. Then he arranged for the bullock to be taken to Windsor Castle where Black Prince was paraded around the Middle Ward in the presence of an appreciative monarch and her consort. Perhaps a photograph was taken to sit alongside Old Grannie's portrait. Perhaps he behaved and did not leave a memento. At Christmas of that year, McCombie had the bullock slaughtered and sent generous cuts of beef to the palace.

When Queen Victoria visited McCombie's farm at Tillyfour, not far from Balmoral, in the summer of 1869, the royal seal of approval was complete. Aberdeen Angus beef became the acme of fashion and no self-respecting restaurant or upper-class dinner table could fail to serve it. Always striving to improve his breeding lines, the enterprising McCombie bought an outstanding yearling heifer which he promptly named The Queen Mother. No royal comment is recorded. But perhaps his most astute acquisition was Hanton, a bull that was a grandson of Old Jock. He, in turn, sired one of the most prolific bulls in Aberdeen Angus breeding history. Black Prince of Tillyfour's bloodlines can be found in almost every bull, cow and bullock in the breed – anywhere.

In 1873, four bulls from the prestigious Ballindalloch herd were transported to the USA. Originally bred from Tillyfour stock, they introduced the Aberdeen Angus bloodlines to an appreciative market, one reared on good beef. The imported bulls were crossed with Texas longhorns (but their progeny remained polled) and farmers found that their offspring were hardy and able to winter out on the unfenced range. Between 1878 and 1883, more than 1,200 Aberdeen Angus bulls and cows were shipped across the Atlantic and, in the grassy vastness of the Midwest, they thrived. But their name shrank. Now they are called Black Angus and burgers made from their excellent beef are sold by all the major chains.

The Aberdeen Angus breed and its international success may be seen as the high point of early modern farming in the northeast of Scotland. If its name has endured, the fame and sheer pungency of another product of the same landscape has faded somewhat. As they worked long and back-breaking hours at repetitive tasks in the fields and steadings, farm labourers often sang. And some of them composed. The bothy ballads are their legacy. A rich, rough-and-ready canon of simple songs about farm life and work, they were made up by men from the bothies. These were outbuildings where unmarried men lived communally. Usually very basic, even primitive, the bothies were nevertheless a fertile ground for the making of music – and of history. For once, the ballads supply a version of events seen from the base of the social pyramid and not the routine perspective from the apex.

Some of the most fondly remembered are reminders that the men and women who toiled in all weathers and seasons to produce food occasionally lifted their heads and looked at the glories of the countryside around them. The Gadie Burn runs through the centre of ancient history, through the battlefield of Mons Graupius, but the fieldworkers who composed and sang of it were more interested in celebrating its beauties:

> O gin I war whaur the Gadie rins,
> Whaur the Gadie rins, whaur the Gadie rins,
> O gin I war whaur the Gadie rins,
> At the fit o' Bennachie.
>
> I've roamed by Tweed, I've roamed by Tay,
> By Border Nith and Highland Spey,
> But dearer far to me than they
> Are the braes o' Bennachie.
>
> When blade and blossoms sprout in spring,
> An' bid the birdies wag the wing,
> They blithely bob an' soar an' sing
> At the fit o' Bennachie.
>
> When simmer cleads the varied scene
> Wi' licht o' gowd and leaves o' green,
> I fain wad be whaur aft I've been
> At the fit o' Bennachie.
>
> When autumn's yellow sheaf is shorn,
> An' barnyards stored wi' stooks o' corn,
> 'Tis blithe to toom the clyack horn,
> At the fit o' Bennachie.

When winter winds blaw sharp an' shrill
O'er icy burn an' sheeted hill,
The ingle neuk is gleesome still
At the fit o' Bennachie.

As farms consolidated and grew large, what were known as 'fermtouns' grew up. Around the farmhouse and steading (where the clyack horn or harvest drinking cup was drunk), rows of cottages were built and, in an age before contraception, families flourished. Food was usually plentiful, if a little monotonous, and a brood of children could be useful around a farm for tending to the hens and looking for eggs, mushrooms and other wild fruits and roots. And, when they were old enough to roar and wield a stick, they could help herd beasts in and out at milking time. Some of the great fermtouns of the North-east had a hundred souls or more living around them.

It could be a transient life. Farm workers of all degrees were hired on the fee system. At the hiring fairs held in market towns at intervals of six months, they would gather and present themselves for inspection and interview. Still just within living memory, it was sometimes a humiliating process and some farmers could be thoughtless, even arrogant. 'No better than a cattle market,' said Jenny Corbett, recalling the hiring fairs of the early 20th century in the Borders. But good workers were sought after and could strike a reasonable bargain. An annual or six-month sum was agreed on a handshake and a drink in a nearby pub. The cash was important but so were the payments in kind known as gains. These were usually several tons of potatoes, peat or coal, oatmeal, flour, pasture for a cow, a pigsty and other items. Gains were popular because they were inflation-proof and, with the free tenancy of a cottage, farm workers could subsist easily without spending scarce cash. But sometimes there was disappointment, even disingenuousness on the part of farmers. In another famous ballad, 'The Barnyards o' Delgaty', a young ploughman accepts a fee at the hiring fair at Turriff.

As I went doon to Turra market,
Turra market for to fee,
I fell in with a market farmer,
The barnyards o' Delgaty.

He promised me the ae best pair
I ever set my e'en upon;
When I gaed hame to Barnyards,
There was naething there but skin and bone.

The auld black horse sat on his rump,
The auld white mare lay on her wime,
And a' that I could hup and crack,
They wouldna rise at yokin' time.

James Small's revolutionary swing plough needed horsepower to pull it and, in the 18th century, another famous Scottish breed came into being to meet that need – something more reliable than the pair at Delgaty. But the new breed was not initially developed for farming. In Lanarkshire, the Dukes of Hamilton were growing wealthy on the proceeds of coal mining but, as industry began to demand more, they were unable to keep up. The central difficulty was that their draught horses could only pull small cartloads and, since profit depended on bulk transport, more powerful animals were urgently needed.

The Hamiltons had been supporters of William of Orange in 1688 and their connections with the Low Countries supplied a solution to their haulage problems. Here is an informative entry in *The First Statistical Account* of 1793.

Rutherglen Fairs are famous for the finest draught horses in Europe . . . About a century ago an ancestor of the Duke of Hamilton brought six coach horses from Flanders . . . They were all handsome black stallions. The surrounding farmers gladly bred from them, and the cross with the Scotch horse procured a breed superior to either, which has been improved by careful breeding. Great attention is paid to colour, softness and hardness of hair, length of body, breast, and shoulders of their breeders [stallions]. Every farm has four or six mares. The colts are mostly sold at the fairs of Lanark or Carnwath. They excel in the plough, the cart and the wagon.

Good Clydesdales made good ploughmen and their size and stamina made the work easier and faster. With big feet and legs able to generate great power under well-muscled hindquarters and shoulders, they could pull the plough through even boggy or frosty ground with ease. Breeding became big business and perhaps the most famous and prodigious stallion was a wonderfully made horse called Dunure Footprint. Black with white, feathered socks, he was neat with his feet but took a good grip of the land and was highly intelligent and tractable with a calm temperament. Like every good sire, he stamped his foals with these characteristics and, because they were easy to train and manage, Dunure Footprint was in great demand.

Long before artificial insemination, all covering was natural. And it could be dangerous. Dunure Footprint's own sire, Baron of Buchlyvie, had to be put down when a mare he was covering kicked him and broke one of his legs – a very costly accident. But his son was luckier. At the beginning of the 20th century, his owner, William Dunlop, took him all over Lowland Scotland by train. In whichever locality he stood at stud, farmers would bring their mares to be covered and they paid Dunlop a huge fee, £60, for the privilege. Over the season, fortified by frequent feeds of milk mixed with beaten eggs, Dunure Footprint would mount a mare every two hours and, in what must have seemed like a long career, he sired more than 5,000 foals. At the end of the summer, he could still service a mare but sometimes fell off her, exhausted. His progeny dominated Clydesdale breeding for decades.

Daintiness of foot was important for these huge horses (very often they weighed more than a ton and stood 19 or even 20 hands high) because of the need to turn at the end of the furrow and leave as little land unploughed as possible. When Archibald Grant complained about the S-shaped rigs left by teams of oxen at Monymusk, it was the waste of good land that frustrated him. Clydesdales, by contrast, could turn tidily, stepping inside each other, changing their leading leg, and, when potatoes began to be grown commercially, their neatness was amazing to see. Early 20th-century film shot in Angus shows a team of two ploughing out weeds between dreels of potatoes and not one green leaf is touched by the massive hooves even when they turn.

Ploughmen and horsemen grew very fond of their paired teams. When the day's work was done and lowsin time came, they unhitched a plough or harrow and left it in the unfinished field before riding back to the farm. How they got on is a mystery. Once in the stables, they groomed the sweat off the horses' flanks, brushed and combed out their manes, washed the mud off their legs and picked out muck and small stones from their hooves before feeding and watering them. These are verses from a bothy ballad called 'Harrowing Time':

> So on we drive until the sun
> Ahint yon hills does hide;
> And syne we loose our horses tired,
> And homewards we do ride.
>
> And homewards we do ride fu' keen
> To get our horses fed;
> We kaim them weel baith back and heel,
> Their tails and manes we redd.

Ploughing, harrowing and carting were the main work for horses but much else was done on the fermtouns. Cattle were looked after by the bailies and women did manual jobs like weeding, shawing and milking. The harvest was both the culmination and the crisis of the year. Not only did everyone on the fermtoun lend a hand, for time and the weather were of the essence, but itinerant harvesters were also often employed. Mostly women, many came in groups from the Highlands with their sharpened sickles in late summer. Since the corn ripened first in the south, they would begin in Berwickshire and the Tweed Valley before moving north to Lothian, Fife, the Mearns and the Moray coastlands. When they bent to their work, they sang Gaelic songs and sometimes farmers hired a piper to play as they swung their sickles in what was a rhythmic movement through the fields. Bandsters followed them, tying the sheaves together by twisting stalks of straw around them. One of the very best of the bothy ballads, 'Johnnie Sangster', describes the hard work as well as the fun, the daffin', of the harvest when men and women worked together late into the sunlit summer evenings.

> O a' the seasons o' the year
> When we maun work the sairest,
> The harvest is the foremost time,
> And yet it is the rarest.
> We rise as seen as mornin' light,
> Nae craters can be blither;
> We buckle on oor finger steels,
> And follow oot the scyther.
>
> A mornin' piece to line oor cheek,
> Afore that we gae forder,
> Wi' clouds o' blue tobacco reek
> We then set oot in order.
> The sheaves are risin' thick and fast,
> And Johnnie, he maun bind them.
> The busy group, for fear they stick,
> Can scarcely look behind them.
>
> I'll gie ye bands that winna slip,
> I'll pleat them weel and thraw them.
> I'm sure they winna tine the grip,
> Hooever weel ye draw them.

I'll bang my knee against the sheaf,
And draw the band sae handy.
Wi' ilka strae as straught's rash,
And that'll be the dandy.

Oh some complain on hacks and thraws,
And some on brods and bruises.
And some complain on grippit hips
And stiffness in their troosers;
But as soon as they lay doon the scythe
And pipers yoke their blawvin',
They ane and a' forget their dools
Wi' daffin an wi' tyawvin.

If e'er it chance to be my lot
To get a gallant bandster,
I'll gar him wear a gentle coat,
And bring him gowd in handfu's.
But Johnnie he can please himsel'
I wadna wish him blinkit;
Sae, after he had bred his ale,
He can sit doon and drink it.

A dainty cowie in the byre,
For butter and for cheeses;
A grumphie feedin' in the sty
Wad keep the hoose in greases.
A bonnie ewie in the bucht
Wad help to creesh the ladle;
An we'll get tufts o' cannie woo'
Wad help to theek the cradle.

Though wonderfully well done and smacking of authentic experience, there is a hint of the elegiac in 'Johnnie Sangster', a look back over the shoulder at a sunny Arcadia already fading, the good years of high farming in Lowland Scotland. And indeed they were not to last. Mechanisation progressed and intensified. The first prototype tractors were being made in the early 20th century and, in Europe, a cataclysm was waiting to engulf the world of the ploughmen and the bandsters.

The village of Arbuthnott lies in the centre of the Howe of the Mearns, home to some of the best farming country in all Scotland. South of Stonehaven, not far from the sea, it was the inspiration and the ill-disguised location of one the greatest novels ever written. Published in 1932, *Sunset Song* was the first in a trilogy based around the character of Chris Guthrie, the daughter of a Mearns farmer, John Guthrie. Its author, James Leslie Mitchell, grew up in Arbuthnott and, for most of his short life, he both loved and hated it.

Born in 1901 at Auchterless in Aberdeenshire to Danes Mitchell, an impoverished smallholder, and Lellias Grassic Gibbon, he and his parents moved to the Mearns when Mitchell was very young. A fiery, impulsive and idealistic teenager, he was forced to leave Mackie Academy in Stonehaven after a series of disagreements with the school authorities. In 1917, aged only 16, Mitchell ran away to Aberdeen and the city exerted a profound influence on him.

After persuading a local newspaper to take him on as a reporter, Mitchell became deeply involved in politics. In fraternal sympathy with the Russian Revolution, he founded a soviet in the city and probably joined the British Socialist Party (BSP) at that time. Having moved to Glasgow to work on *Farmers' Weekly*, Mitchell was sacked and then blacklisted by most Scottish newspapers. Apparently he had been fiddling his expenses in order to make donations to the BSP. Unable to find work, the young radical was forced to join the Royal Army Service Corps, which he hated, but it did allow him to travel, mainly to the Middle East.

On leaving the army in 1928, Mitchell and his wife, Rebecca, moved to the relative anonymity of Welwyn Garden City. Determined to devote himself to writing, he began an extraordinary period of almost frantic activity. More than a dozen books flowed, amongst them *Spartacus*, a treatment of the great Roman slave rebellion. But, for his most famous and original work, Mitchell took his mother's and grandmother's maiden names and wrote *Sunset Song* and its sequels, *Cloud Howe* and *Grey Granite*, as Lewis·Grassic Gibbon. In 1935, at only 33 years of age, James Leslie Mitchell died of peritonitis caused by a perforated ulcer.

The essence of *Sunset Song* is elegy, the sunset of a farming way of life, the old life on the land that was swept aside in little more than a decade by mechanisation, economics and, above all, the slaughter of the First World War. From a distance, either from Welwyn Garden City or abroad in the army, Mitchell's home thoughts were sharpened into graphic focus and brought alive with extraordinary skill. The tone, the subject matter and the plot are none of them upbeat or even particularly appealing, especially to a predominantly urban audience. What makes *Sunset Song* sing is magnificent writing, pinpoint precision and an unblinking eye. Written quickly and probably without a break, it has a coherence and a pace that is deeply involving and dazzling in the brilliance of its language. But most of all it comes from the heart, from real experience. Here is an extract from an account of a return to the farmlands of the Mearns:

> Going down the rigs this morning, my head full of that un-accustomed smell of the earth, fresh and salty and anciently mouldy, I remembered the psalmist's voice of the turtle and instinctively listened for its Scots equivalent – that far cooing of pigeons that used to greet the coming of spring mornings when I was a boy. But the woods have gone, their green encirclement replaced by swathes of bog and muck and rank-growing heath, all is left bare in the North wind's blow. The pigeons have gone and the rabbits and like vermin multiplied – unhappily and to no profit, for the farmers tell me the rabbits are tuberculous, dangerous meat. Unshielded by the woods, the farm-lands are assailed by enemies my youth never knew.

The Pass of Leny, where the boggy Lowland flatlands give way to the mountains beyond (© Jim Henderson)

Ben Ledi – the beginning of the Highlands (© Jim Henderson)

Where the mountains rise from the plain: the
Cairngorms near Grantown-on-Spey (© Jim Henderson)

The Battle of Culloden memorial cairn, which marks the site of the
final confrontation of the Jacobite Rising of 1745 (© Jim Henderson)

Fort George, built in the aftermath of the 1745 Jacobite Rising
(© Jim Henderson)

The Sculptor's Cave, Covesea, the scene of
extraordinary prehistoric rituals (© Jim Henderson)

One of the most beautiful of all Pictish carved stones is found
at Hilton of Cadboll (Historic Scotland. Licensor www.scran.ac.uk)

Burghead, the site of a key Pictish fortress known as 'the Bull Fort'
(© Jim Henderson)

On his state visit to Scotland in 1822, George IV refused to drink any
other whisky other than that produced at Glenlivet (© Jim Henderson)

Bennachie, where the Caledonian kings gathered their armies to face the Romans in AD 83 (© Jim Henderson)

Tank traps on the Cowie Stop Line, thought to be the most complete of any of the stop lines built in the early years of the Second World War (© Jim Henderson)

Stonehaven, which was expected to see intensive street-fighting in the event of a Nazi invasion (© Jim Henderson)

The countryside around Arbuthnott, where Lewis Grassic Gibbon was brought up (© Jim Henderson)

Ploughing was one of the main activities
for horses in the North-east fermtouns

The J.M. Barrie memorial, Kirriemuir (© Jim Henderson)

J.M. Barrie, whose *Auld Lichts Idylls* is a brilliant satire on the mores of small-town life (© National Trust for Scotland. Licensor www.scran.ac.uk)

Schiehallion, the 'magic mountain of the Caledonians' (© Jim Henderson)

Dunkeld Cathedral, which still displays damage caused
by musket-balls during the siege of 1689 (© Jim Henderson)

The site of the Roman fort at Inchtuthil, Perthshire (© Jim Henderson)

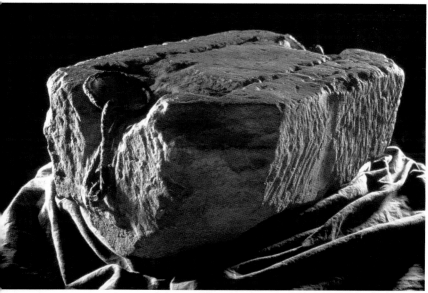

The Stone of Destiny featured in the coronations of the kings of Alba. Removed to Westminster Abbey by Edward I, it was (officially) returned to Scotland in 1996 (© Historic Scotland. Licensor www.scran.ac.uk)

Dunadd, where the kings of Dalriada were inaugurated (© Jim Henderson)

Lower North Inch, Perth, where Clan Chattan and
Cameron warriors fought to the death in 1396 (© Jim Henderson)

Birlinns – small, highly manoeuvrable warships – were the key to control of the Isles and North-west Scotland

Loch Katrine, made famous as a tourist destination after Sir Walter Scott published *The Lady of the Lake* in 1810 (© Jim Henderson)

James Macpherson, 'translator' of Ossian and described by Dr Johnson as a 'mountebank, a liar and a fraud' (Licensor www.scran.ac.uk)

Rob Roy Viewpoint, Loch Lomond, where the Highlands and Lowlands meet (© Jim Henderson)

Balmoral Castle, where Queen Victoria spent increasingly
long periods after the death of Prince Albert (© Jim Henderson)

The crew of the *Vital Spark* sailed over geological and cultural frontiers
every time they made their regular trip from Broomielaw up the Argyll coast
(The Scotsman Publications Ltd. Liceonsor www.scran.ac.uk)

Colonel Alistair MacDonell, looking every inch the Highland chief, and who ruthlessly evicted the clansmen and their families from Glengarry. Painting by Sir Henry Raeburn. (© National Galleries of Scotland. Licensor www.scran.ac.uk)

The seasons, the weather, the unchanging rhythms of farming and above everything a beautifully realised and utterly original sense of place all animate *Sunset Song*. The farms and people of Kinraddie (Arbuthnott) are lovingly, sometimes amusingly, described but it is the character of Chris Guthrie who represents Mitchell's own feeling for the place and the changing attachments to it. Chris's father, John Guthrie, farmed Blawearie. A dark, dour and angry man, he made life almost unbearable for his daughter. To escape from his moods, Chris found refuge at 'the Standing Stones up there night after night and day after day by the loch of Blawearie', where 'around them there gathered things that wept and laughed and lived again in the hours before the dawn'. And it was 'the only place where ever she could come and stand back from the clamour of the days'. Society, people changed, died and moved on and Chris knew that 'nothing endured at all, nothing but the land she passed across, tossed and turned and perpetually changed below the hands of the crofter folk since the oldest of them had set the Standing Stones by the loch of Blawearie'.

At the close of *Sunset Song*, after many of the men of Kinraddie, including Ewan Tavendale, Chris's husband, had died in the trenches of the First World War, a memorial to them is carved on one of 'the Standing Stones'. The minister has organised an unveiling ceremony.

And then, with the night waiting out by on Blawearie Brae, and the sun just verging on the coarse hills, the minister began to speak again, his short hair blowing in the wind that had come, his voice not decent and a kirk-like bumble, but ringing out over the loch

'FOR I WILL GIVE YOU THE MORNING STAR'

'In the sunset of an age and an epoch we may write that for epitaph of the men who were of it. They went quiet and brave from the lands they loved, though seldom of that love might they speak, it was not in them to tell in words of the earth that moved and lived and abided, their life and enduring love. And who knows at the last what memories of it were with them, the springs and the winters of this land and all the sounds and scents of it that had once been theirs, deep, and a passion of their blood and spirit, those four who died in France? With them we may say there died a thing older than themselves, these were the Last of the Peasants, the last of the Old Scots folk. A new generation comes up that will know them not, except as a memory in a song, they pass with the things that seem good to them, with loves and desires that grow dim and alien in the days to be. It was the old Scotland that perished then, and we may believe that never again will the old speech and the old songs, the old curses and the old benedictions, rise but with alien effort to our lips.

'The last of the peasants, those four that you knew, took that with them to the darkness and the quietness of the places where they sleep. And the land changes, their parks and their steadings are a desolation where sheep are pastured, we are told that great machines come soon to till the land, and the great herds come to feed on it, the crofter is gone, the man with the house and the steading of his own and the land closer to his heart than the flesh of his body.'

A piper then played the lament, 'The Flooers o' the Forest' and the darkness crept over the land. The great machines did come and, after the Second World War, they came in great numbers. When the brilliant Ulsterman Harry Ferguson designed an affordable and adaptable small tractor with a three-point linkage that could not only pull machinery but give it power, the fermtouns finally emptied of their people and their horses. The Standard Motor Company sold more than half a million of these well-made machines known as 'the Wee Grey Fergies' and, by the mid 1950s, the Clydesdales had all but vanished. Far from being the work of many hands, farming became a solitary activity usually run by one man with help from outside contractors for haymaking and harvest time. Leslie Mitchell saw that future coming and his achievement was to give a fitting epitaph in *Sunset Song*.

Across the Highland Line, crofting turned out to be more tenacious – a way of life that has outlasted what one observer called 'a bad attack of history'. Culloden broke the political and cultural hold of the clans and set in motion a cycle of consequences that were to become known as *Fuadach nan Gaidheal*, 'the Highland Clearances'.

Increasingly absent and anglicised clan chiefs came to value their estates not for the number (and loyalty) of the people they could support but for how much of an income they could produce. Forced evictions from the fertile glens to free them for more profitable sheep farms drove tenants down the seashore, to more marginal land. There, many failed to scratch a living from poor soil and, to subsist, they became involved in kelping, a near-forgotten industry. Seaweed was gathered and burned. The ash was rich in chemicals, such as magnesium, sodium and potassium, but, when cheaper sources became available after the end of the Napoleonic Wars, the industry collapsed.

It was then that emigration gathered pace. Brutal landlords forced tenants off the land entirely. Many moved south to the growing industrial cities and others left Scotland for a new life in North America and elsewhere in the Empire. The USA was also a popular destination – precisely because it was no longer a British possession. The bitterness and heartbreak of exile left an indelible scar.

The ignorance and careless contempt of some landowners was startling. In the early 19th century, the Countess of Sutherland employed the notorious Patrick Sellar as her factor to clear people off her estates. Amidst scenes of starvation and pitiful suffering, she wrote to a friend in England, 'Scotch people are of happier constitution and do not fatten like the larger breed of animals.' It was all done in the spirit of progress – to make the land more productive – and the Countess remarked of her husband, Lord Stafford, that 'he is seized as much as I am with the rage of improvements, and we both turn our attention with the greatest of energy to turnips'.

John Prebble

Scotland's greatest popular historian was not a Scot. John Prebble was born in Edmonton in North London and raised in Saskatchewan in Canada. He returned to London to complete his education at the Latymer School. His close affinity with Scotland and the Highlands came about in Canada where he grew up in the township of Sutherland in rural Saskatchewan. Mainly inhabited by emigrant Scots, many of them Highlanders, stories of Glencoe, Culloden and the Highland Clearances were told to Prebble at an impressionable age. After serving in the Royal Artillery in the Second World War, he began a career as a journalist and an author. First published in 1961, his account of the Battle of Culloden was the first in the Fire and Sword *trilogy – the other two deal with the Massacre of Glencoe and the Highland Clearances. Prebble's wide-ranging and meticulous research allowed him to see the battle from many standpoints but, in particular, he foregrounded, where he could, the experiences of the soldiers who fought at Drumossie Moor. Beautifully structured and written with real verve, his account of Culloden has not only remained in print for more than 50 years and sold hundreds of thousands of copies, it has yet to be bettered. Written for the common reader, the book has, like much popular history, drawn the ire of academics. The former Historiographer Royal in Scotland, Professor Gordon Donaldson, was particularly intemperate when he described Prebble's* Culloden *as 'utter rubbish'. This sort of remark is not untypical and is a symptom of an uneasy relationship. On the one hand, academics require history to be popular in order to keep the study of it in curricula – and it is often threatened. On the other hand, popular historians often depend on the spadework of academic research from which they can fashion a coherent story that will appeal to the reading public. However, the vitriol appears to flow in only one direction.*

Those tenants driven out of their homes by Patrick Sellar and others who settled on the coasts were often let a holding known as a croft. Essentially a smallholding, the term 'croft' actually refers to the land rather than the house or any outbuildings on it. Often set out in long strips, these parcels of land were intended to support a single family. Grazing rights on common land were attached and sometimes the right to cut peats from the moor. In his beautifully written memoir *Night Falls on Ardnamurchan*, Alasdair Maclean explains that these arrangements could be very detailed. At Sanna on the Ardnamurchan peninsula, the crofters had customary rights to cut peats at different mosses because the quality was variable. In this way, each family shared the best and worst sources of fuel equally. Co-operation was at the centre of crofting life but strict rules were enforced. Here is Maclean's summary of the conventions of the peats: 'The criterion was the common good. Our crofter, for example, might cut as many peats as he had time and energy for and fireplaces to absorb. He might come at last to despise the ordinary cubed form and hack out his fuel in the shape of pyramids or octahedrons. He might consume his handiwork himself or warp each block in tartan cellophane for the tourist trade. What he might not do was to open up new working wherever he felt inclined: his peats would be cut only in the place appointed to him.'

In 1979, there were 17,997 registered crofts and approximately 13,000 crofters. Tenants now enjoy an absolute right to buy their croft for 15 times the annual rental, which is generally low. Despite many difficulties and the unlikelihood of ever becoming wealthy on the proceeds, it is a way of life that appears to be growing in popularity. With effect from February 2010, Arran, Bute, the Cumbraes, Moray and those parts of Highland region not already inside the boundaries of the traditional crofting counties have all been formally recognised as new crofting areas. Landowners and certain sorts of tenants in the new areas were also given the right to apply to the Crofters' Commission to create new crofts. It seems that a way of life has indeed survived a bad attack of history and that the Highland Line is moving.

Alasdair Maclean

In 1984, one of the most elegiac, deeply personal and occasionally funny book ever published on the crofting way of life was published. Night Falls on Ardnamurchan *is subtitled* The Twilight of a Crofting Family *and the author, Alasdair Maclean, captured with extraordinary precision the pain of crossing the Highland Line never to return. Here is a poem that appears near the beginning of this remarkable book:*

> *Glasgow is not for me.*
> *I do not see the need for such a crowd,*
> *All jumping and biting like fleas in a great blanket.*
> *How long is it since I met myself?*
>
> *The people lock their faces every morning*
> *Before they go to work,*
> *For fear, I think, of having a good look stolen.*
> *Who knows where the key is?*
>
> *Here nothing grows but memory and that crookedly.*
> *That sitting-rock by the ford on the way to Plocaig*
> *I can feel its roughness on the back of my legs.*
> *Our folk had a name for it. What was it?*
>
> *I was a good man with spade once.*
> *The houses are too high:*
> *The streets too narrow.*
> *Who could dig himself out of so deep a ditch?*
>
> *I'd give all I own: my good name,*
> *The linings of my pockets, that kiss you gave me*
> *When I left (you'd replace it surely)*
> *If I could go home once more to Ardnamurchan.*

9

The Auld Lichts, Peter and Wendy

PETER PAN WAS BORN close to the Highland Line. In the winter of 1866, he went skating, suffered a terrible accident and, two days before his 14th birthday, he died. Peter, the Boy Who Wouldn't Grow Up, was, in reality, David Barrie, the older brother of J. M. Barrie. Born in the little town of Kirriemuir in the county of Angus, David had been sent to school in Lanarkshire where he was being looked after by his elder brother and sister, Alexander and Mary. When news of the tragedy reached their mother, Margaret Barrie, she resolved to 'get between death and her boy' but admitted that, even before she could board the train, death had taken him.

In his writings, J. M. Barrie confessed that his boyhood was dominated by David's death and his mother's obsession with the son who never grew up. In the biography he compiled, calling it *Margaret Ogilvy*, using her maiden name, Barrie recalled how he tried to fill the yawning gap in her life by dressing in his dead brother's clothes. Once, when he came into her room unnoticed at first, his mother said, 'Is that you?' 'I thought it was the dead boy she was speaking to,' wrote Barrie, 'and I said in a little lonely voice, "No, it's no' him, it's just me."'

All of his immensely productive life, J. M. Barrie enjoyed the company of children – perhaps he and they felt closer because of his height. According to his passport of 1934, Barrie stood only 5 foot 3 inches tall. When he moved to London, he met the Llewelyn Davies family. Fond of walks in Kensington Gardens,

Barrie struck up a friendship with George, Jack, Baby Peter and their nanny, Mary Hodgson that was to last a lifetime. The boys enjoyed Barrie's stories and playing with his big St Bernard dog, Porthos. The cast for Peter Pan was slowly assembling.

When Barrie met little Margaret Henley and her mother, another friendship blossomed and this time it created a popular Christian name. A photograph of the 1890s shows a plump-cheeked girl wearing a long cloak and a hood. Margaret adored Barrie and called him My Friendy. But, as with many small children, she had trouble pronouncing her Rs and the nickname came out as Fwendy, and sometimes Fwendy Wendy. Aged only six, Margaret Henley died and, out of that terrible loss, Wendy was born. She first appeared in a story, 'Sentimental Tommy', in 1895 but, in 1904, she was immortalised as Wendy Darling in the play *Peter Pan, or The Boy Who Wouldn't Grow Up*.

In his superb, sympathetic biography of J. M. Barrie, Andrew Birkin understood how Peter's character and story grew out of tragedy and a series of warm friendships with children. Originally invented as an entertainment for George and Jack Llewelyn Davies, the tales first revolved around Peter who was still a baby. He could fly, said Barrie, because babies were birds before they were born and, to prevent them from escaping, parents had bars put on nursery windows. This grew into a story about one baby who did escape and who flew through the nursery window – and eventually reached Neverland, never to grow up. The stage set for the opening of Peter Pan was almost complete.

In 1904, the play was an instant success and the indelible, original image of Peter Pan entered the pantheon of children's – and adults' – heroes. Part of the appeal was that Barrie cleverly gave him a darker, anarchic aspect. When the statue of Peter Pan was planned for Kensington Gardens in 1912, it was thought he should be modelled on photographs of Michael Llewelyn Davies in costume. But the sculptor, Sir George Frampton, had other ideas and used a more conventional-looking child. When the statue was unveiled, Barrie was not impressed: 'It doesn't show the devil in Peter.'

The success of the play was enormous and enduring but by no means Barrie's sole literary achievement. For the stage, he wrote *What Every Woman Knows*, *Dear Brutus*, *The Twelve Pound Look* and several other beautifully crafted pieces that are still regularly performed and have been translated into many languages. His novels are perhaps less well read now and, shamefully, his first is out of print. *Auld Licht Idylls* is a brilliant, hilarious satire on the mores of small town Scotland and it is based on what Barrie observed in Kirriemuir, the place he calls Thrums in the novel. In contrast to Lewis Grassic Gibbon's elegy to the old life on the land in *Sunset Song*, it focuses on a curtain-twitching community, creates a pungent, even claustrophobic atmosphere and reveals Barrie as a truly prodigious talent. As much as the influence of childhood tragedy and his close friendships with children helped create Peter Pan, it is the sheer quality of the writing that makes the boy fly into every imagination.

Auld Licht Idylls is not only wonderfully well written, it is also a powerful piece of social history but it may be that its present obscurity is understandable. The tensions in the narrative and much of the satire themselves derive from an obscure series of episodes in the tumultuous history of Scottish religious life. These affected both Highlands and Lowlands but probably had greatest impact in towns like Kirriemuir. To understand something of the power of this superb novel, its references, indeed its title and also something of what drove the tremendously ambitious and industrious J. M. Barrie, history needs to rewind a little.

Central to the Scottish Reformation of the 16th century was literacy. John Knox, his supporters and those who carried on and deepened the effect of what was achieved after the revolution of 1560 believed absolutely in a doctrine known as the priesthood of all believers. This insisted that each Christian was responsible for his or her own salvation and, in order to gain that, they had to be able to read the Word of God for themselves. The old role of priests as interpreters and readers of the Bible would be swept away as mass literacy was introduced all over Scotland. It would usher in what the reformers called a 'Godly Commonwealth'. A school in every parish! That was the clarion cry and, over the course of the 17th century, in the face of great hardship, much was achieved.

J. M. Barrie was not born into wealth or privilege. His father was a weaver in Kirriemuir and he was aware that this his cottage industry was dying as industrialisation took hold. Nevertheless, he and his wife somehow managed to find the money to have all of their eight surviving children educated and not just at an elementary level. Barrie was sent to Glasgow Academy, Forfar Academy, Dumfries Academy and Edinburgh University. By a mixture of scholarships and bursaries to add to the spare means of the family, the modest fees were paid. The Reformation ultimately succeeded in ushering in era of mass literacy because the 900 parishes of the Church of Scotland provided schools with competent teachers and, in contrast with England's two, there were four universities. Education was not free in early modern Scotland but it was cheap and widely available.

Scalan

Despite the fervour of the reformers in Scotland after 1560, Catholicism survived in isolated pockets, most of them in the north and in the Highlands and Islands. The complete eclipse of the Catholic Church had only been prevented by the bravery and piety of a handful of Irish Franciscans. In the 1620s and 1630s, when persecution was a constant threat, they baptised more than 10,000 people and returned them to the Holy Mother Church but, to sustain even that partial recovery, priests were needed urgently. In a remote glen deep in the mountains above Glenlivet, Scalan College was finally set up in 1716. At first little more than a very basic farmhouse built almost entirely of turf, the secret seminary continued to train young men for the priesthood until 1799. By then, the laws banning the Catholic Church had been repealed and colleges could be openly founded. Scalan has now become a place of pilgrimage.

If the promotion of literacy was one of the glories of the Scottish Reformation, the mania for witch-hunting was a disfigurement. During the last quarter of the 16th century and for the whole of the 17th, thousands of Scots, most of them women, suspected of witchcraft were hideously tortured, hanged or burned. Part of the motivation for these grisly episodes was rooted in the preservation and purity of the Godly Commonwealth. Satan was thought to be everywhere and his agents on earth both polluted and endangered society. All over Lowland Scotland, appalling atrocities were perpetrated as suspects were subjected to 'pricking', having been stripped naked and hung from a beam or a hook. It was thought that witches derived their power from contact with the earth. The witch prickers – and there were men who made a profession of this – drove long brass needles into any unusual marks found on the naked bodies of victims. Searching for the 'Devil's Nip' or the marks of Satan, they inflicted terrible injuries and generally extracted confessions. Most convicted witches were strangled before being burned at the stake but others suffered the dreadful fate of being burned 'quick' or alive. In *Auld Licht Idylls*, Barrie recounts a historical episode when a minister absented himself form the parish at Thrums to attend a witch burning.

It was different in the mountains, glens and islands of the north and west. These horrific acts and attitudes did not cross the Highland Line. Between 1570 and 1720 there were only 89 indictments for witchcraft in the Highlands compared with many thousands in the Lowlands and almost all of these were tried in the English-speaking areas of Caithness, Ross, Sutherland and Bute. The Gaelic language was the greatest, most robust defence against the horrors of the witch finders. Zealots anxious to root out the creatures of Satan were met with incomprehension and a refusal to translate and the reason for this was a straightforward determination to preserve something integral and valuable in Gaelic culture.

Most Lowland women condemned for witchcraft were, in reality, folk healers, people who practised and passed on traditional remedies. Many of these were associated with childbirth. In 1590, Agnes Sampson of Keith in Banffshire was brutally tortured and burned at the stake because she had used 'develisch prayers' to relieve the pains of labour. In the Highlands, such women were admired and their skills prized, their medicine often founded on the use of plant derivatives or therapies designed to ease the discomfort of the sick. And, since these traditions were not written down anywhere and uttered only in Gaelic, they were beyond the twisted reach of monoglot Lowland inquisitors. Since the witch craze infected most of northern and western Europe, the ancient traditions of folk medicine in the Highlands were some of the few to survive the purges.

As the mania subsided, British politics began to grip the Church of Scotland in unwelcome ways and its splits and secessions supplied J. M. Barrie with the source of much of his satire in *Auld Licht Idylls*. Even though the Union of 1707 explicitly enshrined the independence of the Church of Scotland, it nevertheless threatened it almost immediately. In 1712, the Toleration Act badly dented the universality of the Godly Commonwealth when it allowed the Episcopalian Church to be established in Scotland. Instantly dubbed 'the English Kirk' or 'the Chapel', its ungodly interest in ceremony and music set it apart from Presbyterian austerity. Because they installed organs to accompany hymn and psalm singing, Scots still talk of the 'whistlin' kirks'. In his novel, Barrie commented wryly and probably accurately that 'to the Auld Licht of the past there were three degrees of damnation – auld kirk, playacting, chapel'.

Also enacted in 1712, the Patronage Act was an even more serious threat to the Church of Scotland. In the long struggle for independence, congregations had won the right to choose their ministers for themselves. Composed of elders appointed for life, the Kirk Session was mandated to fill a vacancy by, in essence, holding auditions for applicants. In *Auld Licht Idylls*, standards of evangelism were high and exacting. Ministers should be able to deliver a sermon without notes, as though it rose up almost unbidden from the depths of their piety and the profundity of their learning. Written texts were anathema. 'To follow a pastor who "read" seemed to the Auld Lichts like claiming Heaven on false pretences.' When one unfortunate candidate preached outdoors to the congregation in Thrums, he used an ingenious stratagem to conceal his written sermon. But a sudden gust of wind blew up and away went his pages that had been trimmed precisely to fit with the same size of the pages of his Bible. Ever after he was known as 'Paper Watts'.

The Marrowmen

In 1699, Thomas Boston became the minister for the tiny parish of Simprim near Coldstream. There were only 90 communicants. While visiting one of his sparse flock, he picked up a copy of a book entitled The Marrow of Modern Divinity, *which had been brought north by a soldier who had fought in Oliver Cromwell's armies. Written by Edward Fisher, it was a compendium of the views of various radical thinkers of the Reformation but it dealt particularly with the notion of grace. Thomas Boston was greatly taken with Fisher's belief that what mattered in a Christian life was not repentance or even personal reformation but the complete and absolute acceptance of Christ and his teaching. Once that state was achieved, repentance and a new life followed. The book was republished in 1718 and like-minded ministers were dubbed The Marrowmen. Boston and his supporters were attacked by conservatives in the Kirk and their zealous and highly effective preaching was thought to be excessive and intemperate. The Marrowmen were distressingly popular with their congregations. Boston himself appears to have been surprisingly self-effacing. The distinguished Canadian writer, Alice Munro, was attracted to him: 'In his autobiography he speaks of his own recurring miseries, his dry spells, his sense of unworthiness and dullness even in the act of preaching the Gospel, or while praying in his study.'*

The Patronage Act of 1712 removed the right of the Kirk Session to choose ministers and vacancies were to be filled by the choices of the lairds and other potentates who could 'intrude' their own candidates. Dissent rumbled and, in 1732, the First

Secession took place. Led by ministers from Perthshire and Stirling, congregations left the Church of Scotland, believing that they were returning to its founding principles.

In 1747, a new oath of loyalty was required from burgesses after the upheavals of the Jacobite Rebellion. Those who controlled and prospered in Scotland's burghs were compelled to swear allegiance to a secular authority. Many churchmen believed that this compromised their first commitment to their faith and so another split occurred, this time between the Burghers and the Anti-Burghers.

Only five years later, a controversy over the intrusion of unacceptable ministers to vacant parishes set in train the creation of the Relief Church. In 1761, this new and more liberal faction was constituted and it quickly grew popular, with more than 100,000 members. Meanwhile, trouble was brewing in the Burgher Church and, in 1799, they divided into two groups – the New Lichts and the Auld Lichts or what might be subtitled the Progressives and the Traditionalists. Six years later, the Anti-Burghers followed suit and the New Licht Anti-Burghers distanced themselves from the Auld Licht Anti-Burghers.

By 1820, to the relief of many, no doubt, a new spirit of harmony was in the air and the New Licht Burghers and the New Licht Anti-Burghers found common ground and united. Two years later the Auld Lichts Anti-Burghers joined the United Original Secession Church (the version that originated in 1732) and, in 1847, the United Secession Church united with the Relief Church. This flurry of accord left one dogged faction, the Auld Licht Burghers, determinedly un-united – much to the delight of J. M. Barrie, and his readers.

Seeing themselves as the keepers of the flame of an austere reforming zeal, the Auld Lichts held fast to tradition. In Barrie's opening chapter, the parish schoolmaster, the hero of the story, is snowbound in a severe winter. Only the Auld Licht congregation struggled through the drifts to hold a Sunday service. The competition between denominations is one of the themes of the novel and enmities remained sharp. In Thrums there were two main churches, the Free Kirk (the product of another rift) and the Parish Kirk (Church of Scotland) 'both of which the first Auld Licht minister I knew ran past when he had not the time to avoid them by taking a back wynd'.

Jacobite Cricket

Scotsmen and the quintessentially English game of cricket may seem unlikely bedfellows. But the reality is surprisingly different. J. M. Barrie adored cricket and founded his own team of enthusiastic amateurs. He called them the Allahakbarries, believing it was the Arabic for 'Heaven Help Us' as well as being a partial pun on his own surname. In fact, the phrase means 'God Is Great'. Team members included other literary greats who were also Scots. Arthur Conan Doyle, A. A. Milne and Jerome K. Jerome and P. G. Wodehouse all bowled and batted for the Allahakbarries. But they were not the most feared XI to adorn a cricket pitch. When asked to describe how quick his own bowling was, Barrie replied that, after delivering the ball, he usually sat down to wait for it to arrive at the other end, 'which it sometimes did'. He tried to encourage teammates by saying, 'You scored a good single in the first innings but were not so successful in the second.' Barrie forbad his team from practising on an opponent's ground before a match 'because it will only give them confidence'. He believed that his own worst performance was the time he was clean bowled by an American actress. Other Scots did a little better. Mike Denness and Tony Greig both captained England in recent times but perhaps the most fascinating figure was Richard Nyren. Captain of the fabled Hambledon Cricket Club, the forerunner of the MCC who regularly defeated All England XIs, Nyren was involved in the evolution of the rules of the game in the later 18th century. He and his team proposed a bat of uniform width. Noted as a left-arm bowler, he specialised in sending down deliveries overarm. The term bowling originally referred to the old-fashioned underarm action, like bowls. Richard Nyren's origins are uncertain. One scholar believes that his surname is an anglicisation of Nairn and that he was a Jacobite refugee who took up cricket because it was quintessentially English and good cover.

Ministers were feared as well as revered. In the severe setting of the Auld Licht Kirk ('white is not a religious colour and the walls are a dull grey'), they would bang the Bible and rail directly at sinners cowering in the pews. Horrified members talked of the time when 'a laddie whistled when he went past the minister' in the street. Others were awestruck at the familiarity shown by Hendry Munn, the Kirk Officer, towards Mr Dishart, the minister: 'he was the only man in Thrums who did not quake when the minister looked at him. A wild story, never authenticated, says that Hendry once offered Mr Dishart a snuff from his mull.' Barrie strikes a deep chord when he exaggerates – only a little – the deep-seated masochism of the poor sinners in the Auld Licht congregation: 'Old wives grumbled by their hearths when he [the minister] did not look in to despair of their salvation.'

Light comedy might be made out of their traditions but it was a turbulent and hard-won history that brought the thrawn, obdurate and deeply pious Auld Lichts into being and they never forgot the sacrifices and the martyrs. More than anything, it was the time of the Covenanters that inspired them, the middle years of the 17th century when Scotland was aflame with dreams of a religious utopia and was determined to defend them.

The idea of a special covenant between God and the people of Scotland (or at least those Scots who were true believers) grew out of the Godly Commonwealth. Famously, at Falkland Palace in 1596, the great reformer Andrew Melville pointed out to James VI that, while he may be king of Scotland, he was only 'God's sillie vassal'. And, in Christ's kingdom of Scotland, he was not a king or a lord but merely a member. Forty years later James's son, Charles I, by then installed as king of Great Britain and Ireland, attempted to bring Scotland into conformity with England and the Anglican Church by imposing bishops on the Kirk. The response was emphatic. In 1638, a National Covenant reinforcing the particular bond between God and Scotland was drawn up and, in a public ceremony in Greyfriars kirkyard in Edinburgh, it was signed by many powerful men.

When open war broke out between Charles I and the English parliament and spread to Ireland and Scotland, the Covenant became an instrument of unity and, in the 1640s, the Lords of the Covenant in effect governed the nation. After defeat at Dunbar in 1650 at the hands of Oliver Cromwell and his New Model Army, their power was temporarily diminished. And, when the Stuart dynasty was restored in 1660, an even more serious threat materialised. Again, bishops were to be imposed in Scotland and, this time, Covenanters were actively pursued and persecuted. Martyrs began to be made.

Covenanting congregations were forced out of their churches and, across the countryside, many held regular open-air services known as 'field conventicles'. A young preacher from Fife, Richard Cameron, quickly made his mark. But, when Charles I's government insisted that the Kirk submit to High Anglican governance and accept the king (and not Christ) as Head of the Church of Scotland, he and many others fled abroad. In 1679, Richard Cameron was formally ordained at the Scots Kirk at Rotterdam by the Rev. Robert Ward:

> Richard, the public standard of the Gospel is fallen in Scotland; and, if I know anything of the mind of the Lord, you are called to undergo your trials before us, and go home and lift the fallen standard, and display it before the world. But, before you put your hand to it, you shall go to as many of the field ministers as you can find, and give them your hearty invitation to go with you; and if they will not go, go your lone, and the Lord will go with you. Behold all you spectators! Here is the head of a faithful minister and servant of Jesus Christ, who shall lose the same for his Master's interest; and it shall be set up before sun and moon in the public view of the world.

It was a ghoulish prophesy, perhaps even a fate Cameron himself sought. When he returned to Scotland, the fiery young preacher joined with two others, Donald Cargill and David Hackston, and they issued the Sanquhar Declaration. It was a manifesto of the Kirk Militant from the outset. Accompanied by twenty armed men, Cameron walked into the market square in the village in the Galloway Hills and read out what amounted to a call to arms. After disowning Charles Stuart, he announced, '[W]e, being under the standard of our Lord Jesus Christ, Captain of Salvation, do declare a war with such a tyrant and usurper'.

Cameron did not have to wait long to meet his grisly fate. Soon after setting out his intentions at Sanquhar, he was killed near Cumnock in a sharp skirmish with government soldiers, the hated dragoons. Cameron's body was decapitated and his head and hands spitted on the Netherbow Port in Edinburgh. Calling themselves Cameronians, his followers multiplied, especially in Lanarkshire, Ayrshire and Dumfries and Galloway and throughout the 1680s, the period known as the Killing Times, they attempted to protect Covenanters from persecution.

By 1688, the feckless Stuart dynasty had run out of support and been forced to flee and, in what is called The Glorious Revolution, the Protestant William of Orange succeeded. Persecutions ceased immediately but peace did not descend. In the Highlands, the clans were raised in the very first Jacobite Rebellion by John Graham, Viscount Dundee. Supported by Clan Cameron and only a few other chiefs, he led a small army south to Blair Atholl. On 27 July, they caught a slightly larger government army in the narrow pass at Killiecrankie and defeated them after a downhill charge. Dundee had waited until the evening sun had moved around behind his position and the Highlanders swept General Hugh Mackay's dazzled army off the field. In the immediate aftermath, more clansmen rallied to the royalist standard and a force of 5,000 or so would have presented a much more potent threat had Dundee not died of wounds on the battlefield.

Meanwhile, the followers of Richard Cameron had come together to form a regiment of foot. In April 1689, more than 1,200 men had enlisted near Douglas in South Lanarkshire. Each company of twenty had an elder assigned to organise worship and prayer and each recruit was given a Bible. The Cameronians placed themselves in the service of King William III and marched north to Perth to meet the growing threat from the Highlands. The Scottish Privy Council was terrified at the news from Killiecrankie and, while it made preparations to abandon Edinburgh, it ordered the new regiment to move to Dunkeld and hold the town against the rebels at all costs.

Lying precisely on the Highland Line, where the River Tay emerges from its narrow valley threaded through the mountains, the douce little town has a long, intriguing and turbulent history. The name of Dunkeld derives from the Dun (or Fortress) of the Caledonians, the ancient confederacy that faced the Romans at the Battle of the Graupian Mountain. Such a name implies not only importance but also a frontier place, somewhere so called by neighbours who were not Caledonians. Nearby, Schiehallion rises up and reinforces that sense of the south-eastern edges of Caledonian territory because its name translates as the Magic Mountain of the Caledonians. Clearly a place of some long-forgotten spiritual significance, the magic of Schiehallion may come from the fact that it is a shape shifter, a mountain that looks very different from a variety of aspects.

Christian belief replaced paganism at Dunkeld and, on the flat haughland on the banks of the Tay, an early monastery was planted. Dating from the 6th or early 7th century, its foundation was inspired by a missionary expedition from Iona, led by St Columba. Its reputation for sanctity grew and, in the 9th century, Constantine I, probably the first to rule over both Picts and Scots, caused stone buildings to replace the primitive cells of the Celtic monks. The medieval cathedral of the 13th and 14th centuries remembered the simple faith of the earlier churches and it was dedicated to St Columba. Before the reformers did away with such things, the saint's relics were displayed and revered in the side chapels of the great church by the river.

When the Cameronians marched into Dunkeld on Saturday 17 August 1689, their captains saw immediately that its flat site would be very difficult to defend. Led by Lt Col. William Cleland, the soldiers mustered around the cathedral precinct and many of the 1,200 men found shelter in the church. Even though he was only 28, Cleland was an experienced officer, having fought in the Covenanter armies at the battles of Drumclog and Bothwell Brig in 1679. Like Richard Cameron, he had been forced to flee abroad. Surprisingly, he was also a published poet, the author of a mock epic 'On the expedition of the Highland Host who came to destroy the western shires in winter 1678' and, in the this lengthy composition, Cleland made his feelings about Highlanders very clear.

The Cameronian regiment was organised into 20 companies of 60 men apiece, each commanded by a captain, supported by a lieutenant and an ensign. Armed only with muskets and without any artillery, the soldiers would clearly have to create a makeshift defensive perimeter. There was no town wall, only a dyke around the cathedral precinct. The Marquis of Atholl's house stood close by and it was quickly fortified. A single street (now Cathedral Street) with lanes leading off it ran eastwards from the precinct gate to a wider area where the market cross stood. Some of the houses were of two storeys, although most were thatched cottages. To the south of the cathedral flowed the River Tay and a little way downstream there was a ford. To the north-east of the precinct lies Stanley Hill, covered, then as now, with tall trees. After a rapid reconnaissance, Cleland's captains posted sentries and the regiment settled for the night, bivouacking in and around the cathedral.

The following morning, despite it being the Sabbath, the soldiers set to and worked hard to dig defensive ditches and repair the wall around the precinct. To act as lookouts, a detachment climbed the steeple. They quickly reported sightings of small groups of Highlanders in the surrounding hills and, at 4 p.m. in the afternoon, a large company of several hundred armed men emerged ominously from the trees on Stanley Hill, very close to the town. From the vantage point in the steeple, lookouts called down to Cleland that they could see a messenger approaching, carrying a halberd with a white cloth attached. He handed a letter to the Cameronian commander. It presented him with what amounted to an ultimatum: 'We, the gentlemen assembled, being informed that you intend to burn the town, desire [to know] whether you come for peace or war, and to certify that if you burn one house, we will destroy you.'

Cleland replied defiantly that he would not retreat and, at the same time, he got a horseman away, splashing across the Tay fords towards Perth and its garrison. Reinforcements were desperately and immediately needed. Perhaps, after sending out two of his Gaelic-speaking officers, Dhu and Roy Campbell, Cleland had gathered intelligence that the large body of armed men on Stanley Hill were clansmen from the surrounding area anxious to protect Dunkeld and who had risen to join the rebellion. The town was seriously threatened and the Highland army had yet to reach it. No doubt the Cameronian colonel hoped that his messenger was galloping hard down the Perth road.

To the relief of the defenders of Dunkeld, Lord Cardross arrived the day after with five troops of cavalry who had been able to move quickly across country. They quickly engaged with the groups of clansmen around the town and drove them back into the hills, well out of musket range. But no sooner had they arrived than an urgent order came for Cardross from Col. Ramsay, the commander of the Perth garrison. The troopers were to return to him without delay. Cleland objected strongly but the cavalry were forced to obey a direct order and, on 20th August, they crossed the Tay and rode south. That afternoon, scouts reported that the van of the Highland army had been seen upriver at Dalguise and was approaching fast.

As dawn broke on the morning of 21 August, the lookouts in the cathedral steeple watched as their enemies drew themselves up in battle order on the hillsides above Dunkeld. They counted more than 5,000 and, sheltering behind the tumbledown walls and ditches of the precinct, the Cameronians saw that they were badly outnumbered by four to one. And no retreat was possible. Col. Alexander Cannon, the commander of the Highland army, had sent detachments across the Tay to block the fords and more of his troops closed the ring to the west of the cathedral. The defenders of Dunkeld were completely surrounded.

At 7 a.m., the war pipes skirled out the battle rants and the Highlanders swarmed down off the hills and poured into the town. Cleland's ring of outposts was quickly overwhelmed and his men ran for the redoubts behind the precinct wall. Protected by a bristling wall of their long pikes and halberds, the company led by Lieutenant Stewart managed to hold the barricade at the market cross at the east end of Cathedral Street. Raked by supporting fire from the musketeers behind the precinct wall, the Highlanders were driven back several times. But the sheer press of numbers eventually told, Stewart was shot dead and his men turned and ran for the sanctuary of the cathedral. No further retreat was now possible and Cleland knew that his men would fight to the last. They could expect no mercy.

The Cameronians may have been badly outnumbered but they had one advantage. The narrow street and lanes of Dunkeld much reduced the effectiveness of the Highland charge, what had swept Hugh Mackay's army off the braes of Killiecrankie only a few days before. If the Cameronians could keep their discipline and maintain volley fire by rank, then they could hold their ground. But they began to run low on musket balls.

The Highland captains realised that the charge would simply fail repeatedly across such a narrow front and they changed tactics. Having broken into the houses on Cathedral Street and others overlooking the precinct, their snipers easily found elevated positions from windows and roofs where they could fire down on the Cameronians. Almost immediately, Lt Col. Cleland was fatally wounded. Such was the depth of his courage that he tried to drag himself out of sight so that his men might not lose heart. Major Henderson assumed command but the snipers were so close that they quickly picked him out and shot him a few minutes later. When Captain Munro took over, he set covering fire for parties of Cameronians to go out into the street with burning faggots speared on the tips of their pikes. They thrust these into the thatched roofs of the houses occupied by the

Highland snipers and where possible locked their doors. Here is an extract from James Browne's *History of the Highlands*:

The whole town was in a conflagration, and the scene which it now presented was one of the most heart rending description. The din of war was no longer heard, but a more terrific [terrifying] sound had succeeded, from the wild shrieks and accents of despair which issued from the dense mass of smoke and flame which enveloped the unfortunate sufferers. The pikmen had locked the doors of such of the houses as had keys standing in them and the unhappy intruders, being thus cut off from escape, perished in the flames. No less than sixteen Highlanders were burned to death in one house. With the exception of three houses, possessed by the Cameronians, the whole town was consumed.

As waves of Highlanders attacked the precinct wall, the defenders' supply of musket balls was diminishing ever more rapidly. Soldiers began to strip lead off the roofs of the Atholl house and the cathedral, melt it and put it into moulds. At one point, the defenders were firing balls as fast as they could be plunged into cold water. More importantly, gunpowder was also running dangerously short and once the last of it had been shaken out of the last flask, the muskets would be no better than clubs. When that happened and the wall was at last stormed, the officers had planned to retreat with their men into the Marquis of Atholl's house and defend it to the death as a last redoubt.

But then, suddenly, the Highlanders drew back. Much discouraged by the blazing town and the appalling deaths suffered by their snipers, they seemed to lose heart completely. Unable to drive them on, Col. Cannon was forced to concede a retreat and, at 11 p.m., after 16 hours of fighting, as the darkness gathered, Dunkeld, lit only by the burning houses beyond the precinct wall, was deserted.

When the exhausted garrison peered into the gloom and realised that their attackers had gone and they had won an unlikely and glorious victory, they threw their caps in the air. And, like the Covenanters they were, they raised their exultant voices in a psalm of thanksgiving. As the drums rolled, the Cameronians unfurled their colours and gave thanks to God. Ever practical, uncertain that the Highlanders had really re-treated, the captains ordered their men to repair the walls. And the following morning work parties were sent out to cut down some of the trees of Stanley Hill that had given such good cover to the Highland musketeers. But others reported that there was no sign of the enemy around the town – they seemed to have fled, to have melted back into the mountains.

The successful defence of Dunkeld stopped the first Jacobite rebellion in its tracks. Three hundred Highlanders lay dead in the streets and in the burnt-out houses and the chiefs withdrew northwards. Less than a year later, a remnant of the Highland army was routed and dispersed by government cavalry at the Haughs of Cromdale on Speyside. Richard Cameron's martyr-dom had not been in vain and the standard of the Gospel was raised once more in Christ's Kingdom of Scotland.

What the dramatic events of 1689 showed was a Highland Line continuing to be a real frontier – a wide cultural, political and religious divide. The holes and chips made by musket balls are still visible on the eastern gable of Dunkeld Cathedral and it would be two centuries before passions had cooled sufficiently to allow J. M. Barrie to poke fun at the heirs of the Covenanters.

10

The First Frontier

IN THE EARLY SUMMER OF 1961, a team of archaeologists dug a trench across a small part of what they knew to be a very large Roman fort. No upstanding features had survived, not one stone had been left standing upon another but the site was unique for under the grass lay the only complete, undisturbed plan of a legionary fortress anywhere in the Roman Empire. It had never been built over and most of its area was rough, old grazing bordered by mature trees. But, over several digging seasons throughout the 1950s, tantalisingly few finds of artefacts had been uncovered.

Once the area of the trench had been marked out and the surface mattress of grass lifted, Ian Richmond, the director of the excavation, noticed a difference in the colour and texture of the soil. There was a definite set of edges so perhaps a pit had been dug. Under six feet of gravel backfill, the archaeologists found the corroded remains of ten iron wheel tyres – what cartwrights fitted around wooden wheels to protect them from splintering or cracking. Beneath these, the diggers came upon something strange. It was a solid crust of rusted iron, what looked like a lid of fused pieces of metal. Having lifted this out very carefully, they discovered something even more remarkable.

In an unparalleled state of preservation, sealed from damp by the lid of fused rust, here was a cache of almost 900,000 Roman nails. All hand-made, ranging from small tacks to secure roof tiles to massive iron spikes for clenching load-bearing timbers, nothing remotely on this scale had ever been found anywhere in the Empire. And the nails told a fascinating story, a sequence of events painstakingly pieced together by a group of patient and dedicated archaeologists working without the aid of metal detectors or any of the sophisticated technology now available.

Ian Richmond's team made their astonishing discovery at Inchtuthil, a flat and slightly elevated plateau of haughland on the banks of the River Tay, about ten miles downstream from Dunkeld. Marked as 'Victoria' on Ptolemy's 2nd-century map of North Britain, it was designed as a legionary fortress and, as the nail hoard showed, conceived on a mighty scale. Covering an area of more than 53 acres, Inchtuthil or Victoria could accommodate 5,400 legionaries and other auxiliaries. Richmond's surveyors plotted 64 barracks buildings, a temporary headquarters in the centre, workshops, 170 storehouses, a hospital, 6 granaries and a large drill hall, all protected by a perimeter wall and a two-metre-deep ditch and counterscarp beyond it. Four heavily fortified gateways stood at either end of two principal streets which quartered the whole layout in a grid pattern. It was an immense building project, something no Caledonian had ever seen, and, after the end of the Roman Empire, work on a scale that would not be undertaken in Scotland for another 18 centuries.

Inchtuthil may have been the site of a marching camp used by Agricola's invasion force in 82 or 83 but the construction of the legionary fortress certainly commenced in 84 after the battle of the Graupian Mountain. It was the military success that gave the fort its Roman name. Victoria was a concrete statement of imperial policy. North Britain was to be at least subdued and the establishment of a huge legionary base told the Caledonian kings that the Romans planned to stay and bring the whole island into the Empire. Perhaps initially they intended to consolidate the more valuable and malleable Lowlands and, for the time being, contain the Highlands.

It may be that the victors of the battle of the Graupian Mountain marched south to Inchtuthil in the autumn of 83. On the eastern edges of the haughland, at least two temporary camps were laid out – one for the officers, one for other ranks. After the sites had been cleared, the ditches dug and the rampart raised, Agricola's own legion, the XX Valeria Victrix, pitched their leather tents and made preparations to overwinter on the bank of the Tay. Raised some time after 31 BC by the first Emperor, Augustus, the XX Legion carried many battle honours. In the wars to subdue the peoples around the Upper Danube, the Twentieth was led by Marcus Valerius Messalla Messallinus and, after defeating rebellious tribes (having been surrounded and cutting their way out), it seems that they took their general's name. Since Agricola had been their commander during Boudicca's Revolt of AD 60, he may have favoured them with the additional title of Victrix after the battle of the Graupian Mountain.

Such moments of military glory are fleeting. Almost 99 per cent of a soldier's life is spent not fighting and sensible generals keep their men busy. Once the temporary defences were secured at Inchtuthil, the legionaries began the hard work of building a new fortress. And as the nail hoard suggests, it was conceived on a massive scale.

Third in command of a Roman legion was the Praefectus Castrorum and his responsibilities revolved around supply and logistics. Inchtuthil stood at a point on the Tay where the river is still tidal and was probably deep enough to be used for barges or rafts to bring in materials. In 83–84, Agricola still had the British Fleet under his command. Once the rations for the legion, its men, horses and draught animals had been organised, the Praefectus's first consideration was a quantity survey. What materials would the great fortress need and where were they to be sourced?

All of the logistical and construction skills required could be supplied by the legionaries themselves. In addition to their fighting abilities, Roman soldiers also had a wide variety of practical skills – some were masons, joiners, blacksmiths, cartwrights or bookkeepers and most were good labourers with a wealth of building experience. The Praefectus's principal concern will have been the availability of timber. The Inchtuthil fortress would need vast quantities of felled trees for the ramparts, barracks, storehouses and other buildings and such a bulky material had to be available locally. There had to have been dense and extensive forest near the construction site. Perhaps that was a factor in the choice of Inchtuthil. No doubt defended by patrols of armed comrades, Roman woodcutters felled many thousands of trees around the new fortress and stripped them of bark and branches before carting them down to the site. It may be that they stockpiled timber, keeping the stacks off the ground on bearers, to allow it to season. When the sap and moisture drains from felled trees, the beams, posts and rails made from it are much stronger and easier to work.

The Price of Victoria

Idle soldierly hands can cause trouble when not fighting and wise generals always tried to keep their men occupied. Otherwise trouble would be inevitable. The Romans understood this well and the legions were trained for all manner of tasks. They were much more often employed in various sorts of construction than in battle. Inchtuthil Fortress, probably plotted as 'Victoria' on Roman maps, was a huge enterprise. In her Building a Roman Legionary Fortress, *Elizabeth Shirley has done some precise calculations – and they are staggering in their scale. Not allowing for mistakes, inefficiencies and changes of mind – all normal features of any building project – Inchtuthil took 6.1 million man-hours to build over less than three years. Had the fortress been completed, it would have taken 16.5 million man-hours. There were many phases that needed detailed logistical planning – site clearance, the building of a temporary camp to house officers, the pre-construction (for enclosure and defence) of ramparts and gateways, assembly of building materials, surfacing, drainage and water supply, timber construction, stonework structures and, finally, the work needed to abandon the fortress.*

Stone had to be sourced for road making, the paving of the parade ground and for the building of ovens while gravel may have been dredged from the bed of the Tay. Clay was dug and limestone ground down for mortar. Fresh water had to be readily available and archaeologists have found evidence of a temporary aqueduct to supply the site, a run of pipework probably extending over two miles to bring water from the Millhole Burn. Men need only one gallon of water a day but horses and oxen require ten and animals were probably led down to the Tay twice a day to drink. Romans were famously fond of bathhouses and that facility at Inchtuthil may have been the thirstiest consumer of all.

One of the Praefectus's most taxing difficulties was stone. It was not only needed for roads but also for the bathhouse. The nearest quarry for usable sandstone lay three miles to the north of the site, on Gourdie Hill. A road was laid down for the heavy carts and, to pull them, only plodding teams of oxen had the muscle power. To keep carriage weight to a minimum, the quarries roughed out blocks of stone to size, their edges only needing to be smoothed off by a chisel to fit. So that the three-mile journey was easier and more productive, the *gromatici*, the surveyors, made it longer. They chose an easier downhill gradient for fully loaded carts (such loads can push a team so hard that they cannot hold it, lose their footing and go down in front of the cart) and a more direct, steeper approach for those returning empty to the quarry. It worked in a loop on a one-way system – and to regulate it properly there must have been Roman traffic policemen.

Inchtuthil may have been of a singular size, no less than a large military town almost in the centre of a Scotland where everyone lived on farms, but it did not stand alone. The legionary base was the lynchpin of what historians have called the Gask Ridge Frontier. Although it was not a continuous barrier or a wall – this would come later – it was the first boundary to be marked out on an edge of the Roman Empire.

Strung along a north-east to south-west axis, the Gask Ridge Frontier exactly echoes the Highland Line and it is the first explicit recognition of it as a political and cultural divide. It is based on a sequence of forts. Some, like Inchtuthil, are located where narrow Highland glens open out into Lowland areas. Once known as glenblocker forts, they extend from Drumquhassle near Drymen and the southern end of Loch Lomond up to Inverquharity in the north-east. Forward posts too small to resist anything except raiding parties, they acted as listening posts in the hope of giving early warnings of hostile movements in the Highlands.

Behind this line lay the staple and spine of Roman military practice – a road. It ran from Doune up on to the Gask Ridge and, from there, to Bertha or Perth. For part of its length, mainly along the ridge itself, the road linked watchtowers, built approximately a thousand yards apart. That meant a close observation of movement. In fact, it may be that travellers were compelled to pay customs dues on any goods they were carrying or a toll for themselves. The Gask Ridge marked the northernmost frontier of the Empire and those who crossed it were entering the Roman world. Imperial frontiers operating in exactly this way were built elsewhere.

It also seems likely that the Gask Ridge system was no accident, no careless stroke of an imperial pen like the straight-line borders of some 19th-century African colonies. It probably lay on an older frontier, the divide between the Caledonians to the north-west and the Venicones to the south-east. The latter were Lowland arable farmers who most likely supplied the Roman army with corn and other sustenance while the former were unquestionably hostile and would probably remain so. So that their grain supply was protected, the Gask Ridge was a sensible strategic precaution. Its location also reinforces the sense of the place-names of Dunkeld and Schiehallion denoting the edges of Caledonian territory.

Ardoch Fort lies at the southern end of the Gask Ridge, nor far from the Gleneagles Hotel. It is an extremely impressive sight. The ditches and banks around the fort are still deep and massive, grassed-over but barely disturbed, it seems. On the north and east sides there are five ditches but these were not intended as extra security in an especially hostile area. Instead, they reflect the shrinkage of the fort as smaller garrisons were posted there. Part of the ground area inside the original ditch was simply dug into more ditches so that the walls could be brought in.

In late 86, new orders arrived from Rome at the legionary fortress at Chester. Their garrison, the Legio II Adiutrix, was to be transferred immediately to Dacia, modern Romania, where a serious rebellion had flared up. That, in turn, meant the posting of the XX Valeria Victrix to the south as a replacement and, after only three years, Inchtuthil, much of it unfinished, was abandoned. Events moved fast. The completed timber buildings were stripped of anything useful and portable before being set alight. Pottery was methodically smashed into useless smithereens and carts and packhorses were quickly loaded. At the workshops, one centurion was faced with a problem. What should he do with the seven tons of valuable iron that had been beaten into the shape of nails? Perhaps because he had no spare transport capacity, perhaps because the legion was already moving out of the gates, he ordered a deep pit to be dug and the nails to be buried so that Caledonian smiths could not turn the iron into weapons. And, until Ian Richmond noticed a discolouration in the soil in 1961, the centurion's decision was the right one.

After the nails were counted, dated and analysed and many of them distributed to interested parties such as other archaeologists, most of them were stored at the Dalzell Steel Mill in Motherwell. Eventually they were recycled as scrap iron and some people may now be driving around in a car made partly by legionary blacksmiths in Perthshire two thousand years ago. Atomic scientists also found a use for them in their calculations for the rate of corrosion for the cylinders used to contain nuclear waste. And, when the archaeologists first pulled these long and wickedly sharp nails out of the pit at Inchtuthil, it may have occurred to some that Roman soldiers had themselves found another use for them. If Christ was indeed nailed to the cross in Jerusalem then it was objects very like these that were hammered through his hands and feet.

No Rome

For almost the whole of the four centuries of the life of the province of Britannia, the Roman imperial government worried about what lay beyond the Highland Line. Agricola campaigned in the north for four years and appeared to defeat the Caledonian confederacy decisively at Mons Graupius. Hadrian and Antoninus Pius had expensive and massive walls built in part to keep the Highlanders out and Septimius Severus invaded with the largest army that ever crossed the Tweed. And yet the archaeological record of Roman artefacts found in the Highlands is so sparse as to be almost invisible. South of the Forth, a great deal has been found but north of the Tay comparatively little. This may be linked to the accident of discovery but that could apply anywhere and it compares very strangely with Rome's European neighbours. The Baltic coastal region of Poland, what used to be East Prussia, lay far from the imperial frontier along the Rhine and Danube and was never invaded by the legions. And yet many more Roman items have been found there than have ever turned up in the Highlands. This may mean a conscious cultural rejection of what must have been seen as luxury goods or, at the very least, a lack of contact across the Highland Line – a very early example of a recurring theme.

Long after the fall of the Western Empire, the ghosts of long-dead Romans swirled around the Perthshire hills. At the foot of Glen Lyon, Fortingall is the home of a famous tree, a yew that has survived for more than 3,000 winters and is the oldest living thing in Europe. And lingering under its ancient shade are shadows of one of the most notorious Romans of them all, an imperial prefect who washed his hands at a turning point in the history of the world. A curiously persistent legend insists that Pontius Pilate was born at Fortingall, the son of Roman soldier and a Caledonian princess. It is of course chronologically impossible, for Pilate was in fact born around 15 BC, probably in the Abruzzo in Italy, and Rome did not penetrate the woods and the glens of Perthshire until the 1st century AD, in the late 70s. Perhaps the answer lies in a tradition of sanctity by association.

Fortingall stands on the site of a very early Christian church founded from Iona in the 8th century and it may be that its priests confected a spurious link to Christ. The fact that St Andrew knew Jesus and followed him is what made his cult and relics so powerful and his church at St Andrews so venerated. The same is true for the shrine at Santiago de Compostela in Northern Spain. And in Germany and elsewhere in Spain there are villages that claim Pontius Pilate. The fact that he effectively condemned Christ to death was less important than the fact that he had seen him, talked to him and been in his divine presence. The glow of Joseph of Arimathea, who had begged Pilate for Christ's body, had the same value for the church at Glastonbury.

Roman soldiers probably did foray deep into the Highlands as far as Fortingall and Glen Lyon but not in 15 BC. They will have come from Inchtuthil, the momentary but massive presence of a mighty empire on the Highland Line. Perhaps that memory of Rome was enough to plant the seeds of legend around the ancient yew tree.

The Hill of Faith

✼

I N THE DARKENING days of November 1950, a conspiracy
was forming in the mind of a young man at Glasgow
University. A great crime was to be committed – something
that would scandalise one nation and delight another – and, after
650 years, a historical wrong would be righted.

Having completed his national service with the RAF, Ian
Hamilton was 25, a little older than most students but no less
idealistic. He joined the Scottish Covenant Association, a forerunner of the Scottish National Party, and became actively
involved in pursuit of its principal goal, the achievement of
independence. This was by no means unrealistic for, in 1948,
more than two million Scots had signed the Scottish Covenant
and Glasgow University was widely seen as an intellectual cradle
of nationalism. With a clear understanding of the power of
symbols and the impact of publicity, Hamilton's idealism was
hardening into determination and circling the notion of sensational coup. He would remove the Stone of Destiny from
Westminster Abbey and return it to Scotland – where it belonged.

At the Mitchell Library, Hamilton began his research. The
Stone of Destiny, also known as the Stone of Scone, had been
used at the coronations of Scottish kings for many centuries. The
last to sit on it had been King John I, crowned in 1292 after
having been chosen by Edward I of England from amongst a

number of claimants. Four years later John I became John Balliol once again when Edward stripped him of his kingdom and humiliated him publicly. 'A man does good business when he rids himself of a turd,' the English king is reported to have said when the royal coat of arms was ripped off Balliol's tabard at a ceremony in Montrose. And so that none of the rival claimants could seize the empty throne and have themselves crowned on the Stone of Destiny, Edward had it removed from Scone Abbey and shipped to Westminster. There, it joined the looted relics and regalia of both Wales and Scotland.

Ian Hamilton's researches related not only history but also valuable information about furniture. Edward had the Stone built into a coronation throne – what became known as the Confessor's Chair. It was used for the coronation of English kings and, as they lowered their backsides on to it, it symbolised their claim to be Lords Paramount of Scotland, the feudal superior of all Scottish kings. For Hamilton it symbolised the domination of Scotland by England.

If the Stone was to be removed – not stolen for it was Edward I who was a thief – from Westminster Abbey, it would need to be broken out of the Confessor's Chair and carried to a waiting vehicle. At three to four hundredweight, the Stone was heavy but masons had fitted two iron rings and, if these were somehow threaded through a stout metal bar or pipe, at least two strong men would be able to carry it. Clearly his researches told Hamilton that he would need at least one accomplice. Bill Craig was the President of the Glasgow University Union, a Liberal supporter but someone with an appetite for adventure. Or so Hamilton believed.

The next approach was perhaps more awkward. As a humble law student, Ian Hamilton had very little money and, for this bold enterprise to go forward, he needed funds. The Chairman of the Scottish Covenant Association and also Rector of Glasgow University at the time was John MacCormick. With what appeared to Hamilton to be a twinkle in his eye, the Lord Rector gave the penniless student £50 and asked to be kept discreetly informed.

Most urgent was a proper recce of Westminster Abbey and, with the cash, Hamilton immediately bought a train ticket to London. Posing as a tourist, he bought a good guide to the abbey, examined the Confessor's Chair carefully and discovered the dimensions of the Stone (but not its weight). He then worked out a route out of the abbey to a place where a car might safely wait and then quickly get away. Through casual conversation with staff, Hamilton found out that no cleaners came in after the abbey closed to the public and that the nightwatchman's office was not close to the Confessor's Chapel and the Stone. That all strongly suggested a night raid. And the best plan was probably for Hamilton to hide in the abbey until it closed at 6 p.m., wait until the nightwatchman had finished his rounds at 2 a.m., then move to break the Stone out of the chair and remove it.

Plans began to take on the characteristics of crime fiction when the young student conceived the idea of two getaway cars. One would carry the Stone south-west out of London as far as lonely Dartmoor where it would be buried in a secret location until the hue and cry had died down. Then it would be repatriated to Scotland. A second car would make a decoy run to Wales to give the pursuing police the idea that the Stone would be handed over to Welsh Nationalists – for some reason.

The plans shifted from fiction to farce when Hamilton told Bill Craig that the best time to raid Westminster Abbey would be Christmas. In 1950, the Scots celebrated New Year rather than Christmas and the latter was seen very much as an English festival. Everyone in London would be focused on the celebrations, argued Hamilton, and distracted. Security at the abbey might be more lax and police pursuit less prompt and less enthusiastic since many officers would be on holiday. Sorry, said Craig, I'm too busy, too many social engagements I can't break. And then there were the celebrations for the 500th anniversary of the founding of Glasgow University on 7 January and, as President of the Union, Craig had to make preparations for those. Sorry.

Hamilton was furious, depressed but still determined. Glasgow University traditionally marks the end of the winter or

Martinmas term with Daft Friday. It fell on 15 December in 1950 and Hamilton invited a young teacher to be his partner at the evening dance. Like him, Kay Matheson was involved in the Scottish Covenant movement and, as a Gaelic speaker from Inverasdale in Wester Ross, she was a fervent nationalist. 'I'm going to London to bring back the Stone of Destiny,' announced Hamilton. After enquiring how much he had had to drink, Matheson agreed to come along. She would never be able to help lift the Stone but she could drive. More conspirators were needed.

Desperate for at least one more recruit and knowing that secrecy was vital, Hamilton despaired when three fellow students turned him down. But, when Gavin Vernon, a 24-year-old engineering undergraduate, counted himself in, the raiding party was complete. Hamilton collected together a burglar's toolkit including a long and heavy jemmy of which he was very proud. Arrangements were made to hire a car.

When the three conspirators met at the garage in Pitt Street in Glasgow to collect the vehicles, they were crestfallen to discover that it was a 1938 Ford with a small engine and no heater. A winter journey from Glasgow to London in a slow and draughty car would chill their bones. When Hamilton emerged from the garage, he saw Gavin Vernon talking to another student, clearly telling him about the trip. He knew that various friends had been informed and sworn to secrecy – but who was this? Alan Stuart was very keen to join the gang and he overcame Hamilton's initial reluctance when he told him that he had a car, a Ford Anglia. The original getaway plan could now work.

It was a difficult, dangerous journey as winter weather quickly closed in. Over the Pennines from Carlisle to Scotch Corner, the cars skidded, the unheated windscreens iced up repeatedly and they had to be scraped clear with nothing better than fingernails. But, in late December 1950, there was very little traffic. There were also no motorways or bypasses, and although it was a trunk road, like the A1, it passed through the centres of all the towns and cities on its route south. Long-distance journeys were still undertaken by train.

When London was at last reached, they split into two groups. In the late afternoon of 23 December, Vernon and Hamilton entered Westminster Abbey as visitors. Under a cleaner's trolley, Hamilton hid himself, pulling his coat over his head, while Vernon left at closing time to take up his position outside. They waited. But not for long.

'What the devil are you doing here? A nightwatchman shone a torch in Hamilton's face and waited for an explanation. The young student improvised brilliantly, claiming he had inadvertently been shut in. And amazingly he was not detained while a call was put through to the police. In fact, the friendly nightwatchman escorted him to the main door with a kind word and a 'Merry Christmas!'

When the group reconvened, holding a cold council of war in the Ford Anglia, they were not deterred. Indeed, Kay Matheson appeared more determined than ever, ignoring Hamilton's embarrassment at being caught so easily. They would break in from the outside, take the Stone, manhandle it into the cars and they would speed away to Dartmoor and Wales as planned.

It was late on Christmas Eve. London's streets were buzzing with groups of revellers and late shoppers and the lights of pubs and restaurants twinkled as four young Scots made their way to Westminster Abbey. Using their jemmy, Hamilton, Vernon and Stuart broke open one of the side doors. No torchlight swept the darkened abbey, no nightwatchman seemed to be on patrol and the students crept towards the Confessor's Chapel. And there it was, under the seat of the Coronation Chair – the Stone of Destiny.

Once they had prised it out of its housing, cracking and splintering the ancient wood, the three young men were forced to put the Stone down immediately. It was tremendously heavy, much heavier than anyone imagined. And, when Ian Hamilton pulled hard on one the rings attached to the sides, it seemed to split into two pieces. The gang was aghast. But it must already have been cracked. When was it last moved? Centuries ago? Hamilton lifted the smaller piece, about a quarter of the whole, and staggered out of the door at Poets' Corner. Kay Matheson backed up the Ford Anglia and the large fragment was bundled into the back seats.

Meanwhile the other two had used Hamilton's overcoat as a kind of sling and then a sledge to drag the main part of the Stone across the floor of the nave. Kay Matheson was waiting outside but when Hamilton ran over to the car, she told him that a policeman had seen her and was coming across the road. Thinking quickly, Hamilton got into the front passenger seat and threw Alan Stuart's coat over the Stone. When the policeman arrived, enquired and pointed out that it was 5 a.m., the student and the teacher pretended to be a couple down from Scotland. They hadn't been able to find a room and were reluctantly spending the night shivering in their car. The policeman relaxed, took off his helmet and put it on the roof of the car, lit a cigarette and began chatting. Behind them, Hamilton could hear Vernon and Stuart dragging the Stone out of the abbey only a few yards away. Arrest was surely imminent. Matheson and he 'engaged the constable in furious conversation' until the other two saw him promptly and hid.

Once the coast was finally clear, Hamilton sent Kay Matheson off with the Ford Anglia and the fragment. She had a friend in the Midlands and would try to make it there. Now Hamilton would bring the second car round to the abbey and get the main part of the Stone away out of London and down to Dartmoor and safety. He put his hands in his pockets. No car keys. Not in any pocket. In all the excitements and exertions, the keys had been lost. Disaster. Worse than arrest, the Stone abandoned in the doorway of the abbey.

Kay Matheson, meanwhile, stopped at traffic lights in Knightsbridge. When they changed to green and she moved away, the boot of the Ford Anglia sprang open and the fragment of the Stone of Destiny fell out on to the road. She heard the crash, backed up the car and, with every ounce of her strength, somehow heaved it back in.

Instead of keys, Hamilton had found a box of matches and he

began searching for them in the black darkness. They had definitely been in the pocket of the overcoat used to drag the Stone but must have fallen out. Lighting matches as he went, the young man retraced his steps. And, near the abbey door, he stood on something hard – the keys.

After bundling the Stone into the 12-year-old Ford, Hamilton and Stuart drove south-east rather than south-west, having become lost in the suburbs of London. Vernon had left them and agreed to rendezvous after the Stone had been safely hidden somewhere in the English countryside. Jubilant that they had managed to remove the Stone of Destiny from Westminster Abbey but with little idea of where they were, the two students drove out of London and deeper into rural Kent. Desperate to find a hiding-place, they passed a large roadhouse built in a mock-Tudor style and two miles beyond that landmark (one they had to remember), they concealed the Stone in a ditch. It would do for the moment.

Hamilton and Stuart drove back to London and telephoned Bill Craig in Scotland. The story of the raid on the abbey was everywhere, all over the papers and, on the radio, Christmas programmes were interrupted with the sensational news. Traffic on all roads leading across the border to Scotland was being stopped and searched by the police. Elated, Hamilton and Stuart later drove down to Kent to find a better hiding place for the most wanted object in Britain. Neither had any idea what had happened to Kay Matheson. At least none of the press and radio coverage had mentioned an arrest.

After a long, freezing, exhausting journey, Hamilton and Stuart returned to Glasgow. Having buried the Stone in Kent, they had no incriminating luggage as they crossed the border. And, despite several fellow students and at least three others knowing the identity of the raiders and the police having encountered them more than once in London, Hamilton, Stuart, Vernon and Matheson were never questioned. To their immense relief and delight, the three men discovered that Kay Matheson had made it back to Glasgow and gone on home to Inverasdale.

It seemed that, even though the whole enterprise had teetered on the brink of disaster time and again, it had succeeded entirely.

However, there was a problem – but not with the authorities. Alan Stuart's father reckoned that the ancient stone would suffer badly from being buried in frosty ground in Kent. After six centuries indoors, under the Confessor's Chair, it would be highly susceptible to damage if groundwater turned to ice and might, literally, fall to pieces. A pile of fragments might turn a triumph into a public relations disaster. Now that the police roadblocks had been stood down, another journey south to bring back the Stone might not be too dangerous. And so, a week after he had dug a hole in the cold ground of Kent, Hamilton, Bill Craig (who had managed to fit the trip into his busy diary) and a fellow student, John Josselyn, travelled south to retrieve what they hoped would be one piece of sandstone.

When they reached the spot, they were horrified to find that a group of Romanies had camped right on top of the hiding place. After a nod, a wink and some oblique discussion, the Romanies looked the other way while the students dug it up. It was undamaged and in one piece. They managed to fit it into the car by removing the front passenger seat and they each took turns to make a royal progress northwards on the Coronation Stone. After a slow but largely uneventful journey, they stopped on the A7, a few miles north-east of the village of Longtown, just inside the Scottish border. Having removed the overcoat concealing it, they produced a 'gill of whisky and poured a libation over the Stone's roughness'.

It was at that moment that the plan began to falter. In his superb account of the events of Christmas 1950, Ian Hamilton admitted that, as they approached Glasgow, they 'had no further ideas of what to do, or where to go'. Eventually the Stone was hidden near Stirling and the police at last questioned some suspects, who included Hamilton, Stuart, Vernon and Matheson. They admitted nothing. Finally, on 11 April 1951, the Stone was left by Hamilton and others in the ruins of Arbroath Abbey at the high altar. It was the place where the famous Declaration was written and seemed appropriate. And, to the disgust of many Scots, the Stone of Destiny was again taken south, back to Westminster Abbey. No prosecutions were ever brought and no martyrs were made.

It is a striking, memorable story – one that made a tremendous impact at the time and it still resonates. In his book, Ian Hamilton claims that it was a first step on the long road to a Scottish Parliament and maybe to independence. Perhaps it was. Certainly, it is a question that only history can answer. But a more obvious and immediate one might be – why all the fuss over a block of sandstone? What was it about the Stone of Destiny that awoke such strong feelings – on both sides of the border? Perhaps answers are to be found at Scone, its original home, a place very close to the Highland Line and where, for centuries, it occupied a central role in Scottish politics.

Names matter in history and especially in early history when documentary evidence is often thin or nonexistent. The Gaelic *An Sgonn* was the original name for Scone and it refers to the low mound now known as 'Moot Hill'. More precisely, it means 'a shapeless mound' – a lump rather than a hill or mountain sculpted by geology and the weather. It has the sense of something manmade and is also the derivation of scone, a baked lump of dough, shapeless in untutored hands, that goes well with jam and butter.

On the flat summit of Moot Hill, close to Scone Palace, the home of the Earls of Mansfield and lying near the banks of the River Tay, sits a replica of the Stone of Destiny. This shapeless lump was Coronation Hill, where Scottish kings sat in their pomp on the ancient Stone and were solemnly crowned before an assembly of leading noblemen, churchmen and as many witnesses as could be gathered.

The Mound, *An Sgonn*, had another, more frequent function as the location for important public political events. In an age before mass media, politics had to be seen to be done. Here is an entry from the *Chronicle of the Kings of Alba* for the year 905: 'And in the sixth year King Constantine and Bishop Cellach vowed on the Hill of Faith near the royal centre of Scone, after the fashion of the Gaels, to keep the laws and disciplines of the faith and also the rights of the churches and the gospels; from this day the hill has received its name, that is, the Hill of Faith.'

Public declarations from political figures on shapeless mounds still take place in Britain – or at least in a part of Britain that has clung on to many ancient traditions. At midsummer reckoned on the old calendar – that is, 5 July and not late June – Tynwald Day takes place at St John's in the centre of the Isle of Man. On Tynwald Hill, the king sat on the top while on lower levels there were magistrates, noblemen and officers of various sorts. The ceremonies first came on record in 979 but are almost certainly older. Modern Tynwald includes an important judicial function, something that echoes across a millennium and more and something that almost certainly took place on Moot Hill at Scone.

Each year the Deemsters stand forward and read out loud the new laws to be enacted. These two bewigged and robed lawyers read the law of Man in Manx Gaelic and it does not come into force until they do so. Known as 'Breast Law', what was once known by heart and not written down, it is a relic of ancient practice. Justice had to be seen to be done and courts sat on Tynwald Hill and the Deemsters handed down sentences which were often carried out there and then. The old meaning of *deem* or *doom* was 'a judgement'.

Before the notables gather on the hill at St John's, there is a procession and it gives some sense of the ceremony that may have taken place at Scone. What this signified was something straightforward. In the 10th century, Scone was the centre of royal power, the place where the elites of the kingdom gathered, not only where coronations took place until as late as the 17th century (with the unusual case of Charles II being crowned King of Scotland in 1651) but also where politics was played out. Here is an extract from John of Fordun's *Scotichronicon* that explains what went on. Malcolm II reigned from 1005 to 1034: 'The histories record that the aforesaid Malcolm was also so lavish or prodigal in gifts that, although he had held all the lands, regions and provinces of the whole kingdom in his own possession in the ancient manner, he kept hold of none of it for himself apart from the Moot Hill on which stood the royal seat at Scone where kings sitting on the throne in royal attire are accustomed to proclaim judgements, laws and statutes to their subjects.'

And yet virtually nothing remains. There are no ruins of a royal palace, no vestiges of a once-great church, no sense of a bustling centre of population, trade or diplomacy. All that can be seen is the shapeless lump of Moot Hill and, nearby, the grand house of an aristocrat. Scone is Scotland's lost capital.

In 2007, Oliver O'Grady led a team of archaeologists to try to find it and he was spectacularly successful. Digging around the base of Moot Hill, the team found a massive ditch, the sort of barrier used to mark off the boundaries of sacred precincts in prehistoric Scotland. And in the bottom of the ditch tiny fragments of burnt wood were discovered. This was precious organic material that could be carbon dated and it turned out that archaeology confirmed history, the sole scrap of documentary evidence for early Scone, the entry from the Chronicle of the kings of Alba about the Hill of Faith. The pieces of burnt wood were firm evidence that the Mound, *An Sgonn*, was piled up as early as the closing decades of the 9th century. O'Grady commented, '[I]t seems entirely plausible to me to suggest that King Constantine II, or at least some of his successors, was responsible for the creation of this mound.'

Scone had become the centre of a kingdom known as Alba, still the Gaelic word for Scotland. In the middle of the 9th century, Kenneth MacAlpin had consolidated his rule over both the Pictish kingdom and that of the Scots or Gaels in the west, what used to be known as Dalriada. History is rarely as clear-cut as the schoolboy soubriquet for Kenneth, the first king of the Picts and Scots. There had been predecessors who had ruled in both kingdoms. But, after his reign, there is a sense of a dynasty taking over the high kingship of Scotland south of the Mounth and sustaining itself. All Scottish kings are numbered from

Kenneth MacAlpin and his great-nephew, Constantine II, reigned for a long time, from 900 to 943. And then he retired, becoming a monk, perhaps abbot of the monastery at St Andrews.

There must have been a 9th- or 10th-century church at Scone but no trace of it has ever been found. This is perhaps not surprising. At that time, the church in Scotland was almost wholly monastic and with an ascetic and hermitical character. Grand buildings and soaring spires did not much interest these pious communities. They sought not so much to glorify God in material ways but to find him in prayer, contemplation and the privations of a frequently harsh life. The early church was much impressed and influenced by the example of the Desert Fathers, Near-Eastern Christians who fled the cities and towns and sought peace and refuge in the deserts of Syria, Jordan and Sinai. In homage to their exemplary lives, the Gaelic word *diseart* is simply a rendering of desert and it meant 'a hermitical community of monks'. At Scone, there is tradition that Constantine II caused the wooden cells and church of the ascetic monks to be rebuilt in stone.

In the Middle Ages, grandeur did eventually arrive on the bank of the Tay. Between 1114 and 1122, Augustinian Canons came from Nostell Priory in Yorkshire to found a new abbey, a building in keeping with Scone's status as a royal centre. The relics of St Fergus were installed and the new church became a focus for pilgrimage. But much more important was the role noted by the English chronicler, Walter of Guisborough: 'In the monastery of Scone, in the church of God, near to the high altar, is kept a large stone, hollowed out as a round chair, on which kings were placed for their ordination, according to custom.'

In 1559 the abbey's ancient importance was suddenly erased from Scotland's history. In the early, frantic and destructive years of the Reformation, a mob from Dundee arrived at Scone and destroyed the church, smashing its idolatrous sculpture and stained glass and severely damaging the fabric of the buildings. When the new owners of the abbey's estates, the Ruthven family, rebuilt the abbot's palace as a grand house, the rubble of Scone was near at hand and, over time, all traces of the ancient home of the Stone of Destiny were effaced. Oliver O'Grady said, 'The importance of Scone – where kings were made and parliaments met – is only matched by how little we know about the reality of the place.'

By July 2007, some of the mists of history had begun to disperse. O'Grady's team made another sensational discovery. With the use of very sophisticated magnetic imaging techniques, they found the precise footprint of the abbey and its associated buildings. At more than 100 metres in length, the abbey was far larger than had been previously believed. The home of the Stone had, at last, been found. And what is more, the location of what amounted to Scotland's first parliaments had also been discovered. Secular business was often done in medieval churches since they were generally the largest buildings available. Following the example of Tynwald on the Isle of Man, Scone Abbey is likely to have been the place where decisions were hammered out and, on formal occasions, the starting point for processions to the mound, Constantine II's Hill of Faith.

When O'Grady's carbon-dated fragments of wood were found to point to an early date for the creation of Moot Hill, he grasped its pivotal importance immediately. 'And that should be seen as a very significant moment in Scotland's history because they are no longer identifying themselves as Picts and they are gathering, as it says in the text "in the manner of the Gaels" and they are holding their most important royal ceremonies on that mound.'

Far to the west, another hill – this time, a dramatic rock rising out of a flat, boggy plain – saw similar ceremonies of inauguration. In the Gaelic-speaking kingdom of Dalriada, kings were made on the summit of the spectacular fort at Dunadd. There, a footprint was chiselled out of the rock and a basin made, and inscriptions in Gaelic as well as what looks like a rock-cut throne. By placing his foot in the footprint, a king asserted symbolic domination over the land and, by sitting on the throne, he entered into a form of marriage with his kingdom and its people.

Those who stood on the summit of Dunadd could see the tip of Ben Cruachan, the sacred mountain of Dalriada, far to the north.

Something similar went on at coronations at Scone, in the centre of the new kingdom of Alba. When kings were made on the Moot Hill, the Stone of Destiny was brought out of the abbey and used as a throne. Here is a passage from the *Scotichronicon* that describes the coronation of Alexander III in 1249. The climax was the appearance of a seannachie and the recital of the king's genealogy, a ritual that reminded the audience of the customs of the Gaels and a moment that echoed down the centuries to the Highlanders who stood on the moor at Culloden:

> With due reverence they installed him there on the royal seat which had been bedecked with silk cloths embroidered with gold. So when the king was solemnly seated on this royal seat of stone, with his crown on his head and his sceptre in his hand, and clothed in royal purple, and at his feet the earls and other nobles were setting down their stools to listen to a sermon, there suddenly appeared a venerable, grey haired figure, an elderly Scot [meaning a Gael]. Though a wild Highlander he was honourably attired after his own fashion, clad in a scarlet robe. Bending his knee in a scrupulously correct manner and inclining his head, he greeted the king in his mother tongue, saying courteously: 'God bless the king of Albany, Alexander macAlexander, macWilliam, macHenry, macDavid . . .'

The royal seat of stone at Scone stood in the centre of Scotland's history and, when Oliver O'Grady dated the creation of the Moot Hill to the reign of Constantine II, King of Alba (or Albany), he may be forgiven for saying, in the excitement of the moment, 'The lab results are in a sense nothing less than a birth certificate for Scotland.' And he was right – the birth of the kingdom of Scotland can be fairly said to have taken place at Scone.

Even though these extraordinary discoveries were made 57 years after Ian Hamilton and his friends mounted their sensational raid on Westminster Abbey, there was nevertheless a widespread, intuitive sense of the central, symbolic importance of the Stone of Destiny. It was present at the birth of Scotland. It was stolen and it needed to be taken back because, as nationalists, Hamilton's raiders wished to see Scotland reborn.

In 1996, their original aims were at least in part fulfilled. A failing, unpopular Conservative government needed to shore up as much support as possible in Scotland and so Secretary of State for Scotland Michael Forsyth, the MP for the marginal seat of Stirling, engineered the return of the Stone of Destiny. In a strange, snapshot moment, television pictures showed the Stone being trundled across the border at Coldstream Bridge in the back of an army Land Rover. With pipers on either side of the bridge and the Secretary of State and his entourage on foot, moving very slowly on a damp November morning, the procession looked more like a funeral than a triumphant homecoming. On 30 November, St Andrew's Day, with a little more pomp and cheer, the Stone was conveyed up the Royal Mile from Holyrood Palace to Edinburgh castle to join the Scottish regalia. The Conservatives lost the election a year later and the new Labour government put in train the legislation to bring into being a Scottish Parliament. It reconvened in 1999.

Republished in 2008, Ian Hamilton's excellent account of his great adventure, *The Stone of Destiny*, included a poignant postscript from the author, by this time 84 years old:

> I began the last chapter of my book by saying I had never seen the Stone again. It had been my intention to wait until Scotland achieved independence before paying it a visit. We are so nearly there that it makes no odds. An occasion is coming up in 2008 when I may break my long abstinence . . . Alex Salmond and the Scottish Government are to give a reception in the Great Hall of Edinburgh Castle . . . If invited, and I am told I will be, I shall go. If my country's First Minister takes my arm and leads me through to the Crown Room to see the Stone I shall go with him. I have never sought an honour, but I can think of none greater.

As for my long life, breaking into a holy place is not good preparation for entry into the most conservative of professions, but I survived. We three survivors of the original four are now very old. This exercise in looking back is not typical of me, nor so far as I know of them. Life is for living and even at my great age I prefer a motorbike to a keyboard.

I repeat myself as old men do. Remember us with some kindness. What we did for Scotland and what we do for Scotland we do for all the world.

When on 25 March 1707 James Ogilvie, Earl of Seafield, Chancellor of Scotland, signed the Act of Union, ending Scotland's ancient independence, and merging the two parliaments of Scotland and England into the United Kingdom Parliament, he threw down the quill with these words: 'Now there's the end of an auld sang'.

It may be, it just may be, that on Christmas Day 1950 four young people wrote a new verse to that old song. Whatever we did, the song is still being sung.

The Wild West

✷

CARPENTERS WERE busy in Perth in the weeks leading up to the appointed day, hammering, sawing, planing and nailing, and the town simmered with anticipation. At the vast cost to the royal exchequer of £14 2s. 10d., barriers were erected on three sides of the North Inch. An open area to the west of the town, the North Inch has the River Tay as the boundary of its fourth side. A grandstand was built around the summerhouse of the great church of the Blackfriars, founded in the 13th century and dedicated to the Blessed Virgin and St Dominic. The Lord Prior had been busy with arrangements, his cellarer ordering the royal apartments to be made ready and provisions for many visitors to be found and brought to the kitchens. It was late autumn 1396 and King Robert III of Scotland and his court were riding to Perth to see justice done in a spectacular fashion. Accompanying his entourage were other notables, the Duke of Albany, who was the king's brother, and many French, English and Scottish lords. All would witness a remarkable event – the resolution of a dispute in a trial by combat on the North Inch.

On the morning of the 28 September, warriors from two Highland clans marched into the town, led by their pipers and their chiefs, Christy Johnson and Shaw Farquharson. Watched by royalty and nobility, 30 men from Clan Chattan would fight 30 men from Clan Cameron on the flat and green haughland by the Tay. And they would fight to the death with the last men standing declared the winners, the dispute between them finally resolved by the spilling of blood.

Arranged by Thomas Dunbar, the Earl of Moray, and Sir David Lindsay of Glenesk, what became known as 'the Battle of the Clans' was reported by several chroniclers. A very famous incident at the time, it was an important moment in the formation of stereotypes. Wild and uncivilised Highlanders had come out of the mountains to Perth to hack each other to death in front of an audience of civilised Lowlanders. Savages from the wrong side of the Highland Line would slaughter each other in a temporary coliseum costing a few pounds for the amusement of their superiors.

Walter Bower's account in the *Scotichronicon* was the first time the word 'clan' occurs in any surviving documentary record and it immediately acquired a negative tone. Each clansman was armed with a crossbow and three bolts, swords, battleaxes and dirks and none was permitted to wear armour. This was to be a final judgement: 'At once arrows flew on either side, men swung their axes, brandished their swords and struggled with each other; like butchers killing cattle in a slaughter-house, they massacred each other fearlessly; there was not even one among so many who, whether from frenzy or fear, or by turning aside from a chance to attack one another in the back, sought to excuse himself from all this slaughter.'

As the huge crowd no doubt roared, bayed and gasped, the killing went on. Men screamed, blood gushed on the grass as arteries were severed and some fell to their knees, bludgeoned into unconsciousness, stabbed to death by dirks. Many must have been badly wounded by crossbow bolts before the hand-to-hand fighting began but killing men with bladed weapons is rarely quick and the gory trial will not have reached a rapid verdict. Bower again: '[It was] a battle of great ferocity, in which out of the sixty all were killed except one from Clan Cameron and eleven from the other.'

It was said that the single survivor swam the Tay to escape the fate of all his comrades. Famous though it became, the Battle of the Clans was not, by itself, a seminal event. Instead, it formed part of a pattern, the culmination of decades of disorder in the Highlands, or so it seemed to Lowland commentators – although, in reality, it was a pattern mixed with paradox and contradiction.

The most notorious, rapacious and destructive Highland lord was known as the Wolf of Badenoch. Hugely powerful and wealthy, widely landed, a king in the north in all but name, he led bands of ferocious warriors known as caterans and, in return for what he saw as a slight from the Bishop of Moray, the Wolf burned the royal burgh of Elgin and destroyed its great cathedral in 1390. This caused outrage and was seen as yet more evidence of the mindless savagery and godlessness of the north. And, only six years afterwards, no one was surprised that more savages descended from the Highlands to slaughter each other on the North Inch at Perth. Such was the atavistic nature of the tribes of the mountains and glens.

This dichotomy, this stark distinction drawn between the lawlessness of the Gaelic-speaking north and the peaceful, civilised, English-speaking south does not bear much scrutiny. The Wolf of Badenoch was no tribal chief, no feral son of the wilderness but none other than Alexander Stewart, the third son of King Robert II of Scotland. Created Earl of Buchan by his father, he married Euphemia I, Countess of Ross in her own right. This combination of titles made Stewart supreme over vast tracts of the north of Scotland – from Buchan, he ruled over virtually all of the old kingdom of Moray on both shores of the firth and as far north as Caithness. Euphemia brought him much of the mainland north of the Great Glen as well as the islands of Skye and Lewis. In 1372, he was made Royal Justiciar. Not only did this give him additional lands in Perthshire for his great domain, it also gave him royal authority from there all the way north to the Pentland Firth. His dominance seemed immovable – but, by the 1390s, he had fallen far.

Lochindorb Castle was known as the Wolf's Lair. Built on a small island in the middle of a loch that lay in the foothills of the

Grampian massif, it was formidably secure, being defended by water and high walls. From there, the Earl of Buchan and Ross ruled but not without challenge. In the 12th and 13th centuries, the old kingdom of Moray had been enfeebled by the Scottish crown and the resulting power vacuum filled by the church. With appointments to the wealthy bishopric of Moray controlled by the kings of Scotland, it supplied a focus for authority but not one that could be passed on as any sort of inheritance. When Alexander Stewart was made Earl of Buchan and Ross, the church bristled. Bishop Bur of Moray complained that the bands of Highland soldiers in the service of Buchan, the caterans, were routinely raiding the lands of his tenants. But no formal protest could be made directly to the king since his viceregal representative in the north was none other than the commander of the unruly caterans, Alexander Stewart.

In any event, King Robert II was weak and ineffective to the point of ridicule. At 55, an old man when he succeeded David II, he attracted the unflattering nickname of Auld Bleary. By 1384, his eldest son, John, Earl of Carrick, had managed to remove his father from power, forcibly exiling him to Dundonald Castle in Ayrshire. For the sake of continuity and the avoidance of any link with King John Balliol, the Earl took the name of Robert III when Auld Bleary finally expired in 1390. But he fared no better. Badly crippled by a kick from a horse and being unable to take part in warfare, Robert III was himself eventually supplanted by his brother, Robert, Earl of Fife. He appointed himself Guardian of Scotland and, in effect, the Wolf of Badenoch became second in line. When Robert II died in 1406, his last, pathetic words were reported, and perhaps embellished a little, by Walter Bower, 'Bury me therefore, I beg you, in a midden, and write for my epitaph: "Here lies the worst of kings and the most wretched of men in the whole kingdom".'

The weakness of central authority had allowed licence both in the south and the north of the kingdom but, in 1388, Robert, Earl of Fife, reined in his rapacious younger brother. Alexander Stewart was summarily removed from his roles as Justiciar of the North and Sheriff of Inverness and replaced by his nephew, Murdoch. In 1389, more trouble boiled over. Perhaps driven by an impulse to adopt what he saw as the Celtic mores of his caterans and the powerful clans of the Highlands or simply because he wished to, Stewart abandoned his wife, Euphemia, and lived with Mairead Inghean Eachann. She may have been the daughter of Eachann of Strathnaver of the Mackay clan. While his power waxed unchallenged, Alexander could afford to ignore the laws of the church, live in sin and father children with Mairead.

But, after Robert of Fife's initiatives began to dent his brother's control of the north, Bishop Bur was emboldened. Since 1370, he had paid protection money to the Earl of Buchan but now he felt the balance of power shift. With the support of the Bishop of Ross, Bur directed Alexander Stewart to give up his sinful union with Mairead Inghean Eachann and return immediately to his legitimate wife. When the errant earl failed to live up to his promises of future fidelity, Robert of Fife encouraged Euphemia to begin the long and expensive process of seeking an annulment of the marriage at the papal court in Avignon.

Stewart was furious at being scolded by the church and his caterans descended from their lair at Lochindorb Castle in May 1390 and began to blaze a bloody trail through Moray. They burned the town of Forres and may have attacked Pluscarden Priory, a monastic house under the protection of Bishop Bur. When the caterans, described by John of Fordun as 'wyld, wykked hielandmen', overran Elgin in June, they wreaked tremendous destruction. The cathedral was torched, its roof blazing as its trusses cracked and fell and masonry tumbled, and the monastery of the Greyfriars, St Giles Parish Church and the Hospital of Maison Dieu in Elgin were all gutted and blackened. The sense of outrage was universal and the shock and sadness at the ruination of the cathedral is patent in Bishop Bur's letter to Robert III: '[M]y church was the particular ornament of the fatherland, the glory of the kingdom, the joy of strangers and incoming guests, the object of praise and exaltation in other kingdoms because of its decoration, by which it is believed that God was properly worshipped; not to mention its high bell towers, its venerable furnishings and uncountable jewels.'

Retribution was immediate. Church and state combined to tame the Wolf. Almost certainly in the smoking ruins of his desecrated cathedral, Bur passed sentence of excommunication on Stewart. A bell tolled as if for the dead, the Bible was slammed shut and a lit altar candle upended and snuffed out on the floor. Condemned by bell, book and candle, the Wolf was now alone, living beyond the church, outcast and bound for the eternal torments of Hell. He had no choice but to repent and seek forgiveness.

At the Church of the Blackfriars in Perth, a court assembled. In front of his brothers, King Robert III and the Earl of Fife, and the royal council, Stewart was forced, on his knees, to beg for the sentence of excommunication to be lifted. After an appropriate process of humiliation, absolution was granted by Walter Traill, Bishop of St Andrews. But the events at Blackfriars were not the beginning of a road to rehabilitation. In 1392, Euphemia I was granted an annulment of her marriage and, at the stroke of a papal pen, Stewart lost the great earldom of Ross. And, in the same year, he was forced to give up the lordship of Urquhart, valuable lands along the shores of Loch Ness.

Disorder did not cease with the daunting of the Wolf of Badenoch. In the same year as Elgin blazed, events on the southern fringes of the Highland Line helped build the stereotype of wild, wicked men from the mountains. Duncan Stewart, an illegitimate grandson of Robert II and nephew of the Wolf, led a raiding party, described as 'ane infamous byke o' lawless lymmers' by John of Fordun, out of the southern ranges of the Grampians to reive cattle in Glen Isla. These lawless rascals drove their plundered beasts to the valley of the Lornty Burn near Blairgowrie where they were caught by a band of pursuers. A series of skirmishes followed and the Angus men were driven back by the caterans. When Sir Walter Ogilvy and Sir David Lindsay arrived with a force of heavily armed cavalry, perhaps as many as sixty horsemen, battle was joined once more. But, against all the logic of war, the Highlanders, armed only with claymores, targes or shields and long dirks, scattered their pursuers once again, killing Ogilvy. One incident became famous – an archetype for savagery. When Sir David Lindsay drove his lance through one of the caterans and pinned him to the ground, the dying man pulled himself up the shaft and slashed at the knight with his claymore. Such was the rage and force of the blow that it cut through Lindsay's stirrup and steel boot, right to the bone. The ferocity of such men was scarcely human, more a force of nature. And, when the wooden coliseum was built around the North Inch in Perth, the combatants were seen as a different, feral breed of men, not of the same race as the Lowlanders who sat in the grandstands.

Like most stereotyping, it was of course a nonsense. Much of the serial disorder that had painted the Highlanders as savages, as 'wyld wykked' men, had been instigated by members of the royal family, much of it by the king's brother. Across most of the Highland massif, on the Atlantic shore and in the Hebrides, the Lords of the Isles ruled and they were a force for stability not anarchy. And, in many ways, their style of governance was a lesson for the weakness and fractiousness of central government in the Lowlands and the Borders. And, in Moray and in Angus, what was visible to Lowlanders and what was eagerly reported by chroniclers was a set of characteristics unfairly applied to all who lived north and west of the Highland Line. But, when the army of the Lords of the Isles marched to do battle at Harlaw in 1411, there was formality, even dignity.

The great Atlantic principality of the Isles was, in its essence, a realm of the sea. Held secure by a linked network of castles that did not look over valuable tracts of land but guarded the sea roads between the islands, it was governed by the leading men of Clan Donald. It was originally the creation of Somerled the Viking, a 12th-century warrior of Celto–Norse descent who made himself King of the Isle of Man and *Dominus Insularum*, Lord of the Isles. In 1164, he led a naval expedition into the Firth of Clyde to challenge Malcolm IV of Scotland but, at Renfrew, Somerled was killed. It was not to be the last time the Lordship threatened a Scottish king.

The principality was strengthened and re-formed in the first half of the 14th century. When John MacDonald of Islay married Amie niRuari, he found himself in control of the coastline and all of the islands from Skye down to the Mull of Kintyre. At Finlaggan in the centre of Islay, the Council of the Isles met regularly and four great men of the royal Clan Donald blood came to consider matters of policy and to resolve disputes. They were the chiefs of Clanranald, MacIain of Ardnamurchan, MacDonald of Kintyre and MacDonald of Keppoch. Four centuries later, their descendants would lead the MacDonald regiments across the heather at Culloden. Four powerful chiefs of other names also had the right to attend – Maclean of Duart, Maclaine of Lochbuie, Macleod of Harris and Macleod of Lewis – and they were joined by four lesser men – Mackinnon, MacNeil of Barra, MacNeil of Gigha and one other who may have taken his place by rotation. Also present was the Church, in the shape of the Bishop of the Isles and the Abbot of Iona, men who were themselves usually aristocrats from the great families.

Laws were codified and administered by a hereditary caste of judges known as 'brieves'. Little was written until much later, all retained in memory and recited just as the Deemsters of Man still do at Tynwald. What guided the principles of the laws of the Isles was the notion of punishment by reparation rather than judicial revenge. Offenders sentenced by the brieves were more likely to have their crimes measured against a tariff of fines or do onerous services rather than have their hands or heads cut off.

Under the Lordship, the Hebrides and the Atlantic littoral prospered. Tiree was the corn basket of the Isles and the tax yield from Islay so substantial that it spoke of a prodigious annual agricultural output. In their beautifully sited sea castles, the MacDonald lords flourished, growing wealthy and powerful. In 1411, Donald of the Isles was at Ardtornish. Reachable overland by only the roughest of tracks, it communicated with the MacDonald realm by sea and dominated the busy mercantile and military traffic between the islands and the mainland. Looking out over the Sound of Mull, it stood above a wide and sheltered bay where a hundred birlinns could be safely beached. Often also called galleys, these small, highly manoeuvrable warships had brought Somerled several naval victories two centuries before. The arms of Clan Donald have a birlinn at the centre for these little ships were at the core of all they achieved. When Donald MacDonald sent out messengers to call for a muster of the army of the Lordship in 1411, many birlinns answered and thousands of warriors and their captains rowed into the bay at Ardtornish. In the east, a great prize waited to be won.

Through his marriage to Mariota, Euphemia I's aunt and the oldest living descendant of the last earl, Donald claimed the huge territories of Ross. It would bring him Lewis, Harris and a great landholding on the mainland. It would make him more powerful than Somerled. With ambition high and perhaps imitation of the audacity of his great ancestor in his mind, the Lord of the Isles concluded a treaty with King Henry IV of England. They would divide Lowland Scotland between them and banish the squabbling Stewarts to a footnote in history. This was no extravagant fancy but a recurring theme. In 1462, John of Islay and Edward IV of England formally attached their seals to the treaty of Westminster–Ardtornish and it agreed that James III would be deposed and Scotland south of the Forth would be absorbed into Greater England.

A victorious campaign in 1411 would bring Donald as much, maybe more, and early success encouraged the army of the Lordship. Unopposed, they marched up the Great Glen and defeated the forces of Clan MacKay of Strathnaver and seized Dingwall Castle. At Inverness, Donald sent out messengers to the men of western Moray to summon them to his standards and his forces swelled. Having swept through the Moray coastlands, the Islesmen closed in on Aberdeen, the Mounth, the hinge of the north and the road to Angus and the Lowlands.

The Earl of Mar had heard news of the fall of Dingwall and the muster at Inverness. Determined to prevent the clansmen from reaching and burning Aberdeen, Mar led a large party of mounted knights and well-armed infantry out to meet the threat from the west. In the shadow of Bennachie, only a mile or so from where the centurions had drawn up Agricola's legions in battle order, the Lowland army halted. It was the morning of Friday 24 July and, on a flat area of haughland by the River Urie, near Harlaw House, perhaps five thousand men stood to and waited.

The Islesmen and their captains knew that victory would open Scotland to them, Aberdeen would be plundered and fired and the road to the south would be clear. They watched the Lowland infantry form themselves into bristling schiltrons – a schiltron is a military formation in which the men stand shoulder to shoulder, with their long spears 'couched' or grounded and the ranks behind pushing their shafts between their comrades to present a dense concentration of sharpened points. Mar may have marshalled three schiltrons with his force of armoured knights behind them, positioned so that they could ride quickly to shore up crises or break open opportunities. And, in the van, in front of the main body of the army, Sir James Scrymgeour of Dundee stood with a small force of men-at-arms.

The forces of the Lordship made no such complicated manoeuvres. They had only one tactic. In preparation for a furious charge of swordsmen, Donald's generals had formed their men into a broad wedge shape with the Clan Donald contingents in the centre, Clan Chattan on the left wing and Hector Roy MacLean in command of his clansmen on the right. Just as they were to do at Culloden, almost 350 years later, the Highlanders began to recite the sloinneadh, the naming of the names of their ancestors, a call down the generations for the army of the dead to come to Harlaw. And then Lachlan Mor MacMhuirich, the bard of the Lords, stood forward. As the ranks of men hushed and a quiet descended on the battlefield, he lifted his voice in the *brosnachadh catha*, the incitement to battle. Lachlan too called on the dead, reaching back through the mists of an immense past to sing of a hero, the ancient Irish ancestor of Clan Donald, the great warrior Conn of the Hundred Battles.

> O Children of Conn, remember
> Hardihood in time of battle,
> Be strong, nursing your wrath,
> Be resolute and fierce,
> Be forceful, standing your ground,
> Be nimble and full of valour,
> Be dour, inspiring fear,
> Be exceedingly fierce, recklessly daring,
> Be spirited, inflicting great wounds,
> Be venomous, implacable,
> Be glorious, nobly powerful,
> Be exceedingly fierce, king-like,
> Be vigorous, nimble-footed,
> In winning the battle,
> Against your enemies.
> O Children of Conn of the Hundred Battles,
> Now is the time for you to win renown,
> O raging whelps,
> O sturdy bears,
> O most vigorous lions,
> O battle-loving warriors,
> The Children of Conn of the Hundred Battles,
> O Children of Conn, remember
> Hardihood in time of battle.

Heroic origins mattered to the men standing in the Highland ranks at Harlaw, nervously checking their gear, turning to their comrades beside them, exchanging reassurance, exhorting each other. Clan captains always set the older men in front. More experienced, they would break into the charge when the order was given and pull the younger men along behind them. They believed absolutely that they were 'the Children of Conn', the High King of Ireland, the progenitor of the Connachta and the

Ui Neill, the pre-eminent kindred of the north of Ireland. He made the Stone of Destiny roar. Long before it was brought to the Moot Hill at Scone, it sat on the Hill of Tara in the centre of Ireland. But, when in a rage-fit the boy-hero, Cuchulainn, sheared it with his sword because it would not roar when his patron, Lugaid, stood on it, the great stone was lost and passed out of memory. Then Conn walked the ramparts of Tara and stepped on it by accident and it roared out that one day he would be High King. And it came to pass.

Myth-history such as this may be scoffed at as ahistorical, even irrelevant. But what people believed at the time mattered and the tale of Conn and the stories of the Stone of Destiny are no harder to accept than Christian miracles or the Virgin birth. They spoke to the warriors at Harlaw of heroic ages, druids, Celtic gods and feats of superhuman courage. The men who stood opposite the Highlanders and the Islesmen had, by partial comparison, no lineage to speak of, no such richness to encourage them into the charge. They did not fight for their names, alongside the army of the dead, but only for land and for wealth – poor things, both of them. Clansmen believed themselves to possess nobility, a substance bestowed by lineage and a long and deep past described in the mouth-filling glories of the Gaelic language. Racing across the heather at Harlaw, the ghosts of Conn of the Hundred Battles and his war bands would charge the Gall, the Lowlanders and sweep them into oblivion, where they belonged.

Known in Gaelic as *Cath Gairbheach*, 'the Wild Battle', Harlaw was bloody in two languages for, in English, it was 'Red Harlaw'. When the pipers blew the battle rant and signalled the *Claidheamh Mor*, 'the Great Sword', the order to charge, the clansmen fell upon Sir James Scrymgeour's formation of men-at-arms. Many were killed on both sides but no momentum was gained as the Lowlanders held their ground. Summoned from the rear, fresh waves of Highlanders crashed against the schiltrons but they could not be moved either. When the Earl of Mar saw an opportunity and rallied his mounted knights into the gallop, they, in turn, could make no impression. Many horses were hamstrung by the claymores hacking at their legs and brought down, their heavily armoured riders pinned and stabbed to death.

By gloaming on 24 July, a great slaughter had taken place at Red Harlaw but neither side could claim the field. Seeing that his forces were too exhausted to retreat a safe distance, the Earl of Mar ordered them to camp on the battlefield, close to rucks of dead and dying men. Amidst the agonies and the cries of those bleeding to death, slipping in and out of consciousness, many with hacked and lifeless limbs, few will have slept more than fitfully. But, when the dawn glimmered over the flat eastern horizon of the Garioch and lit the peaks of Bennachie, Mar was roused to be given startling news. During the starless and dark night, the Islesmen had slipped away and scouts reported them marching westwards, back to where they had come from. Mar could claim to have driven them off. If Harlaw was not a defeat for the Lord of the Isles, then it was certainly a decisive retreat. Donald was forced to give up his claim to the Earldom of Ross and, while the Lordship remained intact, its ambition was badly blunted.

A wide and sheltered anchorage two miles north of Tobermory on the Isle of Mull, Bloody Bay is a peaceful place now. A lighthouse punctuates its northern headland and it looks over to the mouth of Loch Sunart and Ardnamurchan beyond. More than five hundred years ago it earned its name. In 1483, Clan Donald and the Lordship of the Isles tore itself apart at Bloody Bay in one of the largest and most destructive naval engagements in late medieval Europe. No precise numbers were recorded but historians reckon the navy of a united Lordship could have included 500 ships and perhaps as many as 400 birlinns clashed at Bloody Bay.

The Treaty of Westminster–Ardtornish had backfired badly for John of Islay. A decade after it was agreed, Edward IV of England's priorities changed as he turned his attention from the Wars of the Roses to France. When he prepared for war across the Channel, he needed no threat at his back and good relations with James III of Scotland required to be encouraged. An indication of good faith was needed and, without a moment's hesitation, the English king gave instructions that the secret terms of his treaty with the Lordship were to be divulged to James. It was high treason worthy of dire punishment and John of Islay was summoned before parliament to answer for himself. When he failed to appear, his vast territories were declared forfeit to the crown. But the Scottish king had not the means or the inclination to back that decision with action and, in the summer of 1476, a deal was done. With the loss of the earldom of Ross, with the exception of Skye, as well as Knapdale and Kintyre, John was absolved but, crucially, he lost the ability to pass on his title and the right to confer the dignity of the Lord of the Isles passed to the crown, where it remains.

This was a wounding slight and it caused serious domestic discord. With a contracting principality and no guarantee that his heir would bear the title won by Somerled, John's reputation withered and his position grew weak. The heir to the Lordship, Angus Og MacDonald, gathered support amongst the leading figures of Clan Donald and, in a palace coup, had his father removed and marginalised. One tradition has John of Islay forced to live under an upturned boat. But old allies rallied, the boat was righted and, with the support of Clan Maclean, Clan Macleod of Lewis and Clan MacNeil, he mustered a great fleet of birlinns and an army to man the oars. And, to meet them, Angus Og called on Clanranald and the MacDonalds of Ardnamurchan and Keppoch to join him and Macleod of Harris. Only half of the birlinns that sailed into Bloody Bay would sail out again.

First known as 'the little ships', birlinns were based on the design of the Viking longship and it is thought that they evolved during the 12th century in the decades before the rise of Somerled. Their compact size and shallow draft allowed them to outrun larger craft by moving inshore or navigating the many narrow channels along the jagged Atlantic coasts. The principal development was the use of a hinged rudder attached to the stern. The Vikings had relied on the 'steerboard' (the derivation of 'starboard') or steering oar and they made turning slower and wider. Hinged rudders allowed birlinns to be much more manoeuvrable.

Like the longships, they were propelled by single banks of oars and a square sail set on a mast secured amidships. Made from wool woven into small squares and sewn together, birlinn sails were often dyed bright colours so that they were visible from a distance and in a swelling sea. Boat-building skills were well honed in the Hebrides and the woods preferred were oak and yew. Both were durable and flexible. In heavy weather, the gunwales of a birlinn could twist a long way out of true and, if it was not to disintegrate, the long, overlapping wooden strakes needed to flex. *B'e sin fiodh a chur do Loch Abar* is a Gaelic phrase analogous to 'carrying coals to Newcastle'. Meaning 'bringing wood to Lochaber', it shows the source of oak for shipbuilding. An alternative Gaelic word for a birlinn is *iubhreach* and it simply means 'yew built'.

The *Aileach* is very beautiful. Made in 1991 in Donegal, it is a modern replica of a birlinn and, like the boats that went to Bloody Bay, it can glide through the water when rowed on by all hands and is able to go very close inshore. After he had fought on the losing side at Culloden in 1746, Alasdair macMhaighstir Alasdair composed a glorious poem called 'The Birlinn of Clanranald' and his verses, even in translation, catch the elegance of these little ships perfectly.

> The smooth-handled oars, well-fashioned,
> Light and easy,
> That will do the rowing, stout and sturdy,
> Quick-palmed, blazing,
> That will send the surge in sparkles,
> Up to skyward,
> All in flying spindrift flashing,
> Like a fire-shower!
> With the fierce and pithy pelting
> Of the oar-bank,

That will wound the swelling billows,
With their bending.
With the knife-blades of white thin oars
Smiting bodies,
On the crest of the blue hills and glens,
Rough and heaving.

And, when all the oarsmen are seated in the birlinn, Malcolm, son of Ranald of the Ocean, begins the boat song.

Now since you're all chosen,
And ranked in good order,
With a bold stately plunge send her forward!
With a bold stately plunge send her forward!

A plunge quick and handy,
Not reckless, nor languid,
Keeping watch on the grey briny storm-hills
Keeping watch on the grey briny storm-hills.

The discipline and close teamwork so beautifully described by Alasdair macMhaighstir Alasdair converted these little ships into lethal weapons. Naval warfare with birlinns depended on the skill of a crew and their coordinated power in pulling hard at the knife blades of whip-thin oars through the water. Tremendous bursts of speed over short distances enabled birlinns to ram an enemy ship, perhaps sink it, certainly splinter its oars on one side and probably allow warriors to board it. When that happened, swords and dirks could do their work. Many birlinns carried archers and crossbowmen (the short bolts were less affected by the wind) and, earlier in his poem, Alasdair spoke of 'our birchen shafts that split not, cased in grim badger skin'.

In an age before marine cannon, all medieval naval actions were fought at close quarters to make ramming and boarding possible. When the opposing fleets sailed into Bloody Bay in 1483, it is likely that their admirals disposed them in a line abreast formation – that is, a long row of birlinns moving side by side, being careful not to foul each other's oars, all pointing their ramming prows at the enemy. Some birlinns may have been lashed together to create a wider platform for archers and crossbowmen or boarding parties. Less nimble and slower but heavier and more threatening to single boats, these multiple-hulled craft were themselves better defended and more difficult to board.

In common with all sea battles, Bloody Bay was a chaotic affair – a struggle on unsteady, swaying birlinns – and it was difficult to tell after the fleets clashed which side was which and where, if anywhere, advantage was being gained. In the ferocity of the hand-to-hand fighting and the shattering impact of ramming, many men will have gone overboard to drown or even to be attacked while they thrashed helplessly in the water. But the outcome was clear. Those watching from the shores of Mull will have seen Angus Og's captains triumph. And, after the wholesale loss of life and many birlinns having been rammed, broken and sunk, John of Islay lost the Lordship to his son. But he was not to enjoy it for long. Angus Og was murdered in 1490 and John of Islay emerged once more from the shadows, reappearing briefly only to meet more humiliation. James IV of Scotland, a Stewart king with fewer of his dynasty's feckless failings, had tired of the pretension of Clan Donald and especially the raiding of John's nephew, Alexander MacDonald of Lochalsh, and, in 1493, the Lordship of the Isles was declared forfeit to the crown. Reduced to the status of a dependant pensioner at the Scottish court, John MacDonald of Islay, Lord of the Isles, Earl of Ross and the descendant of Somerled, King of Man and *Dominus Insularum*, died a miserable and lonely death in a Dundee lodging house in 1506.

All was not ended. A light still flickered in the west and Clan Donald still dreamed of glory. Between 1494 and 1545, there were six major rebellions against the crown, the last being the most threatening. At Islay, Donald Dubh was able to rally a force of 4,000 warriors and 189 birlinns, only a remnant of the former fighting strength of the Lordship but still very formidable. Before war rumbled eastwards from the islands once more, the last claimant to the old principality of Clan Donald died suddenly of a fever in Drogheda in Ireland.

In the first half of the 16th century, as rebellion after rebellion failed and the Lordship faded, the MacMhuirich bard, Giolla Coluim mac an Ollaimh, could sense the end of the dominance of the MacDonalds and he mourned:

> Ni h-eibhneas gun Chlainn Domhnaill
> It is no joy without Clan Donald,
> It is no strength without them:
> The best race in the round world:
> To them belong every goodly man.
> In the van of Clan Donald
> Learning was commanded
> And in the rear were
> Service and honour and self-respect.
>
> Brilliant pillars of green Alba
> A race the hardiest that received baptism;
> A race who won fight in every land,
> Hawks of Islay for valour.
>
> A race without arrogance, without injustice,
> Who seized naught save spoil of war:
> Whose nobles were men of spirit,
> And whose common men were most steadfast.
>
> It is no joy without Clan Donald.

Part Seen, Part Imagined

✹

I RONIES ABOUNDED at Fontenoy. Like so many battles, the one fought in Flanders fields, near the town of Tournai, saw the Duke of Cumberland lead the army of what was known as the Pragmatic Alliance. A combined force of British, Hanoverian, Austrian and Dutch troops faced the might of the French army under the command of Marshal Saxe on 11 May 1745. It was the decisive engagement of the War of the Austrian Succession, in essence a contest for the hegemony of the continent, and its outcome depended largely on the conduct of two regiments of Gaelic speakers and it led directly to the involvement of a third group of Gaels in a desperate and ultimately fatal adventure.

Fontenoy was won by the French and that reverse for the Duke of Cumberland and the fact that his unsuccessful European expedition had left only 8,000 regular soldiers at home to defend Britain prompted Charles Edward Stuart to raise the Highland clans in rebellion in August 1745. At every twist in this story, the courage of Gaelic-speaking soldiers was enormously influential but it could not save Highland society from a brutal fate after Culloden.

Like Highland furies, the Black Watch almost won Fontenoy for Cumberland and, if they had, Charles Stuart may not have rallied his army at Glenfinnan three months later. But, when they and the allied armies were forced back in a fighting retreat, it was Dillon's Irish Brigade that decided the outcome in favour of the

French. Irish Jacobites in the service of the king of France, they tore into the Coldstream Guards, roaring their war cry, *Cuimhnigidh ar Luimneach agus feall nan Sassunaich!*– 'Remember Limerick and the treachery of the English!' They meant the Treaty of Limerick of 1691 that ended Jacobite resistance in Ireland.

New Maps and Old

One of the more constructive cultural legacies of the 1745 Jacobite Rising was the Ordnance Survey. This series of uniquely accurate maps takes its name from ordnance or artillery and what prompted the process that led to their creation and precision was initially a military motive. Until the second half of the 18th century, the Highlands of Scotland was a remote region, much of it entirely unknown and inaccessible to outsiders. If the Jacobite threat was to be consigned to history, then its geography needed to be mapped and the redoubts of potential rebels understood better. William Roy, a Scot from the Lanarkshire parish of Carluke, was part of a team commissioned to make an accurate map of the Highlands – what became known as 'The Duke of Cumberland's Map'. Roy had grasped the latest mathematical advances of the Enlightenment and, by his careful use of trigonometry and precise formulae, his work broke with the approximations of the past. In particular, he understood the principles of geodesy – how the curvature of the Earth influenced the calculations of surveying and mapping. William Roy rose through the ranks of the British army and became a major general. In 1784, he measured a baseline between Hampton and the tiny hamlet of Heathrow so that he could work out the relative positions of the French and British royal observatories. The Heathrow baseline was the germ of all subsequent surveys of the United Kingdom.

An important part of William Roy's map-making was undermined by forgery. While compiling surveys for his great work, Roy also drew excellent ground plans of surviving Roman camps, some of which would later be destroyed by deep ploughing. But, unfortunately, the army geographer based his understanding of Roman Britain on faulty history. In 1747, Charles Bertram, a writer and teacher of English, announced his discovery of 'De Situ Britanniae', 'The Description of Britain'. Purporting to be an account written by a serving Roman general, it had been miraculously preserved in a manuscript copied by Richard of Cirencester, a 14th-century monk. It was especially imaginative in describing Roman Scotland, listing the name of (fictional) peoples and (fictional) places. Perhaps the most famous invented name is one that survives. Bertram's (fictional) general wrote:

This province is divided into two equal parts by a chain of mountains called the Pennine Alps, which rising on the confines of the Iceni and Carnabii, near the river Trivona, extend towards the north in a continued series of fifty miles.

Taking its name from the Apennines, the mountain range that runs down the spine of Italy, the Pennines now appears on legitimate maps while Bertram's forgery has been forgotten.

A great philosopher stood in the way of the charge of Dillon's Irish Brigade that day and may have fought in the ranks of the Black Watch when they themselves had attacked the French. Adam Ferguson wrote the enormously influential *An Essay on the History of Civil Society*, published in 1767, and his influence on the European Enlightenment was definitive. Believing that civilisation is largely based on the acceptance of laws that restrict the independence of individuals but ensure that society enjoys the collective liberty underwritten by security and justice, he warned that social chaos usually led to despotism. Ferguson especially informed the thinking of Adam Smith and, as Professor of Natural Philosophy at Edinburgh University, he stood at the centre of progressive intellectual life.

Whatever his other great gifts, Adam Ferguson was possessed of tremendous physical courage. Born at Logierait in Highland Perthshire, he was a native Gaelic speaker. This facility and a certain amount of theological study at St Andrews University qualified him for his first paid appointment as chaplain to the Black Watch. Many regiments in the British army have a prayer they recite before battle and that of Ferguson's regiment was one of the earliest. It is known as a Collect and their chaplain led the men of the Black Watch in a brief moment of worship before the

guns boomed out over Fontenoy, a prayer that recalled their
origins clearly:

> *O God, whose strength setteth fast the mountains,*
> *Lord of the hills to whom we lift our eyes:*
> *Grant us grace that we, of the Black Watch,*
> *Once chosen to watch the mountains of an earthly kingdom,*
> *May stand fast in the faith and be strong,*
> *Until we come to the heavenly kingdom of Him,*
> *Who has bidden us watch and pray,*
> *Thy Son, our Saviour and Lord.*

The Highlanders of the Black Watch respected their young
chaplain profoundly. After the Collect was said and the ranks
closed up, Ferguson then spoke briefly about what was expected.
Their conduct as soldiers should encompass four cardinal virtues
and the chaplain expressed them concisely in Gaelic – *coir* was
what was proper, *ceart* was what was right, *dligeach* was what was
necessary for a soldier to do and *dileas* was the need for
unconditional loyalty. And these exhortations were no matter
of theory for Ferguson. He aimed to practise them himself. The
Highland historian, Robert Stewart of Garth, spoke to men who
had been at Fontenoy and this is an incident that remained in
their memories:

> When the regiment was taking its ground on the morning of
> battle, Sir Robert Munro perceived the Chaplain in the ranks,
> and, with a friendly caution, told him that there was no necessity
> to expose himself to unnecessary danger, and that he should be
> out of the line of fire. Mr Ferguson thanked Sir Robert for his
> friendly advice, but added, on this occasion he had a duty which
> he was imperiously called upon to perform.
>
> Accordingly he continued with the regiment for the whole of
> the action, in the hottest of the fire, praying with the dying,
> attending to the wounded, and directing them to be carried to a
> place of safety.

By his fearless zeal, his intrepidity, and his friendship towards the soldiers (several of whom had been his schoolfellows at Dunkeld), his amiable and cheerful manners, checking with severity when necessary, mixing among them with ease and familiarity, and being as ready as any of them with a poem or heroic tale, he acquired an unbounded ascendancy over them.

What is moving is Ferguson's instinctive understanding that wounded or dying soldiers of the Black Watch wished to be spoken to in Gaelic, in the language of their mothers and families, the soft spoken tongue of the mountains and green glens of home. His bravery in battle was not that of earlier churchmen – the warlike bishops and abbots who led men on to the killing fields of Flodden or Bannockburn. It was different and perhaps more difficult to have the courage to ignore the din and chaos of fighting, the roar of the cannon and the snap of musketry and kneel down beside a fallen countryman and console him with a Gaelic prayer or help orderlies take him behind the lines.

Despite his origins in Highland Perthshire, Adam Ferguson was emphatically not a Jacobite. Intellectually and practically he could not support the restoration of a dynasty inclined to absolutism and whose kings had caused widespread and bitter civil war in Britain and Ireland. But he was a man of action and, as one of the greatest minds of the Scottish Enlightenment, not unusual in that. When Prince Charles and his Highland army approached Edinburgh on 15 September 1745, the city's Defence Volunteers mustered at the Tolbooth in the High Street. Amongst the 400 men who formed up in ranks was David Hume, perhaps the greatest philosopher of the age. When they were ordered to man the city gates and confront the Highland hordes, the number of volunteers dwindled drastically to only 42. But one who did not slink off down a close was Hume. Like Adam Ferguson, he was prepared to act in defence of his principles as well as his city and risk his life if necessary.

James Macpherson saw Scotland and the Highlands in particular in a different light – a Celtic twilight. Born the son of a farmer in Ruthven, near Kingussie, he was a Gaelic speaker and, from the first, he was aware of the turns of the troubled history of Highland and Lowland. Macpherson grew up in the shadow of Ruthven Barracks, built after the 1715 Jacobite Rebellion and the site of one of the castles of the Wolf of Badenoch. In 1753, the young scholar matriculated at Aberdeen's two universities, attending King's College before moving to Marischal College. After a year teaching at the school in his native village, ambition stirred in James Macpherson. At Aberdeen, he was said to have written more than 4,000 lines of verse and, as the familiar comforts of home in Ruthven began to fade, the restless young man moved to Edinburgh in 1758 to pursue a life in letters.

'The Highlander', a heroic rendition of deeds done at the obscure Battle of Cullen (in Banffshire), was said to have been so bad that its author tried to suppress it. But some modern scholars are less damning and a recent study has revealed much about Macpherson's method of working. Set in the 10th century, the poem borrowed heavily from John of Fordun's *Chronicle* even to the extent of lifting phrases as well as names and events. Out of the medieval mixture of narrative, tradition and myth-history, Macpherson constructed a plausible plot. And some of the writing is better than the author's own estimate. Here is his description of the clash of battle at Cullen as the Scots attack the Vikings, the Danes:

> The full form'd columns in the midnight hour
> Begin their silent journey t'wards the shore
> Within the womb of night.
> . . .
> Confirm the troops and arm the youth for fight.
> . . .
> Onward they rush, and in a shout engage.
> The swords thro' air their gleaming journeys fly,
> Crash on the helms and tremble in the sky.
> Groan follows groan, and wound succeeds wound,

While dying bodies quiver on the ground.
. . .
The Danes beholding their commander die,
Start from their ranks and in confusion fly.

Later in the narrative comes a fascinating passage, a prophesy
from a hermit.

See Scot and Saxon coalesc'd in one,
Support the glory of the common crown.
Britain no more shall shake with native storms
But o'er the trembling nations lift her arms.

Written only ten years after Culloden by a Gaelic speaker born
in the heart of the Highlands, the poem and its prophesy are an
affirmation of Britishness, the common crown being that on the
head of George II, the native storms the Jacobite Rebellions and
the trembling nations those waiting to be drawn into the
burgeoning British Empire. And more than that, 'The Highlander' was the first step in Macpherson's attempt to discover –
and, if necessary, reconstruct – a national epic not for the
Highlands or for Scotland but for a united Britain. Just as
Imperial Rome had her Virgil to sing of heroic origins and
mighty Greece had Homer, the British Empire would need its
founding heroes. Macpherson's first coherent literary effort also
shows the young writer not as a forger but as a patriotic adaptor.

On a visit to Moffat in Dumfriesshire, James Macpherson met
John Home, a former minister of the Kirk who had, surprisingly,
made a tremendous reputation as a playwright. In 1756, he wrote
Douglas: A Tragedy. The plot began to form in his mind when
Home heard a woman singing an ancient ballad known as 'Gil
Morrice' and he wrote these lines to open the drama:

My name is Norval. On the Grampian Hills
My father feeds his flocks: a frugal swain,
Whose constant cares were to increase his store.

Verses much more alarming than anything written by James Macpherson, they nevertheless launched a hugely successful production in London. Sarah Siddons and David Garrick took leading parts and David Hume enthused, saying that Home possessed 'the true theatric genius of Shakespeare' but was even better. Thomas Gray, the famous author of 'Elegy Written in a Country Churchyard', reckoned that the playwright 'seemed to have retrieved the true language of the stage, which has been lost these hundred years'. And famously, one Scottish member of an ecstatic audience was said to have shouted, 'Whaur's yer Wullie Shakespeare noo?' Such was the immense power of these romantic tales in the second half of the 18th century, a phenomenon that modern tastes find hard to fathom.

When James Macpherson met John Home in Moffat, he recited Gaelic poetry and showed him some manuscripts he said he had found in the Western Isles and the Highlands. Much encouraged by his listener (Did he have Gaelic? It's unlikely since Home was born in Leith.) and perhaps impressed by the famous playwright's dazzling success in London, Macpherson translated these and, in 1760, they were published in Edinburgh as *Fragments of Ancient Poetry collected in the Highlands of Scotland and translated from the Gaelic or Erse Language*. Hugh Blair, Professor of Rhetoric and Belles Lettres at Edinburgh University was a central figure in Scottish intellectual life and he not only endorsed Macpherson's work but raised money for him to carry on recording poetry from the oral tradition in the north. In his expeditions into the interior, he was accompanied by a Captain Morrison and the Rev. Gallie. On a visit to Mull, Macpherson collected some early manuscripts.

Just as Walter Scott was to do in the Borders forty years later, Macpherson wrote down what he heard recited from memory. With rhyme schemes, repeating choruses and familiar conventions, poetry is designed for ease of recall and many women (they were usually the tradition bearers in many communities) could summon up dozens of lengthy compositions. In an age without commonly available printed books, aside from the Bible and other devotional literature, or indeed any other means of transmitting and telling stories, oral traditions in the Highlands – and in the Borders – were very rich. And, like Scott, Macpherson tended to edit and adapt what he heard and, where there were manuscripts, he would sometimes conflate material from different sources. But, in 1761, he took matters a stage further – and, for some, it was a stage too far.

James Macpherson claimed that he had rediscovered a lost epic poem by a bard he called Ossian. Complete and pristine, it told the heroic story of Fingal and its finder announced that he had translated it into English. A British epic poet to rival Homer and Virgil, Ossian's great work was a sensation when it was revealed to the world. And it immediately became wildly and enduringly popular. More poems came to light and were translated and, in 1765, a collected edition, *The Poems of Ossian*, was published. Goethe translated parts of it into German, Napoleon carried a copy as he led the Grande Armée into Russia and great writers such as Blake, Thoreau, Byron, Scott and Arnold either praised or imitated Ossian, or both. Mendelssohn, Schubert and Brahms were inspired to compose music and the name Oscar (it appeared first in Ossian) was widely bestowed. In the USA, the city of Selma, Alabama, was named after Fingal's palace. And of course, his remarkable cave is seen on Staffa by many thousands each year.

There were other reactions. Some literary figures were very suspicious. Dr Samuel Johnson called Macpherson 'a mountebank, a liar and a fraud'. When calls for the ancient manuscripts of Ossian to be produced for examination were ignored, doubt intensified. The problem was that there was almost certainly no single manuscript – Macpherson had inflated and conflated what he had discovered as a sales ploy. David Hume remarked that 'fifty bare-arsed Highlanders' could not convince him. But Hugh Blair stood by the young author and wrote an introduction to the poems that supported their authenticity.

Somewhat embarrassed, the Committee of the Highland Society began an enquiry. What became known as the Glenmasan manuscript eventually came to light. It was certainly old and it contained material resembling some of what was to be found in Ossian. And, crucially, the respected figure of Adam Ferguson realised that the poems were not a fabrication. As a Gaelic speaker whose ear was tuned to the oral tradition of the Highlands, he could discern genuine elements. Modern Gaelic scholars have agreed with Ferguson's general assessment. The problem was that Macpherson over-claimed – there never was a manuscript but the work was full of genuine references. Many of the names had been anglicised or slightly changed. Fingal is from Fionn MacCumhaill, Temora is Tara, Dar-Thula is Deirdre of the Sorrows and so on. It seems clear that, in pursuit of a Homeric creator, Macpherson did a great deal of reorganisation and invention to create a coherent narrative.

Leaving aside the controversy, perhaps the most profound effect of the Ossian poems was to change perceptions radically. From being the redoubt of wild savagery and sedition, the Highlands very quickly became the fount of romance. Instead of the rainswept home of a rabble of cattle-stealing, Gaelic-speaking primitives, the mountains and glens had once seen noble kings, beautiful princesses and great and brave warriors and picturesque palaces. The shades of long-lost heroes loomed out of the mists swirling around the dark heads of the mountains. And, from the 1760s onwards, the Highlands began to fit the romance of its imagined past as the emigrations emptied the glens and straths and a working landscape slowly decayed into scenery, a vacant stage set for epic tales.

A generation after Ossian, Walter Scott accelerated the disconnection between reality and myth-history as he sat down to write the first of his long narrative poems. Drawing on his own work in collecting the oral traditions of Borders poetry and balladry and setting it in print in *The Minstrelsy of the Scottish Border*, Scott brought many historical elements together in *The Lay of the Last Minstrel*. It told the tale of a Border feud and involved the poet's own patrons, the Buccleuchs, and how they sheltered an old bard. Selling 27,000 copies in ten years, the poem was well reviewed and very lucrative. The public demanded more. Scott did not stray far for his next theme. *Marmion* focused on the Battle of Flodden of 1513 and, when it was published in 1808, the first edition of 2,000 copies sold out in two months even though the cover price was thought to be exorbitant. It sparkled with incident and good writing. Stanza 17 in Canto VI contained a couplet that would become famous:

> Yet Clare's sharp questions must I shun
> Must separate Constance from the nun.
> Oh! What a tangled web we weave
> When first we practise to deceive!
> A Palmer too! No wonder why
> I felt rebuked beneath his eye.

These were remarkable sales figures – the statistics of the first true best-sellers. Printers could scarcely keep up with demand as Scott's popularity changed the publishing industry.

For his third major work, the great poet turned away from home and looked to the Highlands, to a location very close to the Highland Line. When Scott and his family took a holiday in the Trossachs, a series of small, beautiful, wooded glens between Loch Venachar and Loch Katrine, his imagination took flight and he began to work on what became *The Lady of the Lake*. A tale of chivalry and of enmity between Highland and Lowland, between the clans and the king, it did not shy away from recently incendiary issues. After resolving some difficulties with character and plot, Scott sent the poem for publication in 1810. It was a sensation. In only eight months, *The Lady of the Lake* sold 25,000 copies and was sent for sale all over the world. Scott became the most famous living author and was lionised from Paris to Washington. It seemed that *The Lady of the Lake* had ignited the romantic interest in the Highlands that had first been stirred by James Macpherson's Ossian.

Franz Schubert set parts of Scott's new poem to music and, in London, it was dramatised, without permission, with its songs set to music by James Sanderson. Versions were staged in the USA and one song, 'The Boat Song', achieved an unlikely pre-eminence. The music was played when President John Quincy Adams opened the Chesapeake Ohio Canal and again at the inauguration of President James K. Polk. After that, it was decided that the song should be heard every time the President of the United States appeared at a formal occasion. The opening line written by Scott was of course 'Hail to the Chief'. The chief in the poem was Roderick Dhu, Black Rory, a warlike character who preferred to use force rather than rely on the rule of law.

Closer to home, the impact of *The Lady of the Lake* on perceptions of the Highlands was radical. Immediately after its publication, tourists turned up in large numbers to visit the Trossachs and Loch Katrine. Robert Cadell, the son-in-law of Scott's publisher, recorded the reaction: 'The whole country rang with the praises of the poet – crowds set off to view the scenery of Loch Katrine, till then comparatively unknown; and as the book came out just before the season for excursions, every house and inn in that neighbourhood was crammed with a constant succession of visitors. It is a well-ascertained fact, that from the date of the publication of The Lady of the Lake, the post-horse duty in Scotland rose in an extraordinary degree.'

A new hotel was built at Callander to accommodate the thousands who ventured, only a very few miles, across the Highland Line to look at the scenery, the slowly emptying backdrop for Scott's imagination. All of this activity took place before the coming of the railways and at a time when travel overland was difficult, slow and sometimes dangerous. And it took place only sixty-five years after the last Jacobite Rebellion. The Highlands had been defeated, pillaged, neutered, romanticised and was in the first stages of being repackaged.

The next stages followed quickly. In 1814, Walter Scott's first novel was published. *Waverley, or 'Tis Sixty Years Since* appeared anonymously but Jane Austen was not fooled and pretended not to be much impressed: 'Walter Scott has no business to write novels, especially good ones. – It is not fair. He has Fame and

Profit enough as a Poet, and should not be taking the bread out of the mouths of other people. I do not like him, and do not mean to like "Waverley" if I can help it, but I fear I must.'

Many others felt similarly compelled and, in only five months, 5,000 copies of *Waverley* were sold and the first best-selling novel was born. It romanticised not only the Highlands but also relatively recent and bloody events. The title counted that it was only sixty years since the last Jacobite Rebellion and, by blending historical fact with fiction, it created a new genre – the historical novel.

Scott's anonymity was a flimsy conceit. When, in 1815, George, the Prince Regent, let it be known that he would like to meet 'the author of *Waverley*' and subsequently invited him to dine, Walter Scott turned up, unblushing and making no protest. It was a meeting of signal importance, an encounter that would accelerate a tectonic cultural shift in the relationship between Highland and Lowland.

Walter Scott deserved his immense success. He wrote with a prodigious energy and application, qualities that have ensured a lasting esteem amongst novelists and, indeed, writers of all sorts – his waning popularity notwithstanding. Rising early, maintaining a steady writing routine, concentrating on the task at hand, paying no heed to questions of inspiration or the lack of it, Scott may be seen as the first truly professional author.

After *Waverley* and the success of *Guy Mannering* and *The Antiquary*, novels set in Galloway and the Lowlands, The Great Unknown, as he was known, returned to a Highland theme and a setting close to his beloved Loch Katrine and the Trossachs – at least eventually.

Rob Roy may be the title of Scott's fourth novel but he is in fact a minor character. Francis, or Frank, Osbaldistone is the hero of *Rob Roy*. Having quarrelled with his father, Frank is sent to stay with his uncle Sir Hildebrand Osbaldistone in Northumberland. With his customary penchant for baroque character names, Scott introduces tension between Hildebrand's son, Rashleigh, and plain old

Frank. In 1714, on the eve of the first major Jacobite Rebellion, the action moves further north, to Scotland and the Highland Line. Rashleigh has made off with documents important to the honour and solvency of Frank's father and a pursuit begins.

This chase brings the hero in contact with Rob Roy Mac-Gregor and both roam around the clan homelands between the head of Loch Lomond and Loch Katrine, the wild and western end of the Trossachs. Scott stretches his plot a little and makes a link between Sir Hildebrand and Rob Roy and the action ratchets up as the '15 summons the clans to its banners. The dastardly Rashleigh meets a suitable and deserved end, Frank inherits Sir Hildebrand's Northumbrian estates (all the other possible heirs having conveniently perished in the 1715 rebellion) and he marries Diana, a sufficiently distant cousin.

If Scott had followed his own recent form and used the name of his hero as a title for the new novel, *Rob Roy* might have been called *Francis Osbaldistone*. And it might not have impressed Scott's publisher, Archibald Constable. Instead, sound marketing instincts prevailed, the much more commercial *Rob Roy* was proposed and its author noted that his publisher's 'sagacity and experience foresaw the germ of popularity'.

What persuaded Constable that his title would sell more books were notoriety and a growing fashion for Highland romance. Rob Roy was famous for being hunted, living like a kilted savage in the heather, armed to the teeth and surviving by his wits, defiant and elusive. This reputation was long-standing, perpetuated by the publication of *The Highland Rogue*, probably by Edmund Burt, in 1723. It purported to be a catalogue of incidents in Rob Roy's life (not yet over as he was still very much alive when the presses rolled) and described him as a feral phenomenon, preternaturally strong, of 'a gigantic size', with a foot-long beard and a face and body completely covered in red hair. In Gaelic, *Raibeart Ruadh* translates as 'Red Robert' but perhaps not quite so red as painted. At about this time, the legend arose that Rob could pull up his stockings without bending his back.

The reality was, as usual, much more interesting and also

emblematic for the story of the Highland Line and the cultures who coexisted either side of it. Rob Roy's father was Donald Glas, a name that stood in a tradition of using colouring as a nickname. Grey Donald was a *duine uasal* (a Gaelic term meaning 'a man of noble birth'), a scion of the gentry who led the various branches of Clan Gregor. There were three – the Lomond MacGregors, the Balquhidder MacGregors and the Rannoch MacGregors. The first was led by Donald Glas and was also known as Clann Dughail Cheir, the Clan or Children of Dark Dougal, yet another example of colouring and of a name-father sharpening identity. At the end of the 17th century, the paramount chief was a weak man, Gregor MacGregor of Stucnaroy, and Donald Glas was regarded as the de facto leader of the clan. Blood conferred status but prowess was needed to enhance it.

And Donald Glas appears to have been daring and active. At the head of a contingent of MacGregors, their grey-haired chief was at the siege of Dunkeld in 1689 with his youngest son. Born in 1671, Rob Roy was 18 and certainly old enough to fight alongside his father as they charged the cathedral enclosure. After the failure to dislodge the dogged Cameronians, Donald Glas led a cattle raid at Cardross in southern Perthshire. The lawful owners of the stolen beasts were evidently supporters of William of Orange and, while some Highlanders needed no second excuse to reive cattle, there seems to have been a political motive at work at Cardross.

In 1690, Donald Glas was arrested as 'a great robber' and brought captive to face justice at Edinburgh. Eventually freed on a promise of good behaviour from himself and on behalf of his sons, the old chief returned to Loch Lomondside unrepentant. Paying little heed to the law or the bond he had given, Donald Glas led a raid on Kippen where his men lifted cattle expressly as a show of Highland and Jacobite support for the Old Pretender, the exiled James II.

All of these criminal acts took place along the edges of the Highland Line and were highly visible to Lowland opinion. As a resort of lawlessness, even savagery, the mountains and glens were seen as sheltering a recurring threat to order and civilisation.

But when stirred to act, government understood how to disable the MacGregors and they took a measure that had been effective in the past. In 1693, Clan Gregor was disnamed. It became a crime to bear the surname of MacGregor and those who persisted could not only be prosecuted, they could also expect no protection from the law. Their property and persons could be seized by force by anyone at any time.

It had happened before. In 1603, Clan Gregor had descended on the Colquhouns of Luss on the western shores of Loch Lomond and slaughtered them. King James VI and I was persuaded to act against the clan and their name was formally proscribed. After almost a century of pressure from their powerful neighbours, Clan Campbell, the MacGregors became reduced, forced to rent land and even reive cattle or blackmail cattle rearers in order to survive – and, worst of all, to take names such as Drummond or Gregory. When the second disnaming came into effect in 1693, Rob Roy took the name of Campbell.

But he was no savage. Unlike the vast majority of Scots, Rob could read, write and speak in Lowland Scots and Gaelic. His surviving letters show a developing fluency in both languages. Literacy mattered because Rob was in the cattle business; contracts were required to be made and clearly understood and English-speaking markets lay close at hand. From the lands of the Lomond MacGregors, Glasgow, Dumbarton and Stirling were less than a day's ride away. And the parish of Buchanan that included Rob Roy's house at Glengyle was divided into Lowland Scots-speaking farms in the south and Gaelic-speaking townships in the north. Geology marked this unequivocally for the Highland Boundary Fault, so visible on the islands and shores of Loch Lomond, runs through the parish.

The cultural contrasts were sometimes stark. In 1702, James Fraser noted that every Highlander seemed to carry arms and 'their games were military exercises, and such as rendered them fittest for war, [such] as archery, running, jumping with and without racing, swimming and continual hunting and fowling'. In addition to the obvious linguistic divide, religion may still have

Brave Clan Cameron

Nicknames can be eloquent. The clan who prospered most in the aftermath of the Jacobite risings of the 19th century was Clan Campbell and their Gaelic name translates as 'Twisted Mouth'. More likely a reference to language than unfortunate facial features, it probably refers to a different-sounding, south-west dialect of Gaelic or the likelihood that, in the Dark Ages, these Gaelic speakers could also converse in Old Welsh. This was the language of Strathclyde, the old British kingdom based on Dumbarton Rock. Clan Cameron also derives from a nickname but in their case it may refer to a shared characteristic. In Gaelic, Cameron means 'Bent or Broken Nose', the unmistakable mark of a pugilist, a fighter. Deeply respected by James Wolfe at Culloden as 'the bravest of the clans', they also made the rising possible. When Prince Charles was being rowed up Loch Shiel to raise his standard at Glenfinnan, he and Colonel John O'Sullivan could see only 50 or so men waiting on the shore to meet them. When Allan MacDonald of Morar joined them with 150 clansmen, it was still no more than an escort and very far from an army. But, in the middle of fretful afternoon, everything changed. Led by their pipers, a thousand men of Clan Cameron came to Glenfinnan, raised the royal standard and began the long road to Culloden. So powerful was their influence that the Duke of Cumberland was not content to pacify the survivors of the clan – he wanted them all deported to the colonies.

separated the two communities. In the more remote glens, the saints' days and celebrations of the Catholic Church probably hung on long after the Reformation of the 16th century. And clothes mattered too. Highlanders and Lowlanders looked very different.

Rob Roy was not only bilingual – he also owned two wardrobes. Here is a translation of a Gaelic epitaph:

> You were the hawk of the people,
> Rob Roy's what they called you –
> You look good wearing a plaid and a sword.
> Well do a hat and cloak
> With trimmings of gold
> Suit your name, and it's no boast to say it.

By the beginning of the 18th century, Rob had established himself as a reputable cattle dealer, his reiving days apparently behind him. He rented more farms and developed his business as southern markets for Highland beef expanded. On the eastern shores of Loch Lomond, at Rowardennan, he took on the lease of a parcel of land probably because it was the point at which Argyll drovers swam their cattle across from Inverbeg. But perhaps he grew his operations too quickly, making unsound deals, suffering some ill luck. And it seems that Rob Roy was robbed. Having been entrusted with cash to buy cows in the north, his chief herdsman absconded and was never seen again. By 1711, Rob Roy realised that he was facing bankruptcy.

To cover his mounting debts and keep cash flowing, Rob conceived a simple confidence trick. Trading on his previous sound reputation, he accepted money in advance to buy cattle for delivery in the spring of 1712 but he had no intention of fulfilling any contract. Instead, he quietly put his property into the hands of his extended family and planned to disappear deep into the interior of the Highlands, somewhere no one could catch up with him and the cash.

As it became clear to the buyers that no cattle would be driven down the trails in the spring and summer of 1712, suspicion festered and then flared. One of Rob's customers was the immensely powerful James Graham, Duke of Montrose, and his Edinburgh lawyers had MacGregor formally declared outlaw. And then the hunt began.

After Montrose's agents seized Rob's property, a blood feud ensued. Living as a fugitive in the heather, he managed to wage a private war for more than thirteen years against a great land-owner whose resources far outweighed anything an outlaw could muster. It was this unequal contest between a savage but resourceful – even noble – Highlander who knew the land and could live off it, like the Native American Indians, and a cultured, wealthy aristocratic Lowlander that caught the public imagination.

When the standard of the Old Pretender was raised in the

Jacobite Rebellion of 1715, Rob and his men joined the forces led by the Earl of Mar. At the inconclusive battle at Sheriffmuir, near Perth, MacGregor would later claim not to have been involved, having arrived too late. Four years later at the Battle of Glen Shiel, the only action in another abortive rising, he was present and destroyed Jacobite munitions and supplies to prevent them falling into government hands.

In an attempt to pacify the Highlands and improve communications, George I sent Major General George Wade north in 1725. Those involved, however tangentially, in the 1715 rebellion were offered unconditional pardons and, on 8 October, Rob Roy and his men came to Finlarig, near Killin, at the head of Loch Tay. There, they surrendered their weapons (or at least those they had with them) and, on 19 October, Rob wrote a formal letter of submission, craving the king's mercy for his treason at Sheriffmuir and Glen Shiel. In it, he helpfully pointed out that he had not actually joined in the fighting at Sheriffmuir. Here is the most entertaining part of Major General Wade's report to George I:

> I take the liberty to inform your Grace that of the arms that were brought to Breadalbane, the famous Rob Roy sent in a greater proportion and in a handsomer manner than his neighbours. I suppose this might be done with a view to pave the way for his submission to his majesty, which he came and made to me yesterday in this town. He assured me he never had the least thought of entering into the rebellion from any dislike he had to his majesty's government, or from any attachment to the Pretender, but to avoid the persecution of his enemy, the Duke of Montrose, with whom he said he had since accommodated matters, and satisfied all his demands. This appears the more probable from the civility with which he treated the king's soldiers, whenever he met with them straggling in the mountains, whom he never used to part without drinking the health of King George. He has just now sent me his letter of submission.

With a mixture of drams, ingratiating words and a sound instinct for the winning side, the famous Rob Roy finally made peace and appeared to escape justice. He also made it clear that he was willing to inform on other, less compliant Highlanders and his sons joined the independent companies, regiments raised for the crown. In a wonderfully apt satire written in 1726 and entitled 'On Rob Roy's Pardon and Preferment', the Edinburgh poet, Alexander Pennecuik mused on the ironies of his hero's behaviour:

> Welcome brave captain to your own banditti,
> Welcome as succour to a besieged city.
> For service done at Sheriffmuir engagement,
> Made captain of an independent regiment,
> Most just for it is known to every clan
> Rob Roy was aye an independent man,
> Depended not on God nor king before,
> But only trusted to his own claymore.
> Long live the king in plenty, peace and joy,
> Who makes a loyal lad of Robin Roy.
> There is a near relation 'twixt the two,
> One steals a crown, the other steals a cow.

After 13 years of being hunted in the mountains and glens for being a conman and a rebel, Rob Roy was 53 years old in 1725 and no doubt anxious for a quieter life. At Balquhidder, he lived for a further nine years before dying peacefully in his bed.

Rob's posthumous reputation grew steadily. In 1743, only two years before the outbreak of the last Jacobite rebellion, a second edition of *The Highland Rogue* was published. When Dorothy and William Wordsworth toured Scotland, they visited what they mistakenly believed was the grave of famous Rob Roy and the great poet was moved:

> A famous man is Robin Hood,
> The English ballad singer's joy.
> And Scotland boasts of one as good,
> She has her own Rob Roy!

Drama followed and, in 1803, the play *Red Roy* opened in London. Set a century before he was born, it recounted the early exploits of 'The Red Robber' and told of his passionate love for the fair Helen (not his wife). Drawn without any redeeming features, Rob's character met his demise in a raging Highland torrent and the curtain closed. The play was very popular.

Walter Scott claimed a longstanding interest in the Highland rogue, collecting stories and even acquiring some of his alleged possessions He bought a gun, a dirk and a sporran, items presumably not handed over to General Wade's men. They are still on display at his house at Abbotsford. When Scott had completed the novel in late 1817, he sent it off to the his publisher with a jaunty verse:

> With great joy
> I send you Roy
> 'Twas a tough job
> But we're done with Rob.

The sales of the novel confirmed Archibald Constable's marketing instincts and it was a runaway best-seller. Copies comprised an entire cargo loaded at the port of Leith on a ship bound for an eager London market. So widespread was its popularity that, by itself, *Rob Roy* fostered an enduring cultural stereotype. Highlanders had long been seen as savage, even subhuman, but Scott added a romantic sheen, a windswept nobility seasoned by a touch of mystery as the mists swirled around the mountains and the men who knew their secret places. With each passing decade, it seemed, Rob Roy grew more and more like Robin Hood. The atmosphere around him was made seductive by the power of Walter Scott's storytelling. Where the Highlands had been a threat, a dangerous source of sedition and barbarism, the novel helped consign all that to a comfortable past, the stuff of novels and plays. A very colourful and distinct version of Scottishness – and one that was harmless and quaint – had been created by a Lowlander.

Five years after the publication of *Rob Roy*, Scott would create an even greater fiction, one whose popularity has grown hugely in recent times – and, remarkably, place the disnamed and formerly reviled MacGregor clan at the centre of a Highland fantasy. At his meeting with the Prince Regent, the future George IV, in 1815, 'the author of *Waverley*' discussed the prospect of a royal visit to Scotland. Not since the Act of Union in 1707 had a reigning monarch ventured north of the Tweed. Scott was anxious about the growth of radicalism in Scotland and keen to foster a sense of national unity, what was needed for peace and good order. Soon after his accession in 1820, the new king had visited Ireland, the scene of a much more recent rebellion, and, for the sake of balance and even-handedness, it was thought that George IV should pay a state visit to Scotland.

Later to become known as 'the King's Jaunt', a state visit had been mooted for some time but, when it eventually came, the decision that it would take place was made suddenly. In July 1822, Edinburgh's town council was horrified to be informed that the king and his retinue would be landing at Leith harbour in two weeks' time. Thrown into paroxysms of dismay and disorganisation (who knew how such a thing should be done?), the councillors quickly resolved to hand over the running of the entire jamboree to an outsider. Walter Scott was to create the programme, look and tone of the state visit. With only days to come up with a workable plan and enact it, Scott fell back on fiction, turned it into fact – or at least ceremony – and set the Highlands, Highlanders, the clans and tartan at the centre of it all. Rob Roy would have been astonished to see the MacGregors leading the celebrations.

At a levee held at the Palace of Holyroodhouse, George IV made a spectacular entrance. Swathed in a bright scarlet sett of tartan that would become known as Royal Stewart, he wore a Glengarry bonnet stuck with eagle feathers, two belts (perhaps to restrain his vast belly – the king tipped the scales at almost 20 stone) – and a silk and goatskin sporran, and the whole outfit was set off by gems, silver buckles, a dirk, a powder horn and diced stockings. His kilt sat well above the knee and, to disguise his grotesquely swollen and veined legs, the king wore flesh-coloured tights. Lady Dalrymple was heard to remark, 'Since he is here for such a short time, it is as well that we see so much of him.'

It was an astonishing bouleversement. Scott's solution to the problem of the Jacobites and the fact that the last royal visit to Edinburgh was by Bonnie Prince Charlie at the head of an army of Highland savages was to embrace it all utterly.

The first act of the royal visit was a procession to conduct the recently rediscovered Scottish regalia from Edinburgh Castle down the Royal Mile to Holyroodhouse. The escort was none other than Clan Gregor. And at one of several banquets in the king's ample presence, the chief, Sir Evan MacGregor, proposed a loyal toast to 'the chief of chiefs'. That arch equivocator and survivor, Rob Roy, would have smiled.

Others scowled. In August 1822, many in Edinburgh did not approve of Walter Scott's efforts 'to turn [them] into a nation of Highlanders', according to his son-in-law and biographer, J.G. Lockhart. This was no exaggeration. In 'Hints Addressed to the Inhabitants of Edinburgh and Others in Prospect of His Majesty's Visit', a pamphlet circulated before the royal visit, allegedly written by an 'Old Citizen', Scott's most emphatic hint sounded more like a direction, a theatre direction: 'We are the CLAN and our King is the CHIEF'. Other stage directions included the burning of a Fiery Cross on Arthur's Seat. This traditional and suitably dramatic call to arms for the clans had featured in *The Lady of the Lake* and it was to become a notorious symbol for the most infamous clan of them all, the Ku Klux Klan. And grim contemporary historical realities sometimes intruded, at least by implication. Scott organised a Gathering of the Clans, the real ones, that is, but only five attended, including, of course, the ubiquitous MacGregors. Others such as a contingent from Sutherland and another from Glen Garry came in response to critical mutterings that the clan chiefs were depopulating their estates – which many were. It was more than a bitter irony that, at exactly the moment when Edinburgh was filled with tartan-clad Lowlanders and a German king all pretending to be Highlanders, the real originators of this bowdlerised version of their culture were being ruthlessly cleared off the land as aristocrats forgot the bonds and obligations of the past and focused on future profit.

The last official engagement of the King's Jaunt to Edinburgh was perhaps the most ironic, not to say most cynical. At the Theatre Royal, a dramatised version of Scott's novel *Rob Roy* had been hurriedly cast and rehearsed for a command performance. The play ended with the actors in a rendition of 'Pardon Now the Bold Outlaw' and a more direct appeal to ignore history and install Scotland fully back in royal favour. The last song was cringingly entitled 'A' That's Past Forget – Forgie'. No one blinked. It was all part of Walter Scott's hypnotic mirage. Earlier in the week, the king himself showed that he had read the script when he proposed a toast to the people who had attempted to remove his grandfather from the British throne and, surprisingly, to Scotland's excellent tradition of baking. To 'all the chieftains and clans of Scotland, long may God bless the Land of Cakes', proclaimed George IV and history faded into nothing more than a colourful, tartan-clad, picturesque backdrop. The recent past was not so much forgotten as transformed into comforting, harmless and politically prudent parody.

Lockhart caught the paradoxes perfectly when he wrote:

It appeared to be very generally thought, when the first programmes were issued, that the Highlanders, their kilts and their bagpipes, were to occupy a great deal too much space . . . With all respect and admiration for the noble and generous qualities which our countrymen of the Highland clans have so often exhibited, it was difficult to forget that they had always constituted a small, and almost always unimportant part of the Scottish population; and when one reflected how miserably their numbers had of late years been reduced in consequence of the selfish and hard-hearted policy of their landlords, it almost seemed as if there was a cruel mockery in giving so much prominence to their pretensions. But there could be no question that they were picturesque – and their enthusiasm was too sincere not to be catching; so that by and by even the coolest-headed Sassenach felt his heart . . . 'warm to the tartan'.

In the developing story of Scotland's sense of herself, the King's Jaunt marked a clear turning point. By accepting a caricature of Highland culture as representative of the whole nation, Scotland self-consciously carved out a very distinctive place in the United Kingdom of Great Britain and Ireland. Kilts were different and, by wrapping them around Lowland back-sides, Walter Scott solved a fundamental difficulty. Those who lived in Lowland Scotland, the vast majority as Lockhart pointed out, had, in truth, much in common with their neighbours in Northern England. Scots was a recognisable northern dialect of English, a clear cousin to what was spoken on the banks of the Tyne and in Durham, and there were close economic and ethnic links. To prevent Scotland becoming little more than a district of England, to make her look distinctive, Scott turned north to the Highlands, frisked the Gaels for their emblems and appropriated them wholesale. And Scots men and women bought into this new and bogus version of Scottishness with great enthusiasm and in near-complete ignorance of the culture that had given rise to it. Tartan crossed the Highland Line but all of the more complex aspects of Highland society, such as language, did not.

Meanwhile the king climbed out of his belts, plaids and flesh-coloured tights to take ship for London and recover from three weeks of banquets and entertainments. And Walter Scott returned home to the Borders a hero. With the help of the literary efforts of his friend, James Hogg, he had already stimulated the textile industry to produce tweeds, checked cloth and the sort of plaid thrown over the shoulder of the romantic heroes of *Waverley* and *Rob Roy*. And, after the immense success of the King's Jaunt, tartan became extremely popular and the mills of Galashiels, Selkirk and Hawick clacked and thrummed as they attempted to keep up with demand.

Perhaps the most obvious and enduring legacy of the visit of George IV can be seen at weddings in Scotland. No matter where the bridegroom was born and raised, he and his best men almost always walk up the aisle dressed as Highlanders. Many other formal occasions pull kilts and sporrans out of the wardrobe – graduations, dinners, Hogmanay and a host of other important moments persuade men to dress like tidy versions of Rob Roy and the men who charged across the heather at Culloden. At the end of the 18th century, no Lowlanders would have been seen dead in a kilt but at the outset of the 21st, few need any persuasion to buckle on the tartan.

After 1822, momentum built as royal reinforcement for Walter Scott's version of Highland culture redoubled and the real thing began to fade from the pages of history. George IV's niece, Victoria, embraced all things tartan with even more enthusiasm, in more than one sense. After the death of Prince Albert and a protracted period of mourning, she began a relationship with John Brown. He was the Gaelic-speaking son of a crofter from Craithenard, near Balmoral, and the surprising object of the widowed queen's devotion. A new image of the Highlander, steadfast and immovably loyal, was constructed around Brown. And the openness of Victoria's affection was striking – she dedicated a book to her 'beloved friend, John Brown' and took a portrait of him on a bracelet to her grave.

And this, in turn, appears to suggest that there was nothing to hide, no hint of a physical relationship. Perhaps such a thing was so far beyond any precedent that it was inconceivable. Nevertheless, it was very significant that an ordinary Highlander could find himself at the heart of politics, beloved by the Queen Empress, her close confidant. The power of the illusion conjured by Walter Scott in 1822 created the possibility of a relationship otherwise unthinkable.

Victoria and Albert first visited Scotland in 1842, taking care to read Scott's *The Lady of the Lake* while touring Perthshire. Summer in Scotland for the royal family quickly became an annual trip (it still is) and, by 1848, the queen and her consort had ventured further north, emphatically crossing the Highland Line. The Balmoral Estate was bought and, in place of the demolished old house, the familiar pepper-pot turrets of the Scots Baronial style rose up. No anxiety existed that the former owners, the Farquharsons of Balmoral, had been enthusiastic Jacobites, fighting against Victoria's dynasty in 1715 and again in 1745. In fact, the queen unblushingly declared that, at heart, she was really a Jacobite – a remark that at least shows how neutered and safe Highland history had become.

The Munshi

John Brown may have been the most famous of Queen Victoria's male companions in her widowhood but he was not the only one. After Brown's death in 1883, an Indian servant known as the Munshi, *'the teacher', became close to the Queen-Empress. Hafiz Abdul Karim's elevation to royal favour infuriated the more conservative members of the household who whispered that he was 'the brown Brown' and often attempted to reduce him to the ranks. The Munshi appears to have been no saint and he contracted gonorrhoea. Surprisingly Queen Victoria was sympathetic and even forgave him when he engineered the publication of a photograph of him and herself in the* Daily Graphic *in 1897. After Victoria's death, he retired to an estate in India she had left to him in her will.*

In the mid 19th century, the royal family was the acme of style and, in imitation of Balmoral, hundreds of shooting lodges were built in the Highlands, many of them very grand. After Albert's death and perhaps because of her attachment to faithful John Brown, Victoria spent increasingly long periods at Balmoral, up to four months each year. This was not popular with her government and several discomfited prime ministers were forced to make long train journeys to attend meetings of the privy council.

In 1867, Victoria published the immensely popular *Leaves from the Journal of our Life in the Highlands*, following it up with *More Leaves* in 1883. As much as Scott's, these book were very influential. They treated the Highlands as scenery, a grandeur to be walked or ridden through, a place of tranquillity and wilderness, somewhere that hunting the four-legged monarchs of the glen for sport was somehow appropriate. Victoria's jottings were, of course, unhampered by much knowledge of history and they certainly made no mention of what was really going on beyond the manicured policies of Balmoral Castle.

The great 20th-century novelist and poet Iain Crichton Smith remembered another narrative. Here is his English translation of part of his own poem, 'The Exiles':

> The many ships that left our country
> With white wings for Canada.
> They are like handkerchiefs in our memories
> And the brine like tears
> And in their masts like sailors singing
> Like birds on branches.
> That sea of May running in such blue,
> A moon at night, a sun at daytime,
> And the moon like a yellow fruit,
> Like a plate on a wall
> To which they raise their hands
> Like a silver magnet
> With piercing rays
> Streaming into the heart.

The emigrant ships that slipped over Atlantic horizons were one of the defining images of *Fuadach nan Gaidheal*, 'the Highland Clearances'. As a brutal aristocracy pushed their tenants off the fertile inland straths and glens they had farmed for generations, the landscape emptied. In place of busy crofting townships, sheep farms and deer forests were established. Many Highlanders left, crowded on to the emigrant ships or clung to marginal and congested pockets of poor land around the coasts. None had security of tenure and they were severely restricted in how they could scratch a living from the thin soil, the shoreline and the sea.

The contrasts between show, or myth-history, and what was actually taking place could be chilling, almost obscene in their cynicism. Sir Henry Raeburn, the great Edinburgh portraitist, painted Colonel Alastair MacDonell of Glengarry in all his pomp and finery – what he no doubt sported during the theatricals of the King's Jaunt. Looking off to his right at an imagined picturesque scene of bens and glens, MacDonell holds a musket and behind him the iconography of clan warfare hangs on a wall – a targe with crossed basket-hilted swords and a powder horn. Wearing the *feileadh mor*, the 'great kilt', with a plaid over one shoulder, a *sgian dubh*, a 'dirk', in his stocking and a sword, MacDonell of Glengarry looks the epitome of a Highland chief, a war leader of his faithful clansmen. Scott was impressed and he used him as a model for Fergus Mac-Ivor, the wild Highlander in *Waverley*.

In reality MacDonell and his tacksmen were ruthlessly evicting the clansmen and their families from the vast Glengarry estates. Timber was felled for ready cash and sheep farms set up on land worked by MacDonell's people since a time out of mind. Hundreds were herded on to the emigrant ships and Allan MacDougall, the blind bard of Glengarry, lamented this disaster, what he called a cross for his kinsmen:

> *Thainig oirnn a dh'Albainn crois,*
> *Tha daoine bochda nochdte ris,*
> *Gun bhiadh, gun aidoch, gun chluain:*
> *Tha 'n Airde-tuath air a sgrios.*

> There has come on us in Scotland a cross,
> Poor people are naked before it,
> Without food, without clothes, without pasture:
> The North is utterly destroyed.

This is an excerpt from 'The Song to the Lowland Shepherds', men who crossed the Highland Line to establish the new sheep farms.

In 1851, a year before Victoria bought Balmoral, the pace and scale of clearance increased. After the potato famine that ravaged Ireland and made Highland life almost impossible for thousands, some landlords grew impatient. 'Redundancy of the population is notoriously the evil, and emigration is the only effectual remedy,' wrote Sir James Matheson, the owner of large estates on the Isle of Lewis. Between 1851 and 1853, he and his factors had pressed 3,200 of the island population on to ships bound for Canada. Amongst them was a young man, Domhnall Ban Crosd, and, forty years later, in 1890, he returned to Lewis to see what had happened to the place where he had been born, the township of Carnish on the Atlantic coast. His nephew, Donald MacIver, took the old man to see it. Carnish was deserted. Domhnall Ban wept, saying, '*Chaneil nith an seo a bha e, ach an ataireachd na mara.*' – 'There is nothing here now as it was, except for the surge of the sea.'

Much moved by his uncle's bitter tears and all the loss, MacIver wrote one of the great modern Gaelic lyrics, '*An Ataireachd Ard*':

> *An ataireachd bhuan*
> *Cluinn fuaim na h'ataireachd ard*
> *Tha torann a' chuain*
> *Mar chualas leam-s' 'nam phaisd.*
> *Gun mhuthadh, gun truas*
> *A' sluaisreadh gainneimh na tragh'd*
> *Cluinn fuaim na h'ataireachd ard*

> The eternal surge of the sea
> Listen to the roar of the mighty surge.
> The thundering of the ocean is
> As I heard it in my childhood,
> Without cease, without pity,
> Washing over the sands of the shore.
> The eternal surge of the sea,
> Listen to the roar of the mighty surge.

Sna coilltean a siar,
Chan iarrain fuireach gu brath.
Bha m'intinn 's mo mhiann
A riamh air lagan a' bhaigh.
Ach iadsan bha fial
An gniomh, an caidreamh's an agh
Air scapadh gun dion
Mar thriallas ealtainn roimh namh . . .

In the woods of the west,
I would not want to wait forever.
My mind and my longing
Were ever in the little hollow by the cove.
But those who were gracious
In action, in friendship and in laughter
Are scattered without protection
Like a flock of birds before an enemy . . .

It is likely in 1851 that the young Domhnall Ban Crosd boarded the *Barlow*, an emigrant ship that dropped anchor in Loch Roag, not far from Carnish. Sir James Matheson's factor, Munro Mackenzie, was frustrated at how slowly the four hundred emigrants boarded and he sent an irritated message on to the next port of call in Lewis, telling those in charge 'to put them on without their luggage'. Not only would that speed up embarkation, it would also leave room where more emigrants could be packed in.

The long transatlantic voyage was often the stuff of nightmares. In the foul and insanitary conditions below deck, disease festered. Smallpox and seasickness were killers and on the ship *Hercules*, that left from Skye and the Uists bound for Adelaide in Australia, 38 died. A passenger noted, 'Some of the emigrants are dreadfully sick . . . some of the mothers have had their children in their arms for five days and nights without intermission.' After 104 days at sea, several very young children arrived as orphans, bewildered, small strangers in a strange land. Some never arrived at all. In the peak years between 1847 and 1853, 49 emigrant ships were lost at sea.

The population of the Highlands declined sharply, especially in the Hebrides and the coastal districts north of the Great Glen, accelerating the conversion of a working landscape into scenery. Between 1847 and 1858, more than 16,000 sailed for the Americas or Australasia, many of them having been forced on to the ships. Sometimes men had to be bound as they were dragged to the quaysides. Written in the 1870s, here is Catherine MacPhee's recollection of what went on: 'I have seen the big strong men, the champions of the countryside, the stalwarts of the world, being bound on Lochboisdale quay and cast into the ship as would be done to a batch of horses or cattle in the boat, the bailiffs and the ground-officers and the constables gathered behind them in pursuit of them.'

With the annual arrival of the royal family at Balmoral setting all sorts of trends, the land left idle by the evictions needed a use and so-called sporting estates were quickly established. Where farmers had once grown food for their families, deer were allowed to breed. They were followed by wealthy men with time on their hands and guns in them. By 1884, almost two million acres of Scotland, most of it north of the Highland Line, was given over to deer forests for the amusement of a privileged few.

Those who watched the white-sailed ships slip over western horizons, those left behind to grub a living from a harsh and barren landscape began to resist the tide of history. It had run against them for more than a century. The 1880s saw economic failure in the Highlands with a series of poor harvests and poor catches at sea. Similar conditions in Ireland had prompted rent strikes and, in 1881, the crofters on Skye refused to make payments to their landlords. A year later, resistance threatened to become violent. Sent from Portree to the nearby district of Braes, a sheriff officer carried a sheaf of eviction notices for tenants who had refused to pay rents to Lord Macdonald. He was stopped on the road by the women of Braes and they forced him to burn the notices. Tension quickly escalated. Police officers from Glasgow sailed into Portree to reinforce the Skye constables and soldiers were promised if required. It must have seemed to the crofters that the British establishment, the so-called forces of law and order, were uniting to attack them.

And they did. At what became known as the Battle of the Braes, crofters' leaders were arrested and subsequently imprisoned. Women took an active part and were driven back by the police. There were many injuries. Widely reported, this incident prompted government action and, for once, it was not of a punitive sort. In Ireland, tenants had begun to arm themselves and more than violent scuffles were to follow. Although it was not tied to nationalism, it was believed that a similar situation might arise in the Highlands and, to forestall it, the government set up a Royal Commission in 1883 to be chaired by Lord Napier.

While evidence was being taken, Highlanders suddenly found their political voice. With the extension of the franchise, five crofter MPs were returned in the general election of 1885 and accounts of injustices and arguments for change found their way into Hansard, becoming a matter of record. Remoteness was no longer a factor that worked in favour of the landlords and allowed them to do as they wished.

The Napier Commission interviewed witnesses from four parishes believed to be representative and, at Farr in Inverness-shire, Duirinish in Skye, Uig in Lewis and Uig in South Uist, they came across many examples of grinding poverty, of people living far below the breadline. This is what the commission reported about the total of 3,226 families living in the four parishes:

Only one tenth are provided with holdings which can afford sustenance to a labouring family. One thousand, seven hundred and seventy eight are in possession of tenancies which imply a divided and desultory form of occupation. At the bottom of the social scale, more than one quarter are without land and without access to local wages.

Side by side with this mingled multitude, so slenderly furnished with the means of life, we find thirty occupiers forming less than one per cent of the whole community in the occupancy of nearly two thirds of the land. These thirty include a factor, a few proprietors and some non-resident tenants.

Legislation was quickly framed. Modelled on the Irish Land Acts of 1870 and 1881, the Crofters' Holdings (Scotland) Act of 1886 arose directly from the agitation, the findings of the Napier Commission and the presence of crofters' MPs at Westminster. Prime amongst its measures, security of tenure was granted and it set up the Crofters' Commission, a land court where disputes could be heard and resolved.

While its great achievement was to remove the summary power of landlords to evict, the act was weak on the resolution of disputed access to land. Agitation continued and what were known as land raids organised. These involved the forced reoccupation of sheep farms and deer forests as common grazing, an attempt to restore rights of access that had been removed for generations.

The Crofters' Act, however, did lead to the recognition of a significant cultural shift. In defining crofting, as it had to, the act designated Scotland's crofting counties. These were Shetland, Orkney, Caithness, Sutherland, Ross and Cromarty, Inverness and Argyll. The effect of this was to realign the Highland Line and push it much further north-west. Most of Perthshire and Stirlingshire and the Highland districts of Angus, Aberdeenshire, Banff, Moray and Nairn were no longer seen as part of a crofting culture and their removal also mirrored the shrinking Gaelic speech community.

Less brutal and usually forced only by economics, the emigrations continued into the 20th century. The *Metagama* and the *Marloch* were still sailing in the 1920s from Hebridean ports with passengers bound for the New World and a new life. Inevitably departure and loss have deeply coloured Highland history of the last 250 years and it is not a disposition to melancholy and

---

Farmer's Boy

John R. Allan wrote two masterpieces. Each focuses on the North-east of Scotland – one is a wide sweep, a survey of the lowland farm country that runs in a coastal strip of varying width from Montrose to Caithness in the north, and the other is a miniature, an account of Allan's upbringing on a farm near Aberdeen. Farmer's Boy *is beautifully realised and written and it recreates perfectly, with a little licence, the atmosphere of the farm at Dungair before the Second World War brought radical change. Sunlight sparkles and warmth and love animate its all too few pages. And yet John R. Allan's story began in a very much harsher light. He was rescued by his grandparents from an orphanage where his mother had abandoned him before emigrating to Canada. His compendium of the geography, history and culture of the north-east lowlands is magisterial – and highly opinionated. Written unequivocally from the Lowland side of the Highland Line, it is much more than a guidebook. The attitudes of the 1950s are occasionally precisely distilled: 'Nothing so annoys a true native of these lowlands than the suggestion that he is a Highlander. Even when it is meant as a compliment – and it always is – we know it as a deadly insult.' Allan was by no means agin Highlanders but he did deeply, and rightly, suspect those versions of Highland culture such as the National Mod and the growing fetish for Highland dress as 'a sad case of a large and vibrant dog being wagged by a moribund wee tail'. But, by contrast, he was often tickled by Highland priorities and relished the tale of a level crossing where the road rather than the railway gates were usually shut because trains were more frequent than cars and sheep more frequent than either. John R. Allan loved the North-east with a quiet passion: 'the care was a sort of religion, perhaps nearer to our hearts than anything the churches can teach'.*

---

sentiment to state it, but no more than the reality. The great bard of departure was Sorley MacLean and here is Hallaig, his haunting poem for those who have gone.

> *Tha tim, am fiadh, an coille Hallaig*
>
> *Tha buird is tairnean air an uinneag*
> *Troimh'm faca mi an Aird an Iar*
> *'s tha mo gaol aig Allt Hallaig*
> *'na craoibh bheithe, 's bha i riamh*

Part Seen, Part Imagined

Time, the deer, is in the wood of Hallaig

The window is nailed and boarded
Through which I saw the West
And my love is at the Burn of Hallaig
A birch tree, and she has always been

Eader an t'Inbhir 's Poll a' Bhainne,
Thall 's a bhos mu Baile-Chuirn:
Tha I 'na beithe, 'na calltuinn,
'na caorunn dhireach sheag uir.

Between Inver and Milk Hollow,
Here and there about Baile-Chuirn:
She is a birch, a hazel,
A straight, slender young rowan.

Ann an Screapadal mo chinnidh
Far robh Tarmad 's Eachunn Mor,
Tha 'n nigheanan 's am mic 'nan coille
Ag gabhail suas ro taobh an loin.

In Screapadal of my people
Where Norman and Big Hector were,
Their daughters and sons are a wood
Going up beside the stream.

Uaibhreach a nochd na coilich ghiuthais
Ag gairm air mullach Cnoc an Ra,
Direcah an druim ris a' ghealaich —
Chan iadsan coille mu ghraidh.

Proud tonight the pine cocks
Crowing on the top of Cnoc an Ra,
Straight their backs in the moonlight —
They are not the wood I love.

Fuirichidh mi ris a' bheithe
Gus an tig i a mach an Carn,
Gus am bi am bearradh uile
O Bheinn na Lice f'a sgail.

I will wait for the birch wood
Until it comes up by the cairn,
Until the whole ridge from Beinn na Lice
Will be under its shade.

Mura tig 's ann thearnas mi a Hallaig
A dh'ionnsaigh sabaid na marbh,
Far a bheil an sluagh a' tathaich,
Gach aon ghinealach a dh'fhalbh.

If it does not, I will go down to Hallaig
To the Sabbath of the dead,
Where the people are frequenting,
Every single generation gone.

Tha iad fhathast ann a Hallaig,
Clann Ghill-Eain 's Clann MhicLeoid,
Na bh'ann ri linn Mhic Ghille-Chaluim:
Chunnacas na marbh beo.

They are still in Hallaig,
MacLeans and MacLeods,
All who were there in the time of Mac Gille Chaluim:
The dead have been seen alive.

The City of the Gael

✹

'NO,' SAID PARA HANDY, 'it iss a low-country song I
heard wance in the Broomielaw. Yon iss the place for
seeing life. I'm telling you it is Gleska for gaiety if you
have the money. There iss more life in wan day in the Broomielaw of Gleska than there is in a fortnight in Loch Fyne.'

'I daresay there iss,' said Dougie; 'no' coontin' the herring.'

'Och! Life, life!' said the Captain, with a pensive air of ancient
memory; 'Gleska's the place for it. And the fellows iss there that
iss not frightened, I'm telling you.'

'I learned my tred there,' mentioned the engineer, who had no
accomplishments, and had not contributed anything to the
evening's entertainment, and felt it was time he was shining
somehow.

'Iss that a fact, Macphail? I thocht it wass in a coal-ree in the
country,' said Para Handy. 'I was chust sayin', when Macphail put
in his oar, that yon's the place for life. If I had my way of it, the
Fital Spark would be going up every day to the Chamaica Brudge
the same as the *Columba*, and I would be stepping ashore quite
spruce with my Sunday clothes on, and no' lying here in a place
like Colintraive where there's no' even a polisman.'

Captain of the *Vital Spark*, a Gaelic archetype for the 20th and
21st centuries, Para Handy seems immortal. Very popular,
genuinely and enduringly funny, the stories about the little Clyde

puffer and its crew first appeared in the *Glasgow Evening News* in 1905. Continuously in print since then, the tales were made into television first with Duncan MacRae as the skipper, then Roddy McMillan and, most recently, Gregor Fisher. And despite the caricature, Para Handy feels as though he was drawn from a recognisable life, the lost world of seagoing trade between small coastal communities on the Firth of Clyde and the Hebrides beyond. His proper name is Peter MacFarlane and the nickname derives from a Gaelic patronymic. Padraic Shandaidh means Peter, son of Sandy. And his views about Glasgow's virtues and how dull is remote Colintraive also chime with real experience.

When the *Vital Spark* slipped her moorings at the Broomielaw and chugged down the Clyde bound for Colintraive, Furnace, Tighnabruaich, Ardrishaig and a dozen other coastal villages with quays and a need for small cargoes of timber, herring boxes or coal, she unknowingly crossed the Highland Boundary Fault. At the hamlet of Craigendoran, a suburb to the south of Helensburgh, it is clearly visible as it crosses the high ground before submerging beneath the Firth of Clyde. Perhaps in a parallel universe, Para Handy might have sounded the *Vital Spark*'s horn in salute as he steered her past.

Not only was the skipper crossing a geological and cultural frontier, he was also passing the home of his creator. Neil Munro was a distinguished journalist and a great novelist whose reputation now, sadly, rests solely on the exploits of the *Vital Spark*'s crew. Literary fashion is notoriously capricious and Munro's more serious work is unjustly neglected. He was innovative, a revisionist in the viewpoints of his historical fiction and a pivotal figure in the changing relationships and perceptions of Highlanders and Lowlanders.

An illegitimate child born in 1863, Munro was raised in a Gaelic-speaking household by his mother and grandmother near Inverary in Argyll. Bilingual by the time he went to school, his ear was always tuned to the nuances of both languages. His rendering of Para Handy's Gaelicised Lowland Scots is pitch perfect, the eccentric word order a precise translation and the emphases and cadences unfailingly correct. The skipper may have been a larger-than-life character but he always sounded very like the real thing.

After a childhood in Glen Aray and a brief apprenticeship as a clerk in a lawyer's office, Munro made a journey familiar to thousands of Highlanders. At the age of 17 he found a job as a cashier in an ironmonger's shop in Glasgow but he seems to have been early set on a career in journalism. Munro's ambitions were quickly realised and, in only four years, he became chief reporter on the *Glasgow Evening News*. In the meantime he had found time to court and marry Jessie Adam, the daughter of his landlady in North Woodside Road.

At the time of his marriage Munro will often have heard Gaelic spoken in Glasgow's streets. The census of 1881 reported 11,000 Gaels and this urban speech community rose to a peak of 18,500 in 1901. Against the background of an expanding population of more than half a million, this may have seemed a tiny island of Gaelic in a sea of English but it was concentrated. North Woodside Road was not far from Partick on the north bank of the Clyde. Immigrant communities often stayed close and tended to nucleate near where they had arrived and, in the case of Partick, that would have been nearby at the Broomielaw.

When significant numbers from the Highlands settled in Glasgow, many of them the victims of forced evictions, they often took the lowliest jobs and occupied some of the worst housing, as often happens with newcomers. In 1846, *The Scotsman* newspaper sneered, 'It is a fact that morally and intellectually the Highlanders are an inferior race to the Lowland Saxon.'

And *The Baillie*, a weekly magazine published in Glasgow, regularly made Highlanders the object of derision. The halting English of 'Auchtray MacTavish, the Hielan Polisman' was laughed at. In fact, the city's police force actively recruited Highlanders, believing them to be big, steady lads not easily riled. And the Clyde Trust, operators of ferries and docks, also favoured men from the Hebrides. Their sea craft was often learned early and well and so many were employed that the ferry services on the Clyde were known as the Skye Navy.

Highland societies were established and they organised such social life as could be afforded, with ceilidhs and mods encouraging the retention of language and cultures, at least in certain versions. In the later 19th century, the Central Station Bridge became known as the Hielanman's Umbrella since so many immigrants were in the habit of meeting under it. In the early 21st century, Gaelic can still be heard occasionally in Glasgow and, of the small surviving speech community of 58,000, 10 per cent live in the city.

Traffic moved in other directions. When Para Handy steered the *Vital Spark* past Craigendoran, he then had to navigate the stretch of water known as the Tail of the Bank. This was a large and very dangerous shifting sandbank but between it and Gourock and Greenock was a deep-water anchorage for ocean-going ships. In the 19th and early 20th centuries, many Highlanders were ferried out to ships riding at anchor at the Tail of the Bank, waiting to cross the Atlantic.

As the *Vital Spark* puffed around Gourock Bay, Dunoon could be seen on the starboard side. From the mid 19th century, when rail and ferry links were made, wealthy Glaswegians began to build grand villas in the town. And when paddle steamers plied a developing tourist trade on the Clyde, what became known as 'going doon the watter', Dunoon was a prime destination. Trippers were also taken up the long sea lochs to the likes of Inverary or Gareloch, Rothesay on the Isle of Bute, Loch Fyne, and Brodick on the Isle of Arran. For the first time the Highland Line was regularly breached by ordinary people as they began to be able to afford holidays. Instead of a wild, romantic resort of the more wealthy or a source of trouble and troubling difference, the Highlands became a welcome destination.

Para Handy helped put a smile on Glasgow's Highland hinterland. The tales in the *Glasgow Evening News* and in book form were a kind of travelogue for doon the watter. While sailing to Lochgoilhead, the crew of the *Vital Spark* first heard of the introduction of the old age pension and the opportunities offered by 'pension farms' or old folks' homes. The skipper mused, 'Wan pensioner maybe wouldna pay ye, but if ye had a herd, like my frien' in Mull, there's money in it.' At Tighnabruaich on the Kyles of Bute, the midgies were famously vicious: 'They're that bad there, they'll bite through corrugated iron roofs to get at ye!' And, on Mull, they were even worse having 'aal the points of a Poltalloch terrier, even to the black nose and the cocked lugs and sits up and barks at ye!'

As well as holidaymaking, history hovered over the Highlands, like dark clouds over the mountains. And it was history more than humour that caught the imagination of Neil Munro. In 1891, he published *John Splendid*, the first really authentic Highland novel. It was written by a Highlander, a Gaelic speaker, who made a story told from the inside of a culture he grew up in and understood. It was unlike anything written by Lowlanders such as Walter Scott.

John Splendid is itself a translation of the Gaelic *Iain Alainn*. It literally means 'John the Beautiful' and, in the Highlands, that was an adjective that could be applied to men. The action of the novel crackled around the spectacular campaign led by James Graham, Marquis of Montrose, in 1664 in support of the failing reign of Charles I. Through the December snows, an army descended on Inverary, the stronghold of the Covenanting Campbells and their chief. He fled, making his escape by sea in his birlinn, and the town was sacked by Montrose's army of avenging Macdonalds and other clans. But, as an Argyll man raised in Glen Aray near Inverary, Neil Munro told the story from a Campbell viewpoint, foregoing the easy temptations of the temporary glory of Montrose and his victory over a Campbell army at Inverlochy the following year. While Iain Alainn, John Splendid, is painted in the traditional colours of the fearless Highland warrior, his chief, Gillesbeg Gruamach, was a moderniser. He did not look backwards to a glorious military tradition but to the future, beyond the ancient ties of clanship to a more peaceful and productive society governed not by warfare and the bonds of service but by the rule of law – a thriving Highland economy built on trade rather than the old staples of cattle rearing and droving. These goals were at the centre of Grua-mach's ambition rather than prowess in battle.

Munro's Highlanders are often nuanced characters capable of the unexpected and far removed from the caricatures created by other authors. Three more historical novels followed *John Splen-did*, all of them revisionist, all linked to the 1745 Rebellion and its aftermath, all beautifully conceived and written. In *Children of the Tempest*, a Captain Dan MacNeil, skipper of the *Happy Return*, makes a prophetic appearance. Munro clearly relished writing the character and he may well be the prototype for Para Handy.

Significantly, Neil Munro felt no awkwardness in writing about Lowland Scotland. Several novels, including the ambitious *Fancy Farm*, deal confidently with agricultural and urban life. Munro had retired from journalism to concentrate on writing but, with the outbreak of the First World War, he returned and became editor of the *Glasgow Evening News* in 1918.

The New Road was Neil Munro's last completed novel and it is his greatest. Revisiting Highland history, he created an epic whodunit only resolved on the very last page. General Wade's new road between Stirling and Inverness gave the novel its title and, in Munro's hands, it became a route out of the darkness of the past to prosperity and improvement rather than repression. He understood that the new road was destined to mean the ultimate end of a separate cultural life for the Gaelic-speaking Highlands and the rapid integration of the lands north of the Highland Line into Scotland but it could also have the effect of improving the lives of ordinary people.

The New Road is now a half-forgotten masterpiece, barely still in print, and yet it was included by one enlightened critic in a recent listing of 100 Best Scottish Books. *The Vital Spark* was not but, if the gentle humour and vitality of the tales keep Neil Munro's reputation alive, perhaps his great novels, stories that uniquely crossed and re-crossed the Highland Line, will come back into fashion.

The following passage from *The Vital Spark* is a wonderful example of Neil Munro's magical ability to write Gaelic-English, to make readers believe that they are hearing dialogue in another language which they could miraculously understand, a language that spoke of another culture. Dougie had persuaded Para Handy to go to the Furnace Ball. Drink had been taken, tempers flared and the Tar was acrimoniously sacked from the crew, something the skipper had forgotten by the following morning as the *Vital Spark* made headway down Loch Fyne. Para Handy believes that a far worse fate had befallen the Tar:

'Weel, there's a good man gone!' said Para Handy. 'Och! Poor Tar! It wass yon last smasher of a sea. He's over the side. Poor laad! Poor laad! Cot bless me, dyin' without a word of Gaalic in his mooth! It's a chudgement on us for the way we were carryin' on, chust a chudgement; not another drop of drink will I drink, except maybe beer. Or at New Year time. I'm blaming you, Dougie, for making us stop at Furnace for a baal I wudna give a snuff for. You are chust a disgrace to the vessel, with your smokin' and your drinkin', and your ignorance. It iss time you were livin' a better life for the sake of your wife and family. If it wass not for you makin' me go into Furnace last night, the Tar would be to the fore yet, and I would not need to be sending a telegram to his folk from Ardrishaig. If I wass not steering the boat, I would break my he'rt greetin' for the poor laad that never did anybody any herm. Get oot the flag from below my bunk, give it a syne in the pail, and put it at half mast, and we'll go into Ardrishaig and send a telegram – it'll be a sixpence. It'll be a telegram with a sore he'rt, I'll assure you. I do not know what I will say in it, Dougie. It will not do to break it too much to them; maybe we will send the two telegrams – that'll be a shilling. We'll say in the first wan "Your son, Colin, left the boat today": and in the next wan we will say – "He iss not coming back, he iss drooned." Och! Och! Poor Tar, amn't I sorry for him? I wass chust going to put up his wages a shilling on Setturday.'

The Vital Spark went in close to Ardrishaig Pier just as the Cygnet was leaving after taking in a cargo of herring boxes. Para Handy and Dougie went ashore in the punt, the Captain with his hands washed and his watch-chain on as a tribute of respect for the deceased. Before they could send off the telegram it was necessary that they should brace themselves for the melancholy occasion. "No drinking, chust wan gless of beer," said Para Handy, and they entered a discreet contiguous public-house for this purpose.

The Tar himself was standing at the counter having a refreshment, with one eye wrapped up in a handkerchief.

'Dalmighty!' cried the Captain, staggered at the sight, and turning pale. 'What are you doing here with your eye in a sling?'

'What's your business?' retorted the Tar coolly 'I'm no' in your employ anyway.'

It is still Scotland's last frontier. The Highland Line remains a barrier, a clear division between two Scotlands. But much has changed. Just as Domhnall Ban Crosd could see through his tears at Carnish in the late 19th century, only the land and the sea endure. The suddenness of the Highland Boundary Fault is an obvious, imperishable geological drama and no one who travels across it can fail to notice the transition to another Scotland.

What has all but perished is the distinctive culture that lay to the north. Over three millennia, the Highlands has slowly emptied. The volcanic winters that followed the eruption of Mt Hekla in 1159 BC accelerated the blanketing of the peat and forced farmers to depend primarily on stock rearing. People were forced to move east and south across the high passes and down the glens to find kinder and more fertile land in the Lowlands.

The storms of battle erupted along the Highland Line for much of that long time. From the epic struggle at the foot of the Graupian Mountain in AD 83 to the slaughter at Culloden in 1746, great imperial powers have marched north to subdue the peoples of the mountains and straths. And, despite a deserved reputation for ferocity and bravery (and an undeserved one for mindless savagery), the Highlanders were ultimately defeated and their culture began a long retreat. One of the insistent themes of the story of the Highland Line is the victory of the more populous and wealthier Lowlanders. Inevitable and unequal, perhaps the most surprising aspect is how long defeat was delayed.

From the Roman road and fort builders to Marshal Wade, soldiers understood that the Highlands could be never held – the hinterlands could only be more or less efficiently policed. Armies usually marched north in response to provocation. And containment rather than conquest was what their generals aimed to achieve. Few came to colonise or settle. To many outsiders, the Highlands seemed a harsh, barren and elemental wilderness that somehow bred fearsome warriors. But, until the 19th century, after the warriors had fled into legend, it was rarely a place to be possessed, not even by the great Agricola.

At about 2 p.m. on Wednesday 16 April 1746, the sound of the last defeat was heard. After beating off a disorganised Highland charge across the boggy Drumossie Moor near Culloden House, the government army was ordered to march forward to take symbolic possession of the field of battle. The Jacobite army had been scattered and, as their drummers rattled out a steady beat, the victorious infantry advanced to where the clans had stood. And then they cheered.

Less than two miles away, Prince Charles could hear the triumphant huzzas. He had reined in his horse and stopped to shelter under a tree at Balvraid. There, the remnants of his routed army mustered around him. Would they regroup, retreat and fight a summer campaign in the mountains? Showing no leadership, perhaps even panicking, the prince shouted that the Macdonald regiments and other survivors should do as they wished. With that he turned his horse and rode away to a life in exile.

Men were still dying on the battlefield. Bleeding slowly and fatally, their legs often broken by grapeshot, men lay trapped under the bloody ruck of bodies. Clan Fraser had suffered badly in the thick of the battle and, when the brutal General Henry Hawley rode up with a party of soldiers, bayonets fixed, he found Charles Fraser of Inverallochie still alive. Captain of his clan, he lay trapped and covered in blood and he looked silently up at the general. When Hawley ordered a young officer, possibly James Wolfe, to shoot Fraser, he refused but another man more willing was immediately found.

When burial parties came to the moor on Thursday 17 April, they reported that many wounded Highlanders had survived the bitterly cold night. Most had been stripped of their clothes the day before and some with broken limbs and severe wounds had crawled for shelter to a drystane dyke to the south of the battlefield. Desperately thirsty, others had dragged themselves to the spring that later became known as the Well of the Dead. Alexander McGillivray of Dunmaglass, a captain of Clan Chattan, was there and, when she found his body, his wife, Elizabeth Campbell of Clunas, saw that a white cloth had been tied to his arm. Someone who knew him had done that so that he might be recognised and found amongst the mangled piles of the dead.

John Fraser of Lovat had been felled in the charge by a musket ball that shattered his kneecap. When the government army advanced, they stripped and beat him as they passed. All through the night of the battle, Fraser lay shivering in the heather. By the grey light of morning, he crawled to the cover of a small wood where other wounded men lay. Discovered by soldiers, they were taken in carts to Culloden House, put up against a wall and shot at close range. But still Fraser survived. Having crawled away once more, he was discovered by Lord Boyd, a government officer. Taking pity, Boyd concealed Fraser near a farm. And miraculously his wounds healed and although dreadfully crippled, he lived until 1796.

As Prince Charles fled westwards, the Jacobite cause fled with him. The clans would not rise again and thousands of their young men enlisted in the British army as the great drive for empire gathered pace. The society they left behind began to wither as romance replaced reality and people were herded on to the emigrant ships.

The distinctiveness of Highland culture is described best by its own language – and Gaelic is dying. When the question was first asked in the census of 1881, more than 250,000 Scots replied that they had Gaelic, around 7 per cent of the population. In 2001 the number had dropped dramatically to 58,552, 1.2 per cent. Many of these respondents were aged 50 or over and few were children. Activists comfort themselves that the rate of decline is slowing but, despite the heroic efforts being made to save the language, the overwhelming likelihood must be that, by the close of the 21st century, Gaelic will no longer have any native speakers. That is the definition of a dead language.

It may take some time for the death of a culture to become apparent. Because of the richness of history and memory mixed with a measure of guilt at the manifest wrongs of the past, the culture and strong sense of identity in the Highlands will seem to survive. Emigrants, Lowlanders and tourists have too much affection for the lands north of the Highland Line to allow its traditions to die. And, in turn, the Highland economy, based on scenery, tartan, whisky, written and filmic romance and all the other unique identifiers, depends on tourism too heavily for that distinctiveness ever to be allowed to wane. But increasingly Highland culture will seem hollow, like a dead Christmas tree, its needles brown and brittle, but with all the tinsel still attached and the fairy lights twinkling.

The positive legacy of all that history seems to be tolerance. Violence between Lowland and Highland has long been consigned to the past and prejudices appear to be waning. All Scots who wish to can cross the Highland Line and walk or sail through the glories of its landscapes and seascapes. It is no longer a barrier and there are signs that immigration from the south to certain parts of the Highlands, like south Skye, is increasing. It may be that a new sort of life in the north of Scotland is in the making – but it will be all the richer if the stories of the old life are remembered and celebrated.

One of Scotland's very greatest poets, Norman MacCaig, was the son of a Gaelic-speaking mother from the Hebrides. It was said that the freshness and simplicity of her English, her second language, opened up the possibilities of writing for the young

MacCaig. For most of his working life, he was a primary schoolteacher and, during the long summer vacations, almost always went on holiday to Achmelvich, Assynt in Sutherland, near the village of Lochinver. Summers in the Highlands were more than a break from work and his home in Edinburgh – they nourished MacCaig's powerful affinity with Gaelic culture and the landscapes it described.

Most of the poems in Norman MacCaig's rich output are short, scarcely more than three or four verses, rarely more than a page. But, when he sat down to write of a return to the island of Scalpay, off the coast of Harris and his mother's birthplace, he had a great deal to say:

Return to Scalpay

The ferry wades across the kyle, I drive
The car ashore
On to a trim tarred road. A car on Scalpay?
Yes, and a road where there was never one before.
The ferryman's Gaelic wonders who I am
(Not knowing I know it) this man back from the dead,
Who takes the blue-black road (no traffic jam)
From by Craig Lexie over to Bay Head

A man bows in the North wind, shaping up
His lazybeds,
And through the salt air vagrant peat smells waver
From houses where no houses should be. The sheds
At the curing station have been newly tarred.
Aunt Julia's house has vanished. The Red Well
Has been bulldozed away. But sharp and hard
The church still stands, barring the road to Hell.

A chugging prawn boats slides round Cuddy Point
Where in a gale
I spread my batwing jacket and jumped farther
Than I've jumped since. There's where I used to sail

Boats looped from rushes. On the jetty there
I caught eels, cut their heads off and watched them slew
Slow through the water. Ah – Cape Finisterre
I called that point, to show how much I knew.

While Hamish sketches, a crofter tells me that
The Scalpay folk,
Though very intelligent, are not Spinozas . . .
We walk the Out End road (no need to invoke
That troublemaker, Memory, she's everywhere)
To Laggandoan, greeted all the way –
My city eyeballs prickle; it's hard to bear
With such affection and such gaiety.

Scalpay revisited? – more than Scalpay. I
Have no defence,
For half my thought and half my blood is Scalpay,
Against that pure, hardheaded innocence
That shows love without shame, weeps without shame,
Whose every thought is hospitality –
Edinburgh, Edinburgh, you're dark years away.

Scattering snowflakes riddling the hard wind
Are almost spent
When we reach Johann's house. She fills the doorway,
Sixty years of size and astonishment,
Then laughs and cries and laughs, as she always did
And will (easy glum, easy glow, a friend would say) . . .
Scones, oatcakes, herrings from under a bubbling lid.
Then she comes with us to put us on our way.

Hugging my arm in her stronger one, she says,
Fancy me
Walking this road beside my darling Norman!
And what is there to say? . . . We look back and see

Her monumental against the flying sky
And I am filled with love and praise and shame
Knowing that I have been, and knowing why,
Diminished and enlarged. Are they the same?

What this beautiful piece of writing shows is something simple
– that it is possible to catch the intimate essence of a culture
without knowing (much) of its language. In other work, MacCaig
claims incomprehension, especially when his Aunt Julia spoke
quickly in Gaelic. A real family link existed, no doubt, but that is
not an uncommon connection and one which would could apply
to many hundreds of thousands of Scots and exiles.

Sorley MacLean so admired Norman MacCaig's Highland
poems that he wrote that, in them, he had given the landscape
of Sutherland new meaning. He had honoured his Gaelic-
speaking ancestors by writing in very beautiful English. Here
is his:

Neglected Graveyard, Luskentyre

I wade in the long grass,
Barking my shins on gravestones.
The grass overtops the dyke.
In and out of the bay hesitates the Atlantic.

A seagull stares at me hard
With a quarterdeck eye, leans forward
And shrugs into the air.
The dead rest from their journey from one wilderness to
Another.

Considering what they were,
This seems a proper disorder.
Why lay graces by rule
Like bars of a cage on the ground? To discipline the unruly?

I know a man who is
Peeped at by death. No place is
Atlantics coming in;
No time but reaches out to touch him with a cold finger.

He hears death at the door.
He knows him round every corner.
No matter where he goes
He wades in long grass, barking his shins on gravestones.

The edge of the green sea
Crumples. Bees are in clover.
I part the grass and there –
Angus Macleod, drowned. Mary his wife. Together.

Perhaps Norman MacCaig's elegant Highland poems point to
a future without Gaelic, a literature in English able to describe a
thoroughly different culture at least adequately. Perhaps it will
simply fade. This is the last verse of MacCaig's 'Praise of a Man',
lines that might make an elegy for Gaelic, for all that experience
on the other side of Scotland's Last Frontier.

The beneficent lights dim
but don't vanish. The razory edges
dull, but still cut. He's gone: but you can see
his tracks still, in the snow of the world.

Select Bibliography

✿

Allan, John R. *North-East Lowlands of Scotland*, Yeadons 2009
Allan, John, R. *Farmer's Boy*, Birlinn 2009
Barrie, J.M. *A Window in Thrums: Auld Licht Idylls*, Classic Reprint 2009
Birley, Anthony *Tacitus, Agricola and Germania*, Oxford Paperbacks 1999
Cameron, David Kerr *The Ballad and the Plough*, Birlinn 1997
Cunliffe, Barry *The Ancient Celts*, Penguin 1997
Daiches, David *Scotch Whisky*, Birlinn 1995
Devine, Tom *The Scottish Nation*, Penguin 2000
Glendinning, Miles and Martins, Susanna Wade *Buildings of the Land: Scotland's Farms 1750–2000*, RCAHMS 2009
Grassic Gibbon, Lewis *A Scots Quair*, Polygon 2006
Hamilton, Ian *Stone of Destiny*, Birlinn 2008
Maclean, Alasdair *Night Falls on Ardnamurchan*, Birlinn 2011
Marsden, John *Kings, Mormaers, Rebels*, John Donald 2010
McGeachie, Lynne *Beatrix Potter's Scotland*, Luath 2010
McKean, Charles *The District of Moray*, Scottish Academic Press 1987
Moffat, Alistair *The Highland Clans*, Thames & Hudson 2010
Munro, Neil *Para Handy*, Birlinn, 2002
Shirley, Elizabeth *Building A Roman Legionary Fortress*, Tempus 2001
Smout, T.C. *A Century of the Scottish People*, Fontana 2010
Stevenson, David *Rob Roy*, Birlinn 2004
Wightman, Andy *The Poor Had No Lawyers*, Birlinn 2010
Williams, Ronald *Sons of the Wolf*, Lochar 1988

Index